Farmscape

Farmscape: The Design of Productive Landscapes situates agriculture as a design practice, using a wide range of international case studies and analytical essays to propose lessons for contemporary landscape architects who are interested in integrating agriculture into their designs. Agricultural processes, technologies, and cycles have long shaped landscape architectural projects, from the ornamented farm of the eighteenth century, to contemporary projects that integrate agriculture and ecological restoration. The book describes the history of agriculture within landscape architecture and reveals the diversity of current design practices that use the rhythms and forms of agriculture to create productive farms that are also sites of beauty, community, ecological conservation, remediation, and pleasure. Highly illustrated in full colour, this book provides essential context, resources, and best practice examples of rural and periurban designed sites for professionals and students alike.

Phoebe Lickwar is an Associate Professor in Landscape Architecture at The University of Texas at Austin. She is founding principal of Forge Landscape Architecture, an award-winning critical design practice based in Austin.

Roxi Thoren is an Associate Professor of Architecture and Landscape Architecture at the University of Oregon. She studies the integration of second nature, productive landscapes, in landscape architectural design through research and design projects around agriculture, forestry, and power.

Farmscape

The Design of Productive Landscapes

Phoebe Lickwar and Roxi Thoren

LONDON AND NEW YORK

First published 2020
by Routledge
2 Park Square, Milton Park, Abingdon, Oxon OX14 4RN

and by Routledge
52 Vanderbilt Avenue, New York, NY 10017

Routledge is an imprint of the Taylor & Francis Group, an informa business

British Library Cataloguing-in-Publication Data
A catalogue record for this book is available from the British Library

Library of Congress Cataloging-in-Publication Data
Names: Lickwar, Phoebe, editor. | Thoren, Roxi, editor.
Title: Farmscape : the design of productive landscapes / edited by Phoebe Lickwar and Roxi Thoren.
Description: Milton Park, Abingdon, Oxon ; New York : Routledge, 2020. | Includes bibliographical references and index. |
Identifiers: LCCN 2019029868 (print) | LCCN 2019029869 (ebook) | ISBN 9781138054646 (hbk) | ISBN 9781138054653 (pbk) | ISBN 9781315166513 (ebk)
Subjects: LCSH: Landscape architecture. | Agricultural landscape management. | Agricultural conservation.
Classification: LCC SB472 .F37 2020 (print) | LCC SB472 (ebook) | DDC 333.76--dc23
LC record available at https://lccn.loc.gov/2019029868
LC ebook record available at https://lccn.loc.gov/2019029869

ISBN: 978-1-138-05464-6 (hbk)
ISBN: 978-1-138-05465-3 (pbk)
ISBN: 978-1-315-16651-3 (ebk)

Typeset in Univers
by Servis Filmsetting Ltd, Stockport, Cheshire

Contents

Acknowledgements

We are extremely grateful to the many people who helped bring this book to completion, from discussing initial ideas, to sharing project documents, images and archival materials, to providing insightful feedback on ideas, conference presentations, and drafts of the various essays.

This book would not have been possible without the support we received from our academic institutions, The University of Texas at Austin and the University of Oregon. We thank our many faculty colleagues. Beyond our home institutions, we would like to thank faculty colleagues who offered advice, guidance, and encouragement at various stages in the process, including Anne Whiston Spirn, Dorothée Imbert, Jane Gillette, and Gina Crandall.

Research for this book was supported through grants and funding from the University of Oregon, The University of Texas at Austin, the University of Arkansas, and the Fuller Center for Productive Landscapes. Several of our students provided research and illustration assistance. We are grateful to rising stars Erin Cox, Hannah Moll, Loren Corey Phillips, Kelly Stoecklein, Katya Reyna, and Ryan Nicholson.

Early versions of several of the case studies were presented at conferences, including the Council of Educators in Landscape Architecture and New Directions in the American Landscape. The feedback we received from colleagues at those presentations strengthened the clarity and focus of the book.

Designers and staff at the many firms represented were incredibly generous with their time and insights on the projects, as well as sharing project images and other documents. Thank you to Judith Phillips Design Oasis, Martha Schwartz Partners, Mithun, Nelson Byrd Woltz, OLIN, Prunuske Chatham, Inc., and Turenscape.

Staff members at libraries and archives helped to locate images for many of the projects. Thank you to the Beineke Rare Book and Manuscript Library; the Elmbridge Museum; Michele Clark at the Frederick Law Olmsted National Historic Site; the Gibbes Museum of Art; the Library of Congress Prints and Photograph Division, Geography and Map Division, and Manuscript Division; Melanie Bump and Maureen Harrison at the Morris County Parks Commission; the Smithsonian

Institute Archives of American Gardens; the South Carolina Historical Society; Henrik Christensen at the Aalborg Stadsarkiv; Louis Sebastian Bo Jensen at the Danish National Art Library; and Regina Rush at the Albert and Shirley Small Special Collections Library at the University of Virginia.

Special thanks are due to the individuals who aided us as keepers of deep expertise and knowledge about the case studies. Dottie Stone at the Middleton Place Foundation; Hilarie Hicks, Matt Reeves, and Jenniffer Powers at the Montpelier Foundation; the Nærum Allottment gardeners; Judy Corbett, Mark Francis, Rob Thayer, Stephen Wheeler, and Jim Zanetto; Hank McNeil; Mary Padua; Sara Tashker at the San Francisco Zen Center; John N. Roberts; Lize Grobbelaar at Babylonstoren; Mort and Sue Fuller; James Gibbs; and Matt Rembe, Jonathan Perno, Wes Brittenham, and Judy Hartline at Los Poblanos; generously provided memories, oral histories and their own research for the projects.

We would like to recognize the dedicated support and assistance of the team at Routledge / Taylor & Francis, especially Grace Harrison, Editor, Landscape Architecture and Built Environment Research, Editorial Assistants Aoife McGrath and Emily Collyer, and Senior Production Editor Elizabeth Spicer.

Lastly, we wish to thank our families for their ongoing support throughout the research and writing of this book.

Image credits

2.0	Woburn Farm Site Plan by Erin Cox and Phoebe Lickwar
2.1, 2.4	Private collection
2.2	"View in the Grounds of Woburn Farm," 21.1910/3, Reproduced by permission of Elmbridge Museum
2.3, 2.7	Joseph Spence Papers. James Marshall and Marie-Louise Osborn Collection, Beinecke Rare Book and Manuscript Library
2.5	"The Grounds of Woburn from the Bourne," 21.1910/6, Reproduced by permission of Elmbridge Museum
2.6	Biblioteca Virtual del Patrimonio Bibliográfico; Naval Museum; Spanish Ministry of Education, Culture and Sport
2.8	"The Ruin in the Grounds of Woburn," 21.1919/5, Reproduced by permission of Elmbridge Museum
2.9	"The Long Walk in the Grounds of Woburn," 21.1910/1, Reproduced by permission of Elmbridge Museum
3.0	Middle Place Site Plan by Erin Cox and Phoebe Lickwar
3.1, 3.4	Middleton Place Foundation
3.2, 3.6	© Vanessa Kaufman
3.3	Frances Benjamin Johnston. Carnegie Survey of the Architecture of the South, Library of Congress, Prints and Photographs Division [LC-DIG-csas-03839]
3.5	Library of Congress, Geography and Map Division [99448840]
3.7	Gibbes Museum of Art
3.8	Frances Benjamin Johnston. Carnegie Survey of the Architecture of the South, Library of Congress, Prints and Photographs Division [LC-DIG-csas-03845]
3.9	Roxi Thoren, Kelly Stoecklein
3.10	Edward Van Altena. Smithsonian Institution, Archives of American Gardens, Garden Club of America Collection [SC002001]

4.0	Montpelier Site Plan by Erin Cox and Phoebe Lickwar
4.1	"Montpelier Blue Ridge" by Calstanhope is licensed under CC BY-SA 4.0 (https://creativecommons.org/licenses/by-sa/4.0/deed.en)
4.2	"Montpelier Slave Quarters" by Mike is licensed under CC BY 2.0 (https://creativecommons.org/licenses/by/2.0/)
4.3, 4.5, 4.8	Courtesy of the Montpelier Foundation
4.4	Carnegie Survey of the Architecture of the South, Library of Congress, Prints and Photographs Division [LC-DIG-csas-05348]
4.6	Reproduced from *Horse-Hoeing Husbandry*, 1733; photo by SSPL/Getty Images.
4.7	George Aikman, from Humboldt's engraving. Reproduced from *Physical Geography. Humboldt's Distribution of Plants in Equinoctial America, According to Elevation Above the Level of the Sea*, 1839
4.9	Library of Congress, Geography and Map Division [2002627460]
5.0	Moraine Farm Site Plan by Erin Cox and Phoebe Lickwar
5.1	Reproduced from *Garden and Forest* magazine, 1892
5.2	Reproduced from *The Cultivator* magazine, 1846
5.3	Frederick Law Olmsted, Library of Congress, Manuscript Division, Frederick Law Olmsted Papers [mss351210564]
5.4	J. A. Haskell, Courtesy of the United States Department of the Interior, National Park Service, Frederick Law Olmsted National Historic Site
5.5	Olmsted Brothers, Courtesy of the United States Department of the Interior, National Park Service, Frederick Law Olmsted National Historic Site
5.6–5.8	Roxi Thoren
6.0	Merchiston Farm Site Plan by Erin Cox, Hannah Moll, and Phoebe Lickwar
6.2	Reproduced from *The Spirit of the Garden*, 1923
6.5	© Phoebe Lickwar
6.7c	Roxi Thoren
all others	Morris County Parks Commission, Martha Brookes Hutcheson archive
7.0	Welwyn Garden City Site Plan by Erin Cox and Phoebe Lickwar
7.1–7.3	Reproduced from *Garden Cities of To-morrow*, 1898
7.4	Courtesy of the United States Department of the Interior, National Park Service, Frederick Law Olmsted National Historic Site
7.5	© Historic England. [EPW022025] Broadwater Road Estate, Welwyn Garden City, 1928
7.6	Hertfordshire Archives & Local Studies, WGC/539
7.7	Hertfordshire Archives & Local Studies, WGC/544
7.8	© Historic England. [EPW047367] Handside Lane and environs, Welwyn Garden City, 1935

8.0	Ziebigk Siedlung Site Plan by Erin Cox and Phoebe Lickwar
8.1, 8.4, 8.7–8.9	Reproduced from *Deutsche Binnen-Kolonisation*, 1926
8.2, 8.3, 8.5, 8.6	Reproduced from *Die Wachsende Siedlung nach biologischen Gesetzen*, 1932
9.0	Nærum Allotment Gardens Site Plan by Erin Cox, Hannah Moll, and Phoebe Lickwar
9.1	Courtesy Aalborg Stadsarkiv
9.2, 9.7	© Danish National Art Library, Collection of Architectural Drawings
9.3–9.6, 9.8–9.11	© Phoebe Lickwar
10.0	Village Homes Site Plan by Erin Cox, Hannah Moll, and Phoebe Lickwar
10.1	Phoebe Lickwar, Hannah Moll, and Erin Cox
10.2a–10.8	© Phoebe Lickwar
11.0	Winslow Farms Conservancy Site Plan by Erin Cox, Hannah Moll, and Phoebe Lickwar
11.1–11.3, 11.5a–11.8	Courtesy Martha Schwartz Partners
11.4, 11.9	© Phoebe Lickwar
12.0	Shenyang Architectural University Site Plan by Erin Cox, Hannah Moll, and Phoebe Lickwar
12.1–12.9	Courtesy Turenscape
13.0	Green Gulch Farm Zen Center Site Plan by Erin Cox and Phoebe Lickwar
13.1, 13.3–13.7, 13.11	© Phoebe Lickwar
13.2	Courtesy San Francisco Zen Center
13.8	© Stephanie Bower
13.9, 13.10	Courtesy Prunuske Chatham
14.0	Babylonstoren Site Plan by Erin Cox and Phoebe Lickwar
14.1, 14.3–4, 14.6, 14.8–14.13	Courtesy Babylonstoren
14.2	© Koninklijke Bibliotheek / Alamy
14.5	Phoebe Lickwar and Erin Cox
14.7	Phoebe Lickwar and Erin Cox
15.0	Overlook Site Plan by Erin Cox and Phoebe Lickwar
15.1, 15.4, 15.5	Courtesy of the Fuller family
15.2, 15.6	Pray and Gallagher, Courtesy of the United States Department of the Interior, National Park Service, Frederick Law Olmsted National Historic Site
15.3	Olmsted Brothers, Courtesy of the United States Department of the Interior, National Park Service, Frederick Law Olmsted National Historic Site

15.7–15.9	Courtesy of Nelson Byrd Woltz Landscape Architects
15.10, 15.11	Roxi Thoren
16.0	Los Poblanos Site Plan by Erin Cox and Phoebe Lickwar
16.1–16.12	© Phoebe Lickwar

Cultivating the field

The premise of this book is that the design of land and the cultivation of crops are mutually reinforcing practices and that each benefits from being considered and conceived together. The case studies that follow provide examples, selected across time and location, of landscapes that produce sustaining food and economic activity as well as experiences that are richly sensual and culturally meaningful.

The English word culture emerged from the idea of food production, an indication of how central the stewardship of land for sustenance is in Western conceptions of community and societal development. The word agriculture is rooted in the Latin words *agros*, field, and *colere*, tending. From them, we also derive the literal sense of cultivate, tending fields for crops, as well as metaphoric ideas of philosophical, intellectual, and artistic stewardship and fecundity – cultivating ideas, cultivating one's mind – and individual and collective advances and identity – becoming cultured, cultural identity, the culture wars.

Yet with the rise of industrial agriculture, the literal and metaphoric senses of cultivation have become distant. Many people in industrialized nations are physically and intellectually removed from the production of food, and that food production is largely mechanistic rather than a mode of cultural production. If it is true, as Denis Cosgrove posited, that landscapes are "an important mode of social, cultural, and political communication,"[1] then the distancing of communal culture from the productive landscapes of agriculture is a matter of concern and a loss of significant cultural literacy. Landscapes are places for dwelling and working, and they are also symbolic expressions of a society.[2] Our understanding of our culture is co-created with our production of our place. The material practice of making and remaking landscapes is a process of shaping places that reflect our culture and provide opportunities to critique cultural norms and suggest new modes of dwelling.

Artists have explored the public performance of agriculture and its ability to reveal, question, and propose cultural assumptions about food systems. Agnes Denes's *Wheatfield: A Confrontation* (1982), "called attention to our misplaced priorities"[3] towards land, food, and development by cultivating two acres of wheat in lower Manhattan. The project questioned what we value – soil, food, practices, buildings, development, capital. And it questioned how we express those values through labor, words, publicity, or money. The seeds grown were exhibited internationally; visitors to the exhibits could take the seeds and plant them, linking the public act of cultivation to a global community of land stewards. Similarly, Amy Franceschini and the Futurefarmers collective have created a series of projects, including *Soil Kitchen* (2012) and several *Flatbread Society* projects (2012–2017), that seek to connect people through the production of healthy soil, land, crops, and food. Through the lens of food production, Futurefarmers' projects foster the transmission of traditional knowledge between people and generations and promote urban and rural regeneration of ecosystems. These works provide models for landscape architects, as changing ideas and ideals of aesthetics, science, and political and economic structures have provided landscape architects with challenges and opportunities to design at the scale of the farm in ways that reconnect physical and metaphoric cultivation, and expand the boundaries of the discipline.

While there is a substantial body of work on policy and planning work for agriculture especially in urban areas,[4] there is less written on the site-scale design of agriculture and what is available often focuses on agricultural urbanism.[5] The projects in this book illustrate the long history of landscape architectural designs that integrate farm and garden and use that hybridity to explore the expansive margins of the discipline.

Figuring figures

"It matters ... which figures figure figures, which systems systematize systems."[6] As Donna Haraway pointedly distills, works matter and works shape our perception of the world. For landscape architects, the work of figuring the landscape, of collaboratively creating the conditions for future systems of use, production, and maintenance, is a daily engagement in the act of culturally conceptualizing our relationship to place, land, and biotic communities. Referring to epochal shifts, Haraway asks, "when do changes in degree become changes in kind?"[7] This book considers the changes in degree of agriculture as a design practice across the Enlightenment and Modern periods into contemporary practice, and proposes that while normative landscape architectural practice may have experienced a change in kind over that period, from a deep integration of design and agriculture to a rift between the two, there has long been a critical *arrière-garde* practice of integrating agriculture which is regaining prominence in the current day. While we are not at a point where farmscapes are a norm or where agriculture is a normative concern in most landscape architectural projects, we have certainly shifted the degree to which landscape architects consider food systems and integrate food production in their projects.

Farmscape resituates agriculture as a design practice with material, formal, cultural and environmental implications, and proposes lessons for contemporary landscape architects who are interested in integrating agriculture into their practice. The case studies that follow describe the history of agriculture within landscape architecture and reveal the diversity of current design practices that use the rhythms and forms of agriculture to create productive farms that are also sites of beauty, community, ecological conservation, remediation, and pleasure.

Agricultural processes, technologies, and cycles have long shaped landscape architectural projects, with roots in the ornamented farm of the eighteenth century and Frederick Law Olmsted's nineteenth-century scientific farming experiments on designed estates in New England and elsewhere. Some contemporary design firms, such as Nelson Byrd Woltz's conservation agriculture studio, seek to integrate farming practices within multifunctional design and to use design as a tool to connect society to the nutritional, economic, social, ecological, and aesthetic implications of food production. But contemporary design practice largely reflects the cultural separation of most people's quotidian landscape from the landscapes of food production. Reintegrating food production with domestic, educational, and recreational landscapes is critical in light of contemporary questions of food security and ecological health. We cannot understand or care about that which we cannot see.

While *Farmscape* considers site-scale designs, the significance of these projects can best be understood within a context of changing agriculture that is global in scope and impact. While global food markets provide stability and resilience to local food supplies, that system faces increasing stresses. The world's population has doubled since the 1960s, approaching 7.5 billion people and with a projected 9.5 billion by 2050.[8] And while the world produces over 2,900 daily calories per capita, that food is unequally distributed, leaving 821 million people, over 10 percent of the world's population, chronically undernourished.

World populations continue to shift towards urban centers, with over 55 percent of people living in cities in 2016. This leaves fewer people to raise crops and livestock in rural areas, and also means most people have little to no daily exposure to agricultural systems. Responding to efficiencies of labor and the optimization of global markets, increasingly mechanized farms tend to contribute to regional monocultures. Half of the world's calories are drawn from three plants: rice, maize, and wheat. This plantation approach to food production leaves the food supply vulnerable, and reduces local and global biodiversity, impacting both local habitat and regional migration capacity. Donna Haraway, Anna Tsing, and others have described this biotic reduction as the Plantationocene, a long-spanning era of global exchange of people, plants and animals, optimizing resource extraction to local soil, climate, and labor conditions.[9] Tsing argues that this approach has led to a near total loss of refugia, places where diverse populations of plants and animals coexist and can reconstitute populations after stresses.[10] While these systems and impacts are regional and global, site-scale responses can provide stepping stones and biodiverse refugia for reworlding.

And agricultural systems are deeply enmeshed in a climate-change feedback loop. Globally, one-third of land is in agricultural production – crops, pasture, or meadow – or related land uses. This varies regionally; in Asia, the amount is over 50 percent, while it is less than 25 percent in Europe. Agriculture and related land uses contribute a quarter of the world's greenhouse gas emissions, with China, India, Brazil, and the United States alone contributing half of the global agricultural greenhouse gases. Climate variability stresses the global food supply system through floods, storms, droughts, extreme temperatures, and unpredictable seasonal variabilities. Extreme climate events have more than doubled since 1990, when there were about one hundred such events annually. For the past decade, that number has been at or above 200, with 275 events in 2007, a disturbing watermark. These events endanger the food supply system, risking the amount of food produced, our access to and ability to distribute that food, and the safety of the food distributed.[11]

These stresses to the food system also stress the local environment. Seventy percent of the world's freshwater is used in agriculture, a nearly seven-fold increase between 1900 and 2016. While this ensures more stable and higher yields, it also decreases water available for human and environmental use. And as noted above, vast swaths of monocrop plantations decrease animals' capacity for seasonal migration. Without adequate food supplies along their migratory routes, birds, bees, butterflies, and other species can't make their seasonal journeys, putting them and the food supply they pollinate at risk.

Responding to this global context requires a variety of scales and modes of agriculture, some large-scale and global, some small-scale and regional or local. Judith Carney has noted the role agriculture long played as the "connective tissue" "linking culture to environment, cultural identity to food."[12] This book focuses on the potential of individual farms, rather than agricultural regions or regional policies, to re-center agriculture on local communities of plants, people, and other animals. Seven of the case studies have explicit scientific agricultural experimentation, ecological restoration, and monitoring as a goal, and the chapters describe some of the potentials and limitations of a site-scale design, ranging from less than 10 to 2,500 acres, to effect a positive impact on wildlife, soils, microclimate, groundwater and surface water systems.

Themes in the case studies

We selected the case studies that follow to highlight a range of themes that recur in farmscape design across several centuries, teasing out agriculture's "connective tissue" between nature and culture. An early and often recurring theme is the connection between nature and health, the Arcadian ideal of restorative rural lands and the wholesome, healthy, and moralizing activities that occur there. A second, closely linked theme is aesthetics and the aestheticization of farm forms, textures, and materials, seen most strongly in the *ferme ornée*, an idea that resurfaces across centuries. Agriculture as a building block of urban form is a third strong theme, expressed in this book in commercial, communal, and individual agricultural neighborhoods or cities. Agriculture as a way of understanding our place and way in the world is a fourth theme, illustrated by the case studies through the Renaissance concept of three natures, with agriculture mediating between wilderness and garden design; through a mechanistic understanding of the world exemplified through scientific agriculture; and through a holistic or ecological ideology described variously as ecological, conservation, or restoration agriculture. And a final theme we wanted to explore was the idea of agriculture as a cultural repository, a way of preserving, in Judith Carney's words, "distinct repositories of knowledge transmitted through practices and technologies to make nature yield… indigenous knowledge systems [that] link … food to cultural identity."[13] Several of the case studies intentionally use, highlight, and transmit regional agricultural practices, combining cultural stewardship with land stewardship.

In many of the earlier case studies, the designers were farmers in some manner and often offered practical advice as well as philosophical, aesthetic, or ideological guidance. James Madison linked his scientific agriculture experimentation to his political philosophy and corresponded globally with other farmers seeking to increase crop yields and improve soils. Frederick Law Olmsted began his career as a farmer, and many of his projects linked crop production to public health. Leberecht Migge connected individual food production to urban and national planning efforts and to economic self-sufficiency. And Martha Brookes Hutcheson used her farm as a praxis exploring women's agency in the labor market. And while practicing farmers are rare today in landscape architecture, some contemporary designers grew up on or around farms. Konjian Yu notes, "My first teacher was my father, a farmer. I was born and raised on a farm and that is a most influential fact because I was able to touch the ground, I know how water flows, how rice grows and so on."[14] Thomas Woltz also grew up on a productive farm, where "the actions and activities of any season had long-term repercussions on the land; the land would remember the quality of the care. And that is central to our practice as landscape architects. Our works are interventions, and our actions this season will reward us or be a burden for years to come."[15] And yet, it is more common in the current day that designers are not farmers, but are part of a large team, combining expertise and melding values to set down forms, but also and more importantly to catalyze processes.

Contemporary designers rely on agricultural, economic, and ecological consultants to propose future conditions at the farmscape, and rely on managers to maintain both the forms and the processes over seasons and years. The team must coalesce around common nutritional, economic, and cultural goals, and must perform and maintain those goals spatially and temporally. This brings to the fore and problematizes the issue of maintenance. To steward and maintain abundance – abundant crops, soils, clean water, microbiota and biotic refugia – relies on a constant reiteration of values at different temporal scales. Crop production iterates seasonally to annually; clean water production operates on an annual to decades scale; forestry iterates at the scale of a generation. Agriculture highlights a central concern and condition of landscape architecture: the choreography of figuring multiple figures and systematizing multiple systems across scales and time frames, the nature of landscapes as synchronic assemblages at a moment in time, always becoming something else. Thinking like a farmer, designing with agriculture, requires collaboration and shared values, as landowners and farmers maintain and steward the farmscape for years, decades, generations.

At this moment of climate change and environmental and social uncertainty, landscape architecture is a discipline in transition, yet it is well suited to propose and choreograph local, resonant connections to the landscapes that sustain culture and the cultural practices that sustain landscapes. The case studies presented here reveal the opportunities and constraints of site-scale design, to deeply engage in the aesthetic debates of the discipline, embrace the technological hope of the early twentieth century, adapt to scientific advances, and create a terrain for social progress.

Notes

1 Staice A. Townsend, "Symbolic Discourses: The Influence of Denis Cosgrove in the Field of Geography," *California Geographer* 54 (2015): 63.
2 Denis E. Cosgrove, *Social Formation and Symbolic Landscape* (Madison: University of Wisconsin Press, 1998), 35; D. W. Meinig, John Brinkerhoff Jackson, *The Interpretation of Ordinary Landscapes: Geographical Essays* (New York: Oxford University Press, 1979), 288–289.
3 www.agnesdenesstudio.com/works7.html, accessed May 5, 2019.
4 N. Claire Napawan, Stacie A. Townsend, "The Landscape of Urban Agriculture in California's Capital," *Landscape Research* 41, no. 7 (2016): 781.
5 Cf. Judith Anger et al., *Edible Cities* (2012), Carey Clouse, *Farming Cuba* (2014), Jennifer Cockrall-King, *Food and the City* (2012), Mark Grogolewski et al., *Carrot City* (2011), Jeffrey Hou et al., *Greening Cities, Growing Communities* (2009), Darrin Nordahl, *Public Produce* (2009), André Viljoen (ed.), *CPULs: Continuously Productive Urban Landscapes* (2005), and many more.
6 Donna Haraway, "Anthropocene, Capitalocene, Plantationocene, Chthulucene: Making Kin," *Environmental Humanities* 6 (2015): 160.
7 Ibid., 159.
8 Unless otherwise noted, data in this section is from: FAO, *World Food and Agriculture Statistical Pocketbook 2018* (Rome, 2018). Population projections from http://population.un.org
9 D. Haraway, N. Ishikawa, Scott F. Gilbert, K. Olwig, A. L. Tsing, and N. Bubandt, 2016, "Anthropologists Are Talking – About the Anthropocene," *Ethnos: Journal of Anthropology* 81, no. 3 (2016): 535–564.
10 Haraway, "Making Kin," 159.
11 Climate change data is from FAO, IFAD, UNICEF, WFP, and WHO, *The State of Food Security and Nutrition in the World 2018. Building climate resilience for food security and nutrition* (Rome, 2018).
12 Judith A. Carney, *Black Rice: The African Origins of Rice Cultivation in the Americas* (Cambridge, MA: Harvard University Press, 2001), 136.
13 Ibid., 5.
14 Kongjian Yu, interviewed by Udo Weilacher, Beijing, China, October 2016, accessed October 15, 2018, www.turenscape.com
15 Thomas Woltz, communication with Roxi Thoren, Eugene, OR, May 2019.

Woburn Farm

Surrey County, United Kingdom

Philip Southcote, c. 1735

0
100
200 ft

In the eighteenth century, garden design in Britain was turning from the influence of the geometric gardens of France and Holland towards a style that imitated the forms found in nature: drifts of vegetation, undulating topography, and serpentine rivers. The *ferme ornée*, or ornamented farm, was one manifestation of this new gardening style and Woburn Farm, west of London, is often described as the prototype. It was designed by Philip Southcote, who is credited with introducing both the term and the aesthetic to England where it became a popular form of estate design. The *ferme ornée* integrated two realms that were previously kept separate in gentlemen's country estates: the park or pleasure ground and the profitable, productive farm. In the *ferme ornée,* highly ornamented walking and riding paths wove across the entire property, providing visitors with views and passage around and through the farm.

Joseph Addison, in a 1712 essay in *The Spectator*, described the practice of the *ferme ornée*, writing,

> why may not a whole estate be thrown into a kind of garden by frequent plantations, that may turn as much to the profit as the pleasure of the owner?... Fields of corn make a pleasant prospect, and if the walks were a little taken care of ... if the natural embroidery of the meadows were helped and improved by some small additions of art, and the several rows of hedges set off by trees and flowers ... a man might make a pretty landscape of his own possessions.[1]

Stephen Switzer, in *Ichnographia Rustica* (1715), reiterated the theme of profit and pleasure, writing that, "By mixing the useful and profitable Parts of Gardening with the pleasurable in the Interior Parts ... and Paddocks, obscure Enclosures, etc. in the Outward: My Designs are thereby vastly enlarged and both Profit and Pleasure may be said to be agreeably mix'd together."[2] Switzer drew on the classical poet Horace to define three key aspects of this style of garden design: *utile dulci*, or the combination of cultivation and pleasure; *ingentia rura*, taking an expansive view of design, and designing the whole property, not just pleasure gardens distinct from the farm areas; and *simplex munditiis*, or simplicity and noble elegance.[3] These elements combine to describe the *ferme ornée* in which the recreational portions of a country estate are integrated into the farm's livestock pastures, hay meadows, and crop fields.

In the *ferme ornée*, cultivated lands were an integral element of garden design and vice versa. Highly ornamental and lavishly planted linear gardens circumambulated pastures and fields. Designers carefully staged views from the paths of the strolling garden to the farm to create scenes that evoked landscape paintings. Designers and visitors understood these views and the life they represented to be physically restorative and emotionally inspiring. The gardens created bucolic scenes like those painted by Claude Lorrain and Nicolas Poussin, whose scenes of idle merriment and joy portrayed shepherds in a pure, idyllic life, separate from the taints of the city, where "all is lovely – all amiable – all is amenity

2.1
Philip Southcote's Woburn Farm, after Luke Sullivan, c. 1759. A walk led visitors through the farm where crops, livestock, and labor were displayed and aestheticized.

and repose; the calm sunshine of the heart."[4] This painterly approach, of course, masked the labor of the working farm, presenting the agricultural landscape and the work that occurred there as a soothing view to be consumed for pleasure. (Fig 2.1)

By the mid-eighteenth century in Britain, this bucolic approach was well established in the "new" garden design, design based on natural forms rather than geometric principles: Batty Langley, in *New Principles of Gardening* (1728), stated that, "the End and Design of a good Garden is to be both profitable and delightful."[5] By the end of the century, Horace Walpole, in his highly influential *Essay On Modern Gardening* (1771), described three types of modern, naturalistic gardens: "the garden that connects itself with a park, ... the ornamented farm, and ... the forest or savage garden."[6] He noted William Kent as the author of the first, and Philip Southcote as the founder of the second, the *ferme ornée*.

Southcote's Woburn Farm was well known in its era, and its forms and plantings influenced the design of other British estates. Southcote's design principles were described in many essays and books, and tourists frequently visited the farm to see the innovative layout and planting scheme.[7] And the farm and others like it influenced American as well as British garden design. Woburn Farm was vividly described in Thomas Whatley's *Observations on Modern Gardening* (1770), which Thomas Jefferson and John Adams carried with them as they toured British gardens in 1786. The two visited Southcote's estate, Jefferson noting that, "all are

2.2
View in the Grounds of Woburn Farm, Charles Stirling, c. 1815. The linear walk staged views of the farm from defined vantage points.

intermixed, the pleasure garden being merely a highly ornamented walk through and round the divisions of the farm and kitchen garden."[8] (Fig 2.2)

Both Thomas Jefferson's Monticello and James Madison's Montpelier have aspects of a *ferme ornée*. In 1807, Jefferson proposed adding "a winding walk surrounding the lawn before the house, with a narrow border of flowers on each side ... the hollows of the walk would give room for oval beds of flowering shrubs."[9] Monticello is laid out with four connected circular drives dividing the plantation into concentric zones of lawn; grove; orchard, vineyard, and vegetable plots; and crop fields, pastures, deer park, and woodlot. The house and lawn sit at the peak of the mountain, looking out over the farm districts below.[10]

Philip Southcote was part of a group of designers radically changing British garden design in the eighteenth century. Alexander Pope and William Kent "practiced painting in gardening," with Kent credited for introducing the new "natural taste" in garden design, and Lord Petre "carried it farther than either of them."[11] Southcote was friends with both Pope and Kent, and considered himself a pupil of the eighth Lord Petre, who was one of the finest botanists of his time, with an extraordinary collection of exotic and regional trees, shrubs, and plants,[12] many likely from John Bartram's expeditions in America, which Petre helped to

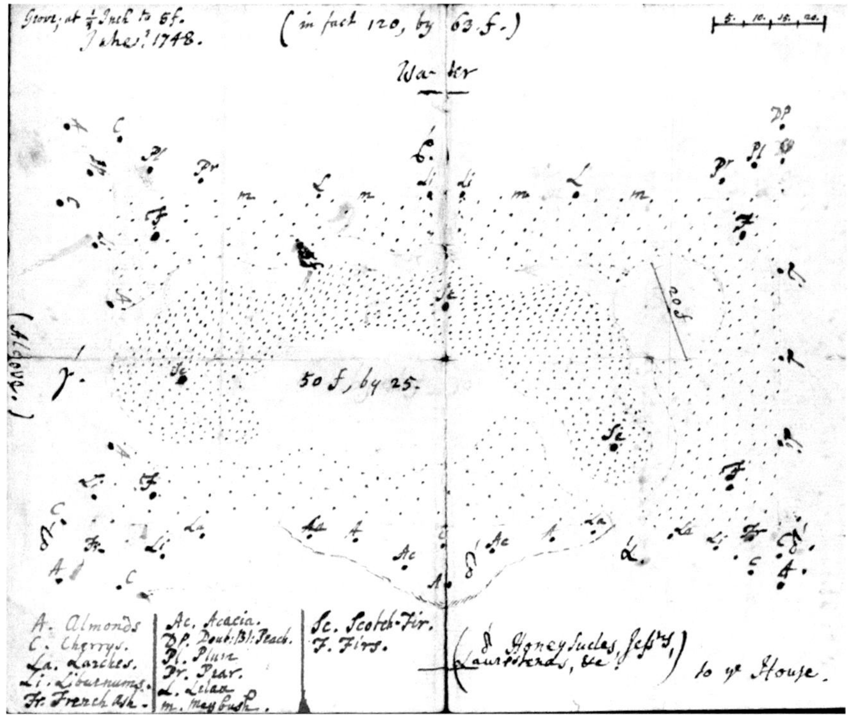

2.3
Plan of a grove, Joseph Spence, c. 1760. Spence used a painterly approach in this composition, framing darker evergreen trees with lighter, fine-textured, and flowering trees.

finance.[13] Southcote described him as, "a nursery-man … [who] understood the colors of every tree, and always considered how he placed them by one another."[14] From Petre, Southcote developed a horticultural approach to garden design that considered in particular the texture and color of trees and shrubs across the year; Petre's gardening papers included a list of trees ordered by foliage color, running from weeping willow to sycamore, titled "Shades of Green; deeper & deeper."[15] (Fig 2.3)

Eighteenth-century English garden design was based in ideas of painterly composition, with a premium on variety, surprise, and delight. Pope neatly summed the aims of the style, "He gains all Ends, who pleasingly confounds, / Surprises, varies, and conceals the bounds."[16] And the author Joseph Spence noted that, "All the beauties of gardening might be comprehended in one word, variety."[17] While William Kent's version of the English garden drew on the Elysian, Classical paradise imagery of Claude Lorrain, with soft, muted colors, Philip Southcote preferred an Arcadian mode, referencing the pastoral countryside through bright, joyful, floral designs. He "prevailed on Kent to resume flowers in the natural way of gardening,"[18] and Southcote's innovations in the English garden style included the extensive and dense use of colorful and fragrant flowers and the creation of an ornamented peripheral walk.[19]

At Woburn Farm, Southcote tested and developed the natural style of gardening. Like Kent and Pope, he believed that gardening was a form of painting, and a good garden design should include one or more principle views, composed

with consideration "of perspective, prospect, distancing, and attracting,"[20] and using clumps of trees, "like the groups in pictures,"[21] arranged to draw the eye from the foreground, toward a "distant clump, building, or view."[22] (Fig 2.4) Serpentine paths created ever-changing views; garden follies surprised and delighted the visitor; and a range of exotic and local plants provided an ever-shifting plant palette. Visual contrast added to the sense of variety; garden designers manipulated light and dark through tree selection, thick and thin groves, and openings in woods. But always, the effect should be natural. "Wherever art is easily discerned by the eye," Southcote said, "the gardener has failed in his execution."[23] (Fig 2.5)

2.4 (page 16–17)
View of Chertsey Bridge from Wooburn Farm, Joseph Stadler after Joseph Farington, 1796. Clumps of trees were planted to draw the eye from the foreground to the middle ground of the farm and distant view of the river and bridge.

Soon after Southcote married Ann, Duchess of Cleveland, in 1732, the couple purchased Woburn Farm as their country seat and Southcote began designing the property. A long hill running east–west bisects the property, with flat lands to the north and south. (Fig 2.6) "All my design at first was to have a garden on the middle high ground and a walk all round my farm, for convenience as well as pleasure," he said.[24] He designed the 150-acre property to include thirty-five acres planted as a pleasure garden, with trees, shrubs, and herbaceous perennials; the remainder was farmland, with two-thirds in pasture and one-third, or about forty acres, in crops.

Whately described the farm in 1770; the pleasure garden connected all parts of the property through a linear walk that encircled the pastures, primarily in the north, and the meadows and crop fields, primarily to the south. "[T]his walk is properly a garden; all within it is farm; the whole lies on the two sides of a hill, and on a flat at the foot of it; the flat is divided into cornfields; the pastures occupy the hill; they are surrounded by the walk, and crossed by a communication carried along the brow, which is also richly dressed, and which divides them into two lawns, each completely encompassed with garden."[25] The walk was typically a serpentine sand or gravel path weaving close to and away from a planted hedgerow filled with "woodbine, jessamine, and every odiferous plant … they replenish the air with their perfumes, and every gale is full of fragrancy."[26] On the pasture side, clumps of evergreens, open tree plantations, thickets of shrubs, or flower beds led the visitor's eye towards pastoral scenes, where "the lowings of the herds, the bleating of the sheep, and the tinklings of the bell-wether, resound thro' all the plantations; even the clucking of poultry is not omitted."[27] In crop areas, the path was mown rather than sand or gravel, with only a hedgerow enhanced by flowering shrubs rather than the more extensive flowering perennial plantings along the pastures.

Southcote's linear garden planting was recorded by Spence; his sketch "after Mr. Southcote's Manner," shows an existing bounding hedgerow, with new plantings layered alongside. First a five-foot planting strip contained three layers of trees and shrubs, with a row of trees such as chestnut, hornbeam, and beech underplanted with a row of flowering trees and shrubs such as lilac, laburnum, and broom. This shrub layer was adjacent to a row of smaller flowering shrubs such as rose, laurel, and sweet briar. Between this densely planted tree-and-shrub

Drawn from Nature & on Stone by C. Stirling

Printed by C. Hullmandel.

THE GROUNDS OF WOBURN FROM THE BOURN.

2.5
The Grounds of Woburn from the Bourne, Charles Stirling, c. 1815. The ridge was planted in natural-seeming woods, accentuating the topography.

2.6
Southcote's Woburn Farm is visible in this detail of *A Topographical Map of the County of Surrey*, John Rocque, 1775. The linear walk is noted on the western and northern edges.

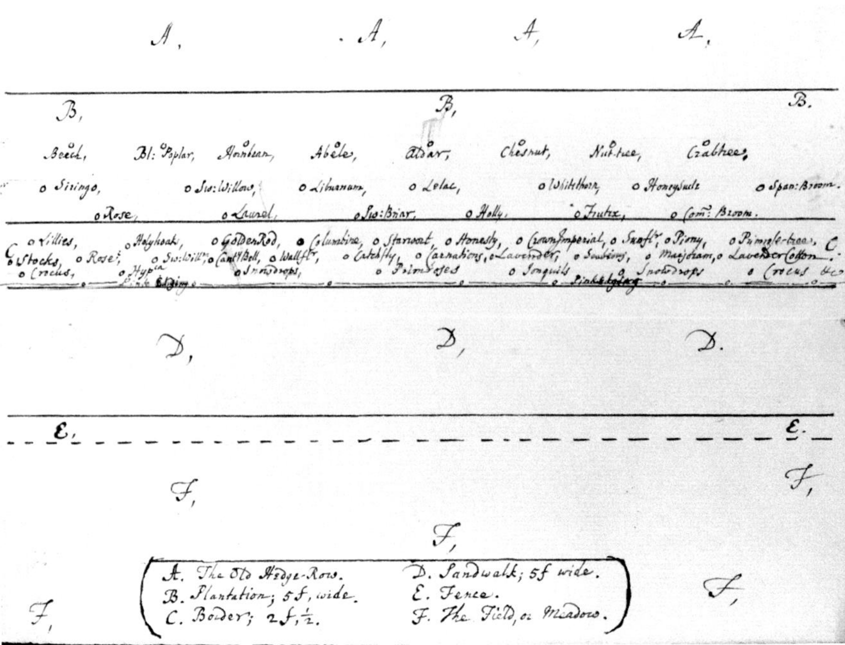

2.7
Order of planting after Mr. Southcote's manner, Joseph Spence, c. 1760. The plantings along the path were intensely dense.

layer and the path was a two-foot perennial border, similarly filled with flowering plants such as lily, stock, and lavender, with smaller plants such as snowdrops and primroses adjacent to the path. Many of these flowers were heavily scented, providing both visual and olfactory delight. (Fig 2.7)

The *ferme ornée* at Woburn Farm was also a site of material exchange. The decorative and exotic plants of the pleasure garden were used throughout the cultivated landscape, and those of the farm were brought in to the domestic grounds, including an extensive potager close to the house. Whately described the lush planting scheme where, "in every corner, or vacant space, is a rosary, a close or an open clump, or a bed of flowers: but if the parterre has been rifled for the embellishment of the fields, the country has on the other hand been searched for plants new in a garden; and the shrubs and flowers which used to be deemed peculiar to the one, have been liberally transferred to the other."[28] While Whately does not specify what plants were transferred from the country to the garden, it is clear that Southcote was using agrarian species decoratively.

To help create primary and secondary views, painterly moments within the farm, Southcote located several buildings, bridges, and follies that formed focal points or moments of surprise on the walk. John Parnell, visiting in 1763, described the "new-contrived" ruin of a church, a little Chinese bridge, a thatched Gothic hut, a Gothic seat set in a recess, a "Rustic cell" and several other elements – bridges, pavilions, grottos, temples.[29] (Fig 2.8) The most prominent was an octagon pavilion at the north end of the hill, overlooking the Chertsey Mead below and the Thames River beyond. A long allée led along the ridge to the pavilion,

2.8
The Ruin, in the Grounds of Woburn, Charles Stirling, c. 1815. Structures and follies created focal points and scenes throughout the farm.

with the trees closer together at the pavilion end to create a forced perspective that extended the apparent length of the so-called Long Walk. (Fig 2.9) Southcote described this distancing as one of the key elements of "painting in gardening," noting that, "by distancing you may make an object look three times as far off as it is. This is done by narrowing the plantation gradually on each side, almost to a point at last."[30] Some of the architectural features were designed by William Kent, and as a group, they reflected the eclectic taste of the era, combining elements from gothic, medieval, neo-Palladian, and Chinese designs.

As designed by Southcote, the *ferme ornée* was expensive to maintain.[31] The horticultural path contained dense, lush plantings of native and exotic species that required pruning, weeding, staking, and deadheading throughout the year. But in varied form, the ornamented farm has had a long shadow. At Woburn Farm, Southcote used a collage approach to overlap and integrate the previously separate domains of the country seat: the pleasure gardens and the productive landscape. Where previous garden design theory had separated the realms of the wild, the cultivated, and the garden, the *ferme ornée* melded second and third nature, with

Drawn from Nature & on Stone by C Stirling. *Printed by C Hullmandel*

THE LONG WALK,

in the Grounds of Woburn.

2.9
The Long Walk, in the Grounds of Woburn, Charles Stirling, c. 1815. Forced perspective accentuated the length of the allée along the central ridge.

two lasting effects. Drawing on the contemporary tradition of pastoral landscape painting, the *ferme ornée* framed the agrarian landscape as a physically, emotionally, and spiritually restorative environment to be included in garden design. And the extension of pleasure gardens into that landscape created a new garden type, the linear park, which, often hybridized with boulevard design, continues to be an important garden type into the twenty-first century.

The nineteenth-century horticulturalist, designer, and tastemaker Andrew Jackson Downing popularized the idea of the *ferme ornée* in the United States. He believed that the United States was a land of individual opportunity and freedom from want, and that this ideology was uniquely expressed through small-scale rural landownership. He wrote *A Treatise on the Theory and Practice of Landscape Gardening* to provide guidance for individuals of "good taste" to design and embellish their rural farms, through the use of tree plantations to frame views, neat and embellished meadows, and roads and paths bordered by lush plantings.[32] Downing and his theories had a lasting influence; after his early death, his business partner Calvert Vaux partnered with Frederick Law Olmsted to enter the competition for Central Park, and in his long career, Olmsted designed estates, parks, and public grounds in the *ferme ornée* style. The idea of a restorative countryside continues into the twenty-first century, although the focus in nineteenth- and twentieth-century works by Olmsted and others tended to focus on the impacts on physical and mental health, rather than on moral or aesthetic development. And increasingly in the twentieth and twenty-first centuries, agricultural land, the once restorative countryside, is perceived as itself damaged and in need of restoration, as seen in later chapters.

Notes

1 Donald Bond (ed.), *The Spectator*, 5 vols (Oxford: Clarendon Press, 1965), III, Paper No. 414 (June 25, 1712): 552.
2 Stephen Switzer, *Ichnographia Rustica* (London: D. Brown, 1715), xvii.
3 Ibid., xvii.
4 R. B. Beckett, *John Constable's Discourses*, (Suffolk Records Society, 1907), 52–53.
5 Batty Langley, *New Principles of Gardening* (London: A. Bettesworth et al., 1728), 193.
6 Horace Walpole, *Essay On Modern Gardening* (Strawberry Hill: T. Kirgate, 1771), 75.
7 For examples, see R. W. King, "The *ferme ornée*: Philip Southcote and Woburn Farm," *Garden History*, 2/3 (1974): 47–50.
8 Thomas Jefferson, "Notes of a Tour of English Gardens, [April 2–14] 1786," Founders Online, National Archives, last modified March 30, 2017, accessed July 20, 2018, http://founders.archives.gov/documents/Jefferson/01-09-02-0328.
9 Rudy J. Favretti, "Thomas Jefferson's 'Ferme Ornée' at Monticello," *Proceedings of the American Antiquarian Society* 103 (1993): 21
10 Ibid., 20.
11 Joseph Spence, Samuel Weller Springer, *Anecdotes, observations and characters of books and men collected from the conversation of Mr. Pope and other eminent persons of his time* (Carbondale, IL: Southern Illinois University Press, 1964), 423, 250.

12 Ibid., 423.
13 King, "The *ferme ornée*," 42.
14 Spence, *Anecdotes*, 424.
15 Ibid., 424.
16 Ibid., 650.
17 Ibid., 251.
18 Ibid., 425.
19 King, "The *ferme ornée*," 54.
20 Spence, *Anecdotes*, 425.
21 Ibid., 252.
22 Ibid., 426.
23 Ibid., 647.
24 Ibid., 424.
25 Thomas Whately, *Observations on Modern Gardening* (London: T. Payne, 1770), 177–178.
26 Ibid., 179.
27 Ibid., 181.
28 Ibid., 180.
29 J. Sambrook, "Wooburn Farm in the 1760s," *Garden History* 7, no. 2 (1979): 83–84.
30 Spence, *Anecdotes*, 425.
31 King, "The *ferme ornée*," 56.
32 Andrew Jackson Downing, *A Treatise on the Theory and Practice of Landscape Gardening, Adapted to North America* (New York: Wiley and Putnam, 1841), 49, 74–76, 389.

Middleton Place

Dorchester County, South Carolina

Unknown, c. 1740–1750

0
0.5
1 mile

3.1
Plan of Middleton Place plantation, Frederick I. Smith, 1885. The rice fields are visible to the west and the residence is to the east overlooking the Ashley River.

From 1750 to 1860, Middleton Place, near Charleston, South Carolina, was understood as the corporate headquarters for the vast Middleton rice and cotton production, and symbolized to visitors the wealth, sophistication, and stability of the family's enterprise. Although the plantation appears to be divided into conceptually clear realms of garden, agriculture, and wilderness, the three realms overlap and comingle. Landscape histories of the plantation have tended to focus on the Le Notre-inspired geometric gardens and the Baroque terraces stepping down from the house to the Ashley River that use a nearly mile-long bend of the Ashley as a water axis at the scale of Vaux-le-Vicomte. But the infrastructure of rice production is essential to understanding this landscape, providing the technology and labor that made it possible while mediating between the gardens and the enclosing rivers, swamps, and forest.

By 1800, the plantation spread over 1,600 acres, bounded by the Ashley River on the east and the Stono River canal on the west.[1] The house and gardens sit on a low bluff twenty feet above the Ashley; the bluff and long axis of the river gave the house a sweeping view that was unparalleled in the South Carolina Lowcountry. In the flat marshes to the west, two dendritic systems meet, one draining northeast to the Ashley, and one draining southwest to the Stono River. This western area is Horse Savannah, a broad, flat, wooded swamp that was well suited to growing rice. (Fig 3.1)

Over its centuries as a rice plantation, Middleton Place followed technological trends in the Lowcountry, moving through three phases of rice production. Providence production, in use from the introduction of rice culture in the Carolina colony around 1690, depended on rainfall for water supply and relied on manual labor for weeding the rice. This system was labor-intensive and prone to crop failures, and was rapidly replaced by reservoir culture. This second phase of rice production used a complex system of dams, dykes, canals, trunk lines, and gates to create rice fields that could be irrigated and flooded as needed from reservoirs that stored water from both rainfall and creek flow. With correct management, weeds could be killed through periodic floods during the growing season, reducing the need for manual weeding and vastly increasing the profits from rice. While most plantations fronted on rivers, these irrigated fields tended to be in the inland swamps, marshes, and savannahs at the "back" of the plantation, and this was the case at Middleton Place. The formal gardens and the house faced the Ashley, while large rice fields were created in Horse Savannah. This inland swamp culture remained the dominant rice production method until around the American Revolution, when tidal culture became the norm.[2] By turning tidal river marshes into rice fields, plantation workers could use the action of the tides to operate flood gates, eliminating the need for manual operation of irrigation trunks, once again increasing the profit from rice production.[3] In 1764, Henry Middleton purchased grants for the marsh lands in front of Middleton Place, as well as those across the Ashley in front of three neighboring plantations; at least one of those properties was immediately "diked, reclaimed and brought under cultivation for rice as annexed to Middleton Place."[4] Like other plantations, Middleton Place

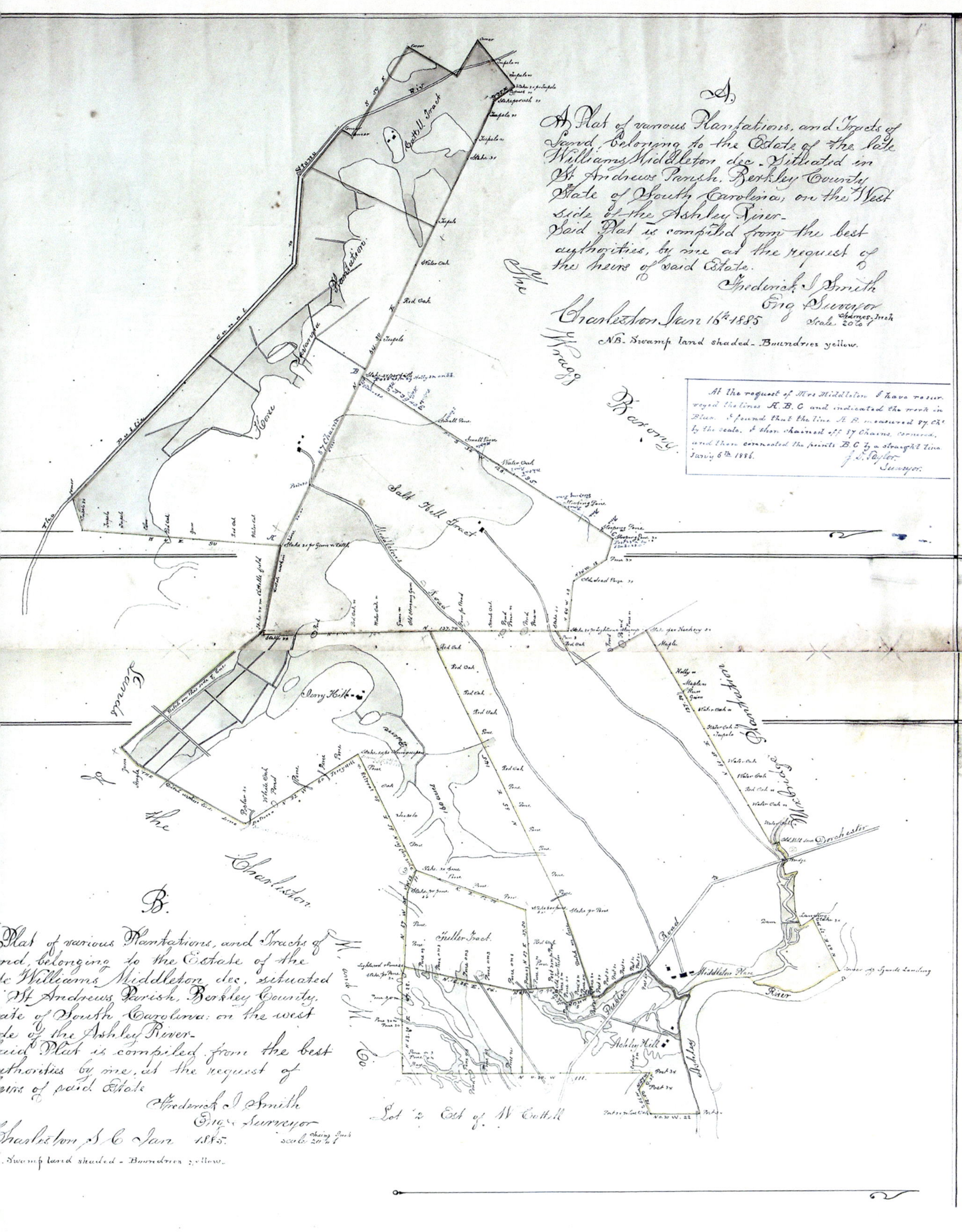
A.
A Plat of various Plantations, and Tracts of
Land, belonging to the Estate of the late
Williams Middleton dec. Situated in
St Andrews Parish, Berkley County
State of South Carolina, on the West
side of the Ashley River.
Said Plat is compiled from the best
authorities, by me at the request of
the heirs of said Estate.
Frederick J. Smith
Eng & Surveyor
Charleston Jan 16th 1885
Scale Chaines Inch 20 to 1
NB. Swamp land shaded - Boundries yellow.
At the request of Mrs Middleton I have resurveyed the lines A. B. C and indicated the work in Blue. I found that the line A. B measured 87 Chs by the scale. I then chained off 87 Chains, cornered, and then connected the points B. C by a straight line
Jany 6th 1886.
J. S. Taylor
Surveyor
Cattell Tract
Stono River
Canal
Horse Savanna Plantation
The Wragg Barony
Salt Hill Tract
Middleton's Road
Dorry Hill
Fuller Tract
Dorchester
Woodbridge Plantation
Middleton Place
Ashley River
Public Road
Ashley Hill
Lot 2 Est of W Cattell
B.
Plat of various Plantations, and Tracts of
nd, belonging to the Estate of the
e Williams Middleton, dec, situated
St Andrews Parish, Berkley County,
ate of South Carolina: on the west
de of the Ashley River.
aid Plat is compiled from the best
thorities by me, at the request of
eirs of said Estate
Frederick J. Smith
Eng & Surveyor
Charleston, S C Jan 1885.
scale Chains Inch 20 to 1
Swamp land shaded - Boundries yellow.

3.2
Strong geometric forms organize the formal gardens.

3.3
The Middleton Oak, seen in 1938, anchors one corner of the rose garden.

began cultivating both the inland swamps and the river marshes of the property relatively early, although the Ashley fields at Middleton Place were probably not tidal culture; an 1857 article notes that "The fields on the western bank were flooded by the ornamental waters of the garden, and from Middleton Creek."[5]

This region was the Rice Kingdom, and in the years before the American Revolution, Charleston was the richest city in British Colonial America and home to the nine wealthiest colonial men.[6] The Middleton family accumulated a vast fortune from their rice plantations; Henry Middleton owned over 50,000 acres across twenty plantations, and his great-grandson Williams Middleton recorded rice sales in fiscal year 1839–40 of just under $400,000 ($11.3 million in 2014 dollars).[7] Middleton Place was not their most productive plantation, but it was their preferred family seat for four generations, and was the heart of a rice empire.

The gardens and rice fields at Middleton Place use distinct structuring systems, creating two formally opposed districts on the property, clearly distinguishing between the productive and aesthetic realms. The gardens impose rational form on the landscape, pure geometry ordering a context perceived as unruly, while the rice fields were inserted into the marsh geomorphology, their forms reflecting topography and the flow of water. (Fig 3.2) With designs from an unknown English garden architect and the off-season labor of fifty enslaved workers, Henry Middleton had the banks of the Ashley River sculpted into twelve miles of Baroque terraces topped with Anglo-Dutch gardens popular in the Stuart reigns.[8] The designer used a tartan grid to organize lawns, parterres, water elements and a bosquet, and used a 45-degree angle to soften the terraced edge. The gardens use some features of the existing landscape as their point of departure – the axis and bend of the river, and apparently the location of the Middleton Oak, a tree that would have already been hundreds of years old when the gardens were laid out around 1740. (Fig 3.3) But the primary ordering system is the clear geometry of square and right triangle, and the river's edge was sculpted to that system for a half-mile upstream. Although no physical evidence remains, Middleton family histories describe the regulating lines of the garden continuing

3.4
Plan of Cedar Grove, c. 1811. Reservoirs and rice fields in the middle of the plantation follow the arcing path of a stream.

into long vistas cut into the forest,[9] in keeping with Le Notre-inspired design. River, forest, springs, and earth were made to conform to a geometric overlay.

In the inland swamps, meanwhile, enslaved workers inserted rice terraces into existing natural forms. A 1795 survey of Cedar Grove, a Middleton property on the east bank of the Ashley River, shows irregularly shaped reservoirs and rice terraces following the course of a local stream. (Fig 3.4) An 1863 Union Army map of Charleston shows the same in the inland swamps at Middleton Place: a series of irregular reservoirs and terraces with irrigation trunks leading to a public canal. (Fig. 3.5) While the gardens adapt the landscape to geometry, the rice fields draw their form from natural systems.

The landscape of rice cultivation provides a mediating space between the domestic gardens and the tidal river beyond. (Fig 3.6) The agricultural fields are second nature, nature regulated, cultivated, and in service to culture, mediating between the perfected third nature of the gardens and the wild first nature of the Carolina Lowcountry. These three natures provide a conceptual framework for the relationship between art and nature, one that in 1740 was a well-established basis for garden design and for forming "a landscape divided into territories in each of which the collaborations of the two presiding figures of Art and Nature will be different."[10]

The designer of Middleton Place used this framework, honed through the Renaissance in European gardens, to structure the landscape into a series of

3.5
A detail of *Map of Charleston and its Defenses,* William A. Walker, 1885, with Middleton Place highlighted. Rice fields and the public canal are visible at the bottom of the map.

nested, related, but clearly differentiated realms. While neighboring plantations would have been visible across the Ashley River, the primary visual axis from the house was downstream, through a tidal margin populated by herons and egrets, fish, crabs, and alligators. Here, nature leads the collaboration, with art found in both the beauty and the sublime of a world beyond human control. As early as 1764, the Middletons were growing rice in the marshes directly in front of the plantation as well as those across the river. The rice fields here and in the savannahs were organized on the logic of second nature, of agricultural efficiency. The Carolina task system, a spatial and temporal system of organizing the labor of enslaved workers into discrete tasks to be completed daily, used quarter-acre land units as a basic module of work. The rice fields between Middleton Place and the river would almost certainly have had this modular structure, subdivided into linear trenches and rows of rice. (Fig 3.7) Water from the garden springs could be released into the fields, or water from the river could be let in or out via trunk dams. The fields conformed to the local hydrology, but then were subdivided into regular geometric patterns, visually and philosophically mediating between wilderness and garden and providing an orderly foreground to the plantation for visitors arriving by river. The rice fields clearly played an aesthetic role in the gardens; a Middleton cousin wrote in 1860, "I can imagine how much the fields at the foot of the slopes and terraces are beautified by the green young rice."[11]

On the terraces above, the gardens exhibit the regular geometry and perspectival axes of Baroque garden design. Their clear forms distinguish them from the two zones beyond, establishing art as the leading voice in the dialogue with nature weaving in and responding to the cultural framework. As John Dixon Hunt notes, gardens "represent within their own area that scale of natures;" gardens simultaneously *are* third nature, but they also *represent* first and second nature.[12] Middleton Place was no exception, with a bosquet representing wilderness, and fish ponds and planting beds representing agricultural patterns. While the three realms were visually distinct, they also related to each other through sightlines. The long axis down the Ashley drew the river into the gardens, with the butterfly lakes at the foot of the terraces echoing the water horizon. (Fig 3.8) Sightlines were carved into the surrounding forests, extending the geometry of the garden into the wilderness of wood lot and hunting grove. While no trace of these sightlines has been located, it is likely that they extended to the north and west, and so would have connected the gardens directly to the first nature of the upland woods.

Though formally and operationally distinct, the agricultural landscape at Middleton Place supported the creation of the gardens, providing both technical expertise and economic resources. The gardens and rice fields are hybrid landscapes that reflect the technology transfer occurring in the colonies incorporating European garden design treatises and African rice husbandry techniques. Between 1749 and 1765, over half the enslaved Africans brought to South Carolina were taken from the Windward and Rice Coast of Africa – present-day Senegal to Liberia – a region where rice had been grown for centuries.[13] They brought with them extensive knowledge required for both reservoir and tidal culture rice husbandry, skills that translated to the creation of the terraces and garden. (Fig 3.9) The enslaved workers at Middleton Place knew how to manipulate water, digging canals and building banks to divide the inland swamps into reservoirs and nearly level rice fields; a well-leveled field would have as little as eight inches of drop over a length of 800 feet or more, a slope of less than 0.1 percent.[14] Rice fields were structured by bounding canals and banks, and organized into quarter-acre units of work with smaller drainage ditches, quarter ditches.[15] Workers also built and installed trunks – box-like wooden pipes – with release gates to irrigate fields, and periodically flood and drain them for sprouting, weed control, and supporting the heavy, ripening, seeded stalks. Planter Theodore Ravenel noted that for a typical

3.6 (pages 34–35)
Rice fields would have occupied the middle band of water, mediating between the pleasure gardens visible to the left and the Ashley River.

3.7
The geometric subdivision of rice fields is visible in Alice Ravenel Huger Smith's 1935 *Ready for the Harvest*, from the series "A Carolina Rice Plantation of the Fifties."

plantation, "each acre has about 650 lineal feet of ditch ...; 500 acres would mean 60 miles of ditch."[16]

The gardens are bounded by the same techniques: terraced earthworks and regulated water. The extensive twenty-acre gardens and sixteen-acre lawn were relatively small in comparison to the plantation's 1,300 acres of rice fields and reservoirs. The river terraces are at a grander scale than the pleasure garden, rising twenty feet above the river in six levels, and continuing north along the Ashley for a half-mile, bounding the gardens and, likely, a hunting grove. (Fig. 3.10) Middleton Place had at least two springs, one feeding the two upper rectangular ponds, and one feeding the butterfly lakes; flowing through the ponds, this water was also used to irrigate the rice fields along the river.[17] The 650-foot-long rectangular pool was stocked with fish. The description of the ponds, where "the trout, the bream, the perch, the mormouth, and other members of the finny tribe, are bred and do congregate,"[18] bears a striking resemblance to descriptions of rice fields: "two ponds, at different elevations, with a dam between them, and a trunk, with a stopper, for the occasional discharge of water from the upper into the lower one." The technical knowledge used to create reservoirs and manipulate the flow

3.8
The butterfly lakes and garden terraces, seen in 1938, echo the river and draw the river axis into the garden.

of water to provide a steady source of irrigation for the cash crop of the Carolina colony was also used in the Middleton Place gardens to create pools that reflect light and sky.

Interwoven with that technical skill was the economic and political structure of slavery in South Carolina. The rice fields at Middleton Place and the Middletons' other plantations provided the necessary wealth and labor to construct the gardens, and the social status that allowed or even demanded a political landscape like Middleton Place. The trip from Charleston would have been considerably faster and more comfortable by river than by road. Most guests would have arrived by boat; as they turned a bend in the Ashley, they would see, across a mile-long water axis, the foreground of rice fields, the terraces stepping up from the marshes, topped by the house and its flankers framed in parterres, shrubs, and trees. Boats landed at the edge of the butterfly lakes, and a sloping road allowed carriages to rise to the top of the bluff. The effect must have been dramatic; the terraces and gardens would delight and awe visitors, reminding them of the cultivation, wealth, and power of the family that sculpted a solid, rational Le Notre-style landscape out of mutable, soggy tidal rivers, cypress swamps, and streams.

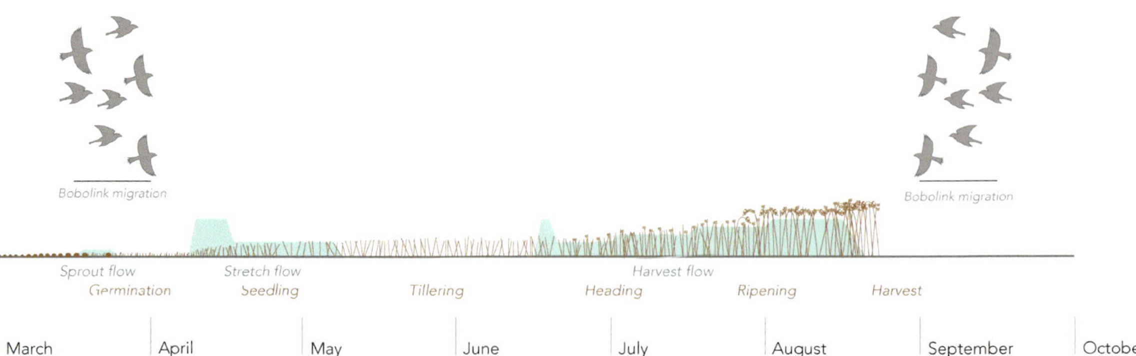

3.9
Coordinating field flooding with tides, rice culture, and the annual migration of rice birds across hundreds of acres of fields required extensive knowledge and skill.

This political landscape returns full circle to the concept of third nature. In the Renaissance, Jacopo Bonfadio correlated first, second, and third nature to the progress of human civilization from "wild, hard people" to "civilized people, gentlemen and *signori*."[19] The Middleton Place gardens, concentrically situated within the territories of agriculture, swamp, and tidal river, adamantly declare a perfection of civilization and gentlemanly mores out of and above the colonial wilderness. From the mutable colonial landscape, through the technology and tactics of plantation agriculture, a rational, and civilized American garden was formed.

Notes

1 See Henry A. M. Smith, "The Ashley River: Its Seats and Settlements," *South Carolina Historical and Genealogical Magazine* 20, no. 2 (1919): 75–122 for a thorough history of the various land grants that eventually comprised Middleton Place from 1741.
2 Richard Dwight Porcher, Jr. and William Robert Judd, *The Market Preparation of Carolina Rice* (Columbia: University of South Carolina Press, 2014), 53.
3 See Porcher and Judd for descriptions of the technology of rice production.
4 Smith, "The Ashley River," 119.
5 Richard Yeadon, byline, *Charleston Daily Courier* (Charleston, SC), April 21, 1857.
6 Porcher and Judd, *Market Preparation*, 3.
7 Information on Henry Middleton from Elise Pinckney, "'Still Mindful of the English Way': 250 Years of Middleton Place on the Ashley," *South Carolina Historical Magazine* 92, no. 3 (1991): 149–171. For information on Williams Middleton, the Middleton papers, University of South Carolina special collections. It is worth noting that calculations of the current value of historic wealth are complex. The $11.3 million is based on a consumer price index comparison, or what the same amount of rice would cost in 2014. In comparison, as a share of the GDP, $400,000 in 1840 corresponds to $4.4 billion in 2014. (Samuel H. Williamson, "Seven Ways to Compute the Relative Value of a U.S. Dollar Amount, 1774 to present," MeasuringWorth, 2018.)
8 Earle S. Draper, "Southern Plantations," *Landscape Architecture* 23, no. 1 (1933): 1–14; Alicia Hopton Middleton, "A Family Record," in *Life in Carolina and New England during the Nineteenth Century*, Alicia Hopton Middleton, ed. (Bristol, RI: Private printing, 1929), 66.

3.10
The garden terraces, photographed c. 1930, rise above the butterfly lakes and would have been capped by the residences.

9 Frances Duncan, "An Old-Time Carolina Garden," *The Century Magazine* 80, no. 6 (1910): 806.
10 John D. Hunt, *Greater Perfections: The Practice of Garden Theory* (Philadelphia: University of Pennsylvania Press, 2000), 40.
11 Henry Middleton to Williams Middleton, 7 May 1860, Williams Middleton papers microfilm, South Caroliniana archives, University of South Carolina, Columbia, SC.
12 Hunt, *Greater Perfections*, 51.
13 Judith A. Carney, *Black Rice: The African Origins of Rice Cultivation in the Americas* (Cambridge, MA: Harvard University Press, 2001), 89.
14 Porcher and Judd, *Market Preparation*, 38.
15 Porcher and Judd, *Market Preparation*, 37.
16 Theodore D. Ravenel, "Planter Pictures Old Rice Culture," *Charleston News and Courier* (Charleston, SC), March 10, 1933.
17 Richard Yeadon, 1857.
18 Ibid.
19 Hunt, *Greater Perfections*, 34.

Montpelier

Albemarle County, Virginia

James Madison, Charles Bizet, 1790–1836

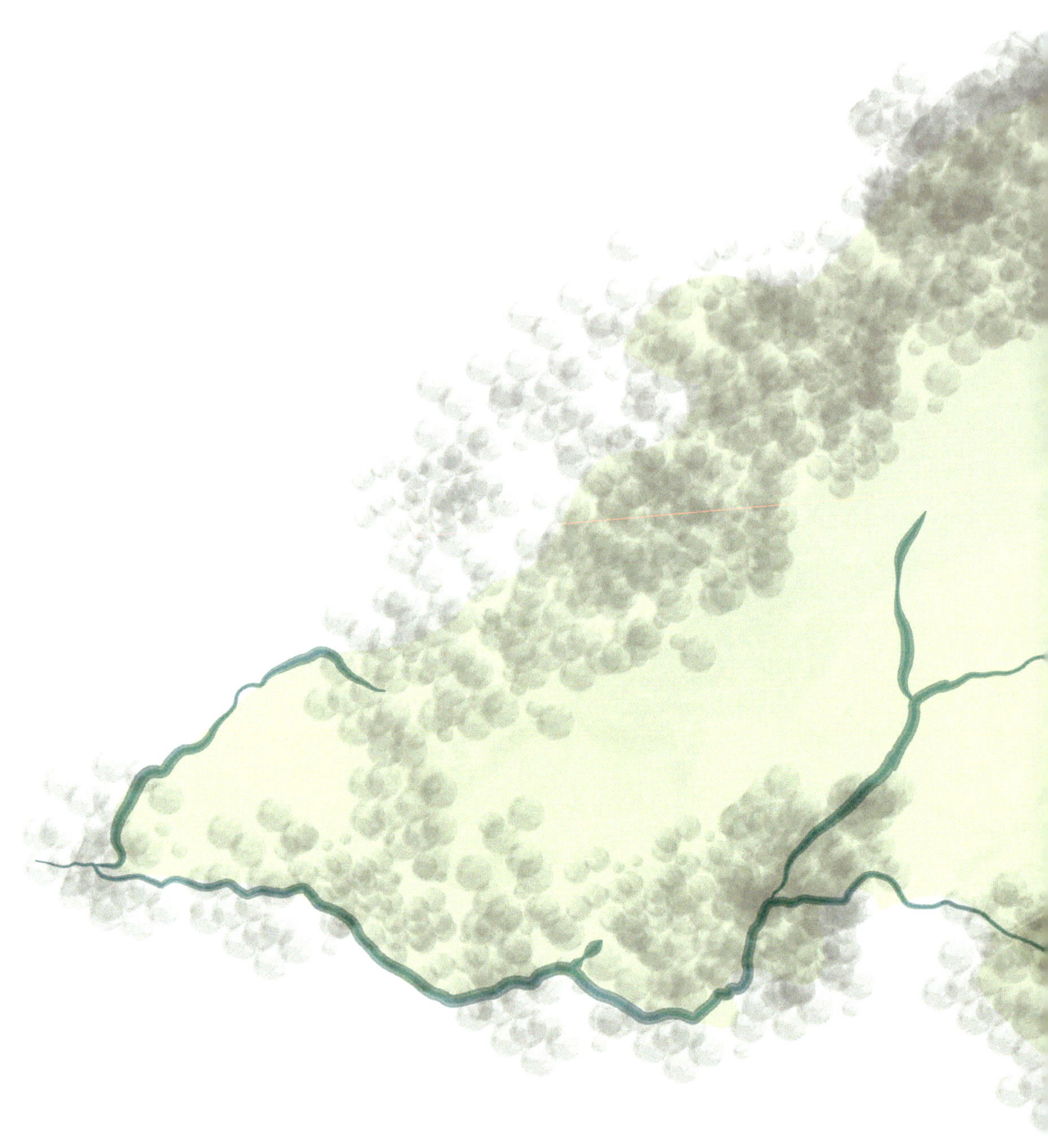

0
100
200 ft

Near the end of his life, President James Madison received a letter that highlighted the contributions of Virginia statesmen to the advancement of agricultural knowledge. Agriculture, pastor Henry Colman said, "has been a favorite pursuit with many of the most distinguished & more intellectual men that have ever lived; ... and [they] often seem vainer of their success in it than in any of the higher concerns of literature, politics or war."[1] For the planter-statesmen of Virginia, including James Madison, Thomas Jefferson, and John Taylor of Caroline, agriculture was a political practice that showed a man's moral standing and connection to *patria*. Agricultural stewardship of land was evidence of a man's capacity for citizenship and for stewardship of the nation.

Madison's Virginia plantation was also a site of experimentation in scientific agriculture. Drawing on his extensive reading and his correspondence with farmers, naturalists, and botanists, Madison used Montpelier as a laboratory to test a range of practices for improving the plantation's productivity. In some ways, the plantation was an early model of ecological conservation, as Madison observed the ruinous state of Virginia farmland, eroded and depleted from centuries of tobacco and corn farming, and advocated limiting field crops and encouraging forest growth to replenish regional soils.

James Madison inherited Montpelier from his father in 1801. At the time, it was a productive tobacco plantation with a spare Georgian landscape, outbuildings around the house, and brick walls separating the entertainment areas from the work areas. James and Dolley Madison expanded the house, and beginning in 1808 they renovated the grounds into a Picturesque landscape.

The house sits on the western slope of a hill, looking over portions of the plantation to the Blue Ridge mountains. (Fig 4.1) Working with Charles Bizet, a French gardener who had designed the White House grounds,[2] Madison created a genteel sequence of experiences reflecting the *ferme ornée* style, leading visitors through framed views culminating in a gracious lawn where Dolley held famous barbeques.

Madison added a terraced formal garden and extensive lawn behind the house, expanded the pleasure grounds around the house, and added trees to frame views to and from the house. Visitors emerged from a wood to view the house across fields and pastures, then were taken on a looped approach road providing cinematic views of the house and property. To the north of the house, a pine allée led to a neoclassical temple over an ice house. The allée tapered from forty feet wide at the house to twenty-five feet wide at the temple end, creating an elongating forced perspective similar to Woburn Farm's Long Walk. To the south of the house was a small cluster of enslaved workers' homes (Fig 4.2), an aspen grove that masked the stable yard and fields beyond, and a six-hundred-foot picket fence that led from the temple to a boxwood grotto to the south, dividing the approach fields from the pleasure garden. (Fig 4.3) Bizet's expertise in grading and terracing was critical in the improvements behind the house, where Madison leveled an expansive 1.25-acre lawn enclosed in a tree border, and had a terraced hippodrome garden built that contained both flowering

4.1
The view west towards the Blue Ridge mountains from the Montpelier house.

plants and vegetables.[3] (Fig. 4.4) Beyond the pleasure grounds, the nearly 1,800-acre plantation contained wheat and tobacco fields, woodlots and forest, pasture and hay fields, and the numerous buildings required to support the plantation and house the one hundred eighty enslaved workers who tended the fields and livestock.[4] (Fig. 4.5)

For nearly four decades, Madison experimented with technologies, plant and animal species, and husbandry techniques, attempting to improve the plantation's yields and decrease the labor required for the annual harvest. Thomas Jefferson once remarked that "the person who united with other science the greatest agricultural knowledge of any man he knew was Mr. Madison. He was the best farmer in the world."[5] Madison was widely read in subjects pertaining to agriculture, including geology, biology, and chemistry, and his notes on agriculture show him seeking to synthesize the latest agricultural science research from the United States and Europe, especially the ways that plants absorb nutrients and which nutrients perform what functions for various plants, processes not well understood at the time. Scientific agriculture emerged as an element of rationalist Enlightenment philosophy, as agronomists sought to understand the science of plant and animal productivity, and propose and test agricultural practices and equipment to increase that productivity. In the seventeenth and eighteenth centuries, agronomists attempted to understand plant growth, working through competing theories about the influence of soil, compost, minerals, and the atmosphere; their studies led to experiments in soil additives and cultivation methods to increase soil fertility and decrease soil and nutrient loss in fields.

Madison's library of over 4,000 books included many treatises on agriculture and natural sciences, as did that of his friend and frequent correspondent Jefferson. Between the two men, they owned M. Duhamel de Monceau's *A Practical Treatise of Husbandry,* Crevecoeur's *Letters from an American Farmer,*

4.2
Enslaved workers' homes, seen here in a 2015 reconstruction, were located immediately southwest of the house.

and the works of agronomists Francis Home and Jethro Tull and naturalists Carl Linnaeus and Alexander von Humboldt.[6] Madison's letters show a familiarity with agronomist Arthur Young's work, including receiving wheat seeds from Young's farm via a correspondent.[7] (Fig 4.6)

Madison was also friendly with Alexander von Humboldt, the Prussian naturalist, meeting him on his 1804 visit to the United States. Humboldt was returning to Europe after five years traveling through South and Central America, where he first developed his theory of *naturgemälde,* a holistic and unified approach to the earth sciences.[8] (Fig 4.7) Humboldt's *Essai sur la géographie des plantes* (1805) outlined his groundbreaking ecological theory of plant communities based on elevation, climate, and microclimate; he proposed a new understanding of the relationship of people and place as global as well as local. In his travels, he had observed the ecological damage caused by indigo farming in Venezuela and sugar farming in Cuba, and he advocated for conservation-based agriculture as a solution.[9] Madison would have been well versed in Humboldt's innovative idea that understanding the global distribution of plants was a branch of physics and geology, and by extension, that improving plant success relied on understanding those sciences.[10]

Agriculture at Montpelier was a process of scientific experimentation more than physical design. Madison tested the theories he read, and proposed new

4.3
A picket fence divided the house, lawn, and formal gardens from the pastures and fields along the approach drive. Engraving after John G. Chapman, c. 1840.

4.4 (pages 48–49)
The terraced flower and vegetable garden, seen in c. 1930, were organized along a central spine.

agricultural hypotheses. Prior to inheriting Montpelier from his father, the two corresponded extensively about the management of both their farms. Their letters show Madison directing experiments with new species of grains, fruits, and vegetables; new technologies such as the moldboard plow; and new tactics such as rotating crops, contour plowing, manuring fields, experimenting with plaster of Paris and salt for soils improvement and pest management, and using cover crops such as clover.[11]

In addition to experimentation, Madison engaged in close observation of his farm, and was part of a global community of citizen scientists seeking to understand the relationship between the earth sciences, agricultural practices, and plant and animal vitality. His correspondence with Jefferson shows them engaged in observational science, monitoring rainfall and temperature, noting soil quality and geomorphology of different fields, recording different planting and harvesting regimes and technologies, and different pest management regimes, and noting the relationship between these factors and crop yields.[12] Madison also recorded plant succession at Montpelier, noting that,

> Within my recollection, there have been three or four changes in the spontaneous herbage of our old uncultivated fields. The same tendency is

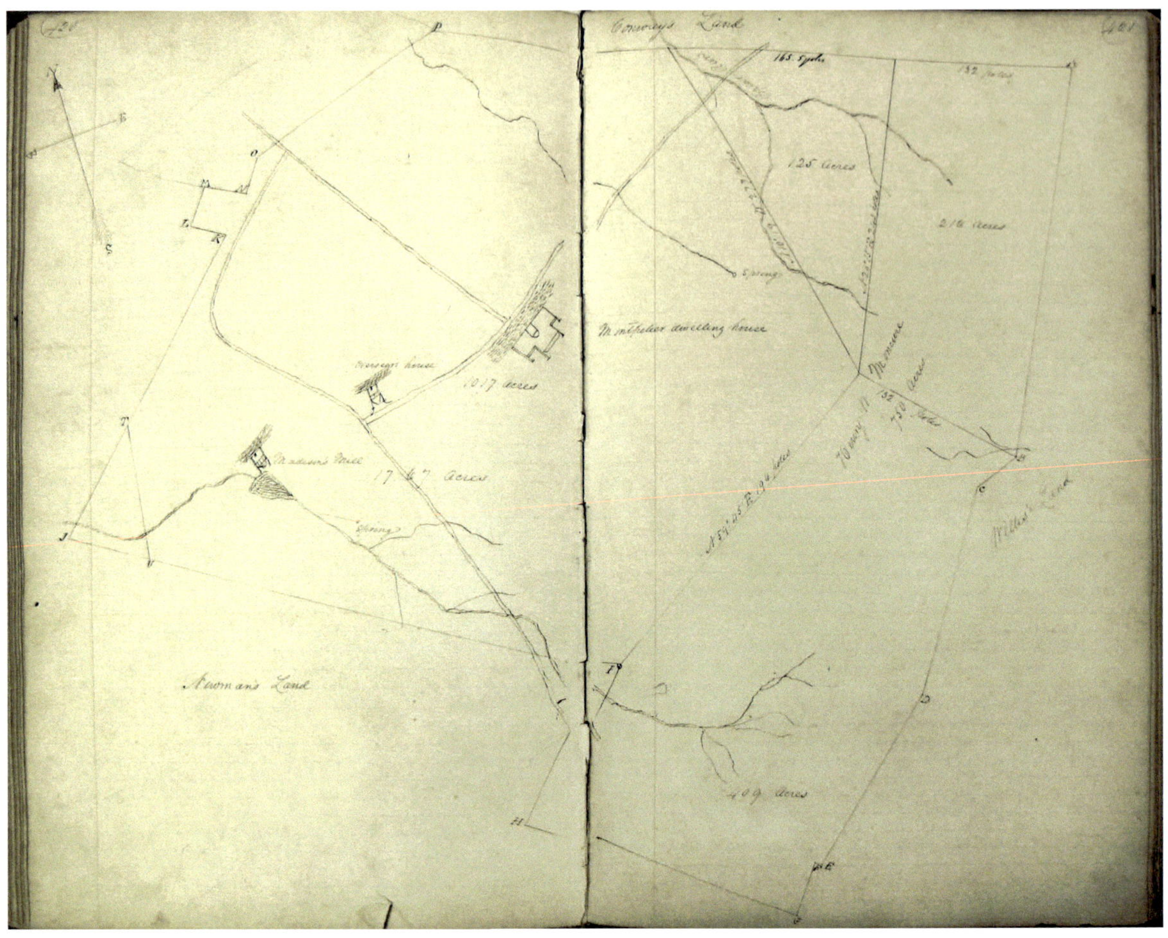

exemplified in the case of Trees. Originally not a pine was seen in our Red mountain forests. Now all our red fields long unplowed, are overspread with pines as thick as they can grow: Whilst the adjacent gray lands, originally clothed with a pine Forest, is gradually losing that kind of Trees, under the depredation of a particular worm, and many years may not pass before the oak & other trees hitherto an undergrowth only, will instead of a new forest of Pines, become Masters of the Soil.[13]

4.5
An 1844 plat of Montpelier shows the estate situated between two spring-fed streams, with the main house at the center, and an overseer's house and a mill to the south.

4.6
Madison's library included Jethro Tull's *Horse-Hoeing Husbandry* (1762), which detailed advances in agricultural tools and techniques.

Madison likely inherited an over-farmed landscape with depleted soils and few trees remaining. Montpelier comprised two large farms;[14] Madison advocated for reducing the actively cultivated area, and seems to have reforested the slopes and river corridors, focusing cultivation and crop rotation in the upper half of the property. Archeological studies indicate that the slopes south and east of the house were cultivated prior to c. 1795, and these areas, now the Landmark Forest, may have been some of the first areas Madison allowed to regrow as hardwood forest.[15] (Figs 4.8, 4.9)

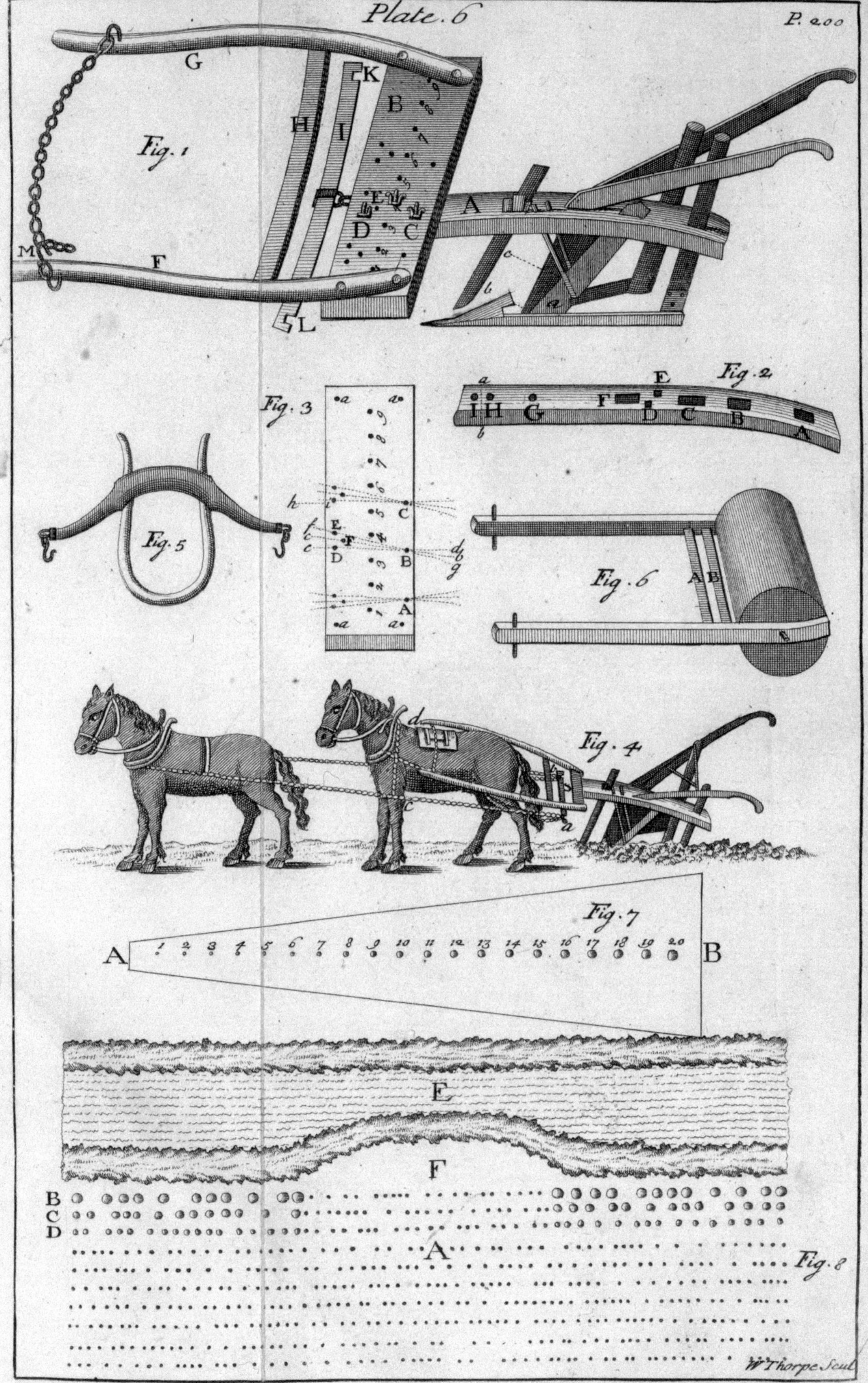
Plate. 6
P. 200
Fig. 1
Fig. 2
Fig. 3
Fig. 4
Fig. 5
Fig. 6
Fig. 7
Fig. 8
W Thorpe Sculp

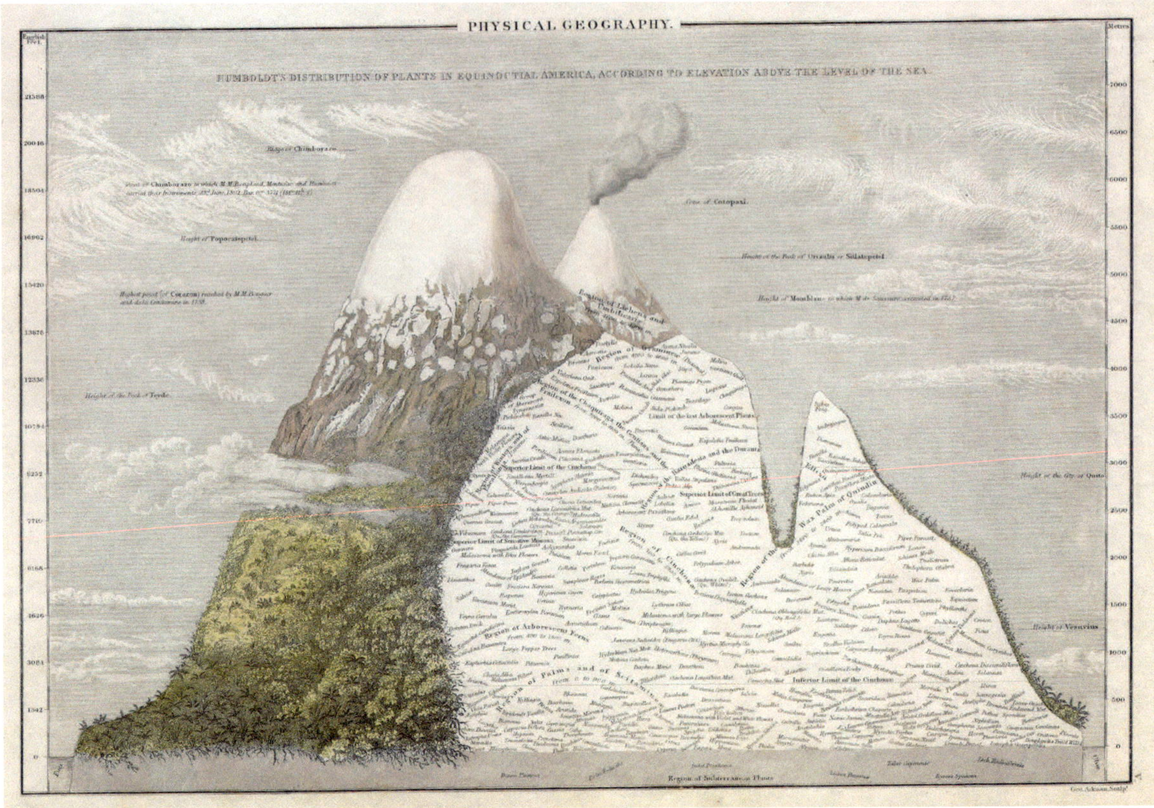

4.7
Humboldt's *Distribution of Plants in Equinoctial America* linked plant communities with climatic and soil conditions.

Madison was part of a regional community of farmers with a nascent ecological conservation agenda, who saw the devastation that extractive models of agriculture had wreaked on the region and who recognized that stewardship of natural systems went hand in hand with agrarian productivity.[16] He farmed Montpelier in a period of agricultural depression. After centuries of forest clearing for tobacco growing, most farms had depleted soils, eroded hills, fallow fields with pine forest regrowth, and as a result, increasingly poor crops of tobacco.[17] Madison observed that "our woods have disappeared, and are succeeded too generally by exhausted fields and gullied hills. The land of our ancestors … must be improved or abandoned."[18] Many farmers switched from tobacco to wheat, even though it was a difficult decision to switch from the known husbandry of tobacco, with its accompanying known weak crops and weak market, to the unknown husbandry of wheat. Madison and others saw the shift from a tobacco-based planter culture to a wheat-based farmer culture, and to soil-improving practices as critical for the survival of Virginia's agrarian economy.

These experiments and observations came together in an address Madison presented to the Agricultural Society of Albemarle in 1818. The address was well received and widely distributed as a booklet and reprinted in newspapers nationally. The first half of the address is a philosophical and political manifesto, in which

4.8
LIDAR analysis of the northeastern property boundary shows historical irrigation ditches and plow scars in current forested lands.

he argues for the nation's agricultural obligation to humanity. He presents three arguments. First, he uses a Malthusian framework of nature's economy to state that while humans can increase their numbers on earth, nature will self-regulate our population within the global carrying capacity.[19] He then argues for our ethical obligation to enhance the well-being of other humans, and that the United States is uniquely positioned within global ecological and economic systems, with an "enviable condition" based on climate, soil vitality, low population density, and "a free people, and the benign influence of a responsible government."[20] Without explicitly making the argument, he frames scientific agriculture as a moral obligation of the young nation, saying that, "the resources of our country may not only contribute to the greater happiness of a given number, but to the augmentation of the number enjoying a greater happiness."[21] Finally, he argues for agriculture as a practice of virtue, and connects agricultural advances with civic advances: "And thus a progressive agriculture, and a progressive population ensue."

The first section also reflects Madison's understanding of nature as a "design," as ordered and systemic and therefore able to be comprehended, and suggests an argument for biodiversity. Without fully explaining, or indeed understanding, why it is significant, he calls for the retention of biodiversity as a critical aspect of nature's function; he notes the exchange of air between plants and

animals as an "admirable arrangement and beautiful feature in the economy of nature" and extrapolates that, if the two kingdoms rely on each other for the air we breathe, so too must the balance of life on the planet rely on the "proportions of each class to the other, and in the species composing the respective classes."[22]

4.9
This 1863 map shows the Montpelier house and "negro quarters" in a band of open farmland with forest to the south.

The second half of the address contains practical advice to planters and farmers: he describes common errors of contemporary agriculture and proposes seven suggestions for improvements based on his reading and experimentation. He suggests reducing the footprint of farms to reduce labor costs, while using better techniques to increase productivity on the smaller footprint. In particular, he suggests reducing the size of cattle herds, seen as both unnecessarily large, overly expensive, and destructive of soils. He describes improved plowing techniques and soil fertilization techniques, proven beneficial at Montpelier, to improve soil fertility and reduce erosion, and although there is as yet little evidence of irrigation at Montpelier, he suggests that it is underused and would be beneficial in Virginia. Finally, he argues for the preservation of forests and replanting them in fallow fields, both as a crop necessary for tools, construction, and firewood, and also as a means to rebuild soils, moving towards long-term crop rotation that includes "a crop of trees" along with hay, grain, and livestock.

Madison's *Address to the Agricultural Society of Albemarle* is a summary of his agricultural thinking based on decades of experimental agriculture at Montpelier. There, he "sweeten[ed] the evening of life with agricultural theory, experiment, and practice," using agriculture to advance both scientific and political thought.[23] Through experimentation, Madison sought to more fully understand the processes of nature, and improve the productivity of regional farms, using and advancing frameworks of natural carrying capacity, soil and water conservation, and conservation agriculture.

Concurrently, he used Montpelier as a model farm and political manifesto for the young nation, where farmers were the most important crop to be raised, and the practice of agriculture helped develop men of virtue suited to democratic life. In this, he drew on models from antiquity that combined "practical agricultural advice with moral reflection."[24] For Madison, the practice of agriculture was an Enlightenment practice clarifying one's connection to nature's order and to rational thought, and producing men of moral and civic virtue, "all with a share in the *patria*."[25] In this agrarian-republican theory, instruction in agriculture was also instruction in environmental and civic stewardship and in moral being, and the capacity to maintain a farm was seen also as the capacity to maintain the republic.[26] This framework of course distanced the landowner from the labor of agriculture. The work of farming at Montpelier and other scientific farms in Virginia was done by enslaved men and women who did not have "a share in the *patria*." And while Madison relied on his enslaved overseer, Sawney, he does not seem to have considered the moral and civic value of Sawney's and other enslaved workers' labor in the same philosophical terms that he used to frame his *Address*. His views on slavery over his life were shifting and conflicting, but in the end, he only freed one Montpelier slave, Billey, and despite his capacity for political and technological innovation, he was unable to rectify his philosophical ethos of liberty with the economic systems of agriculture.[27]

Notes

1 Henry Colman to James Madison, July 24, 1830 (James Madison Papers, Library of Congress, Washington, DC), in Hilarie M. Hicks, "'To Introduce Principle & System into a Profession Hitherto Conducted Without Much of Either:' James Madison's Approach to Agriculture at Montpelier" (Orange, VA: The Montpelier Foundation, December 2012, updated February 2018, MRD-S 41872), 111.

2 Matthew Reeves, *A Brief History of the Montpelier Landscape* (Orange, VA: The Montpelier Foundation, Montpelier Archaeology Department, 2016), 12.

3 Reeves, *Brief History*, 7–13.

4 G. S. Hillard, ed., George Ticknor and Anna Eliot Ticknor, *Life, Letters and Journals of George Ticknor* (Boston, MA: James R. Osgood and Co., 1876), in Hicks, *Madison's Approach*, 95.

5 John Quincy Adams, Diary Vol. 27, January 1, 1803–August 4, 1809 (Adams Family Papers, Massachusetts Historical Society), in Hicks, *Madison's Approach*, 42.

6 Thomas Jefferson to James Madison, September 1, 1785, *Founders Online*, National Archives, last modified June 13, 2018, accessed August 15, 2018, http://founders.archives.gov/documents/Jefferson/01-08-02-0360. "James Madison Book List," unpublished (Orange, VA: The Montpelier Foundation).

7 Thomas Attwood Digges to James Madison, July 11, 1818 (James Madison Papers, Library of Congress, Washington, DC), in Hicks, *Madison's Approach*, 55.
8 Andrea Wulf, *The Invention of Nature: Alexander von Humboldt's New World* (New York: Alfred A. Knopf, 2015), 102–103, 148–149.
9 Ibid., 120.
10 Helmut De Terra, "Alexander von Humboldt's Correspondence with Jefferson, Madison, and Gallatin," *Proceedings of the American Philosophical Society* 103, no. 6 (Dec. 1959): 783–806.
11 On crop rotation: James Madison to James Madison Sr., March 13, 1796 (James Madison Papers, Library of Congress, Washington, DC), in Hicks, *Madison's Approach*, 22; on cover crops and manures: James Madison to James Madison Sr., January 22, 1797 (James Madison Papers, Library of Congress, Washington, DC, MRD-S 11375), in Hicks, *Madison's Approach*, 24; on plaster of Paris: James Madison to James Madison Sr., January 29, 1797 (James Madison Papers, Library of Congress, Washington, DC, MRD-S 11380), in Hicks, *Madison's Approach*, 25; on clover: James Madison to James Madison Sr., March 12, 1797 (James Madison Papers, Library of Congress, Washington, DC, MRD-S 11400), in Hicks, *Madison's Approach*, 26.
12 Hicks, *Madison's Approach*, 28–30.
13 James Madison to Richard Peters, August 15, 1818 (James Madison Papers, Library of Congress, Washington, DC, MRD-S 16204), in Hicks, *Madison's Approach*, 56.
14 James Madison, "Address to the Agricultural Society of Albemarle, 12 May 1818 (Editorial Note)," *Founders Online*, National Archives, last modified June 13, 2018, accessed June 20, 2018, http://founders.archives.gov/documents/Madison/04-01-02-0243.
15 W. Cullen Sherwood, "Soils and Land Use in Montpelier's Landmark Forest" (Report to Montpelier Foundation, 2010), 38.
16 Hicks, *Madison's Approach*, 2.
17 M. E. Bradford, "A Virginia Cato: John Taylor of Caroline and the Agrarian Republic," in John Taylor's *Arator* (Indianapolis, IN: Liberty Fund, 1977), 13. Hicks, *Madison's Approach*, 1.
18 Sherwood, "Soils and Land Use," 41.
19 Thomas Robert Malthus, *An Essay on the Principle of Population* (London: J. Johnson, 1798).
20 Madison, Address to the Agricultural Society.
21 This framing draws on Jeremy Bentham's political utilitarianism, in which the "greatest happiness of the greatest number is the foundation of morals and legislation." *The Works of Jeremy Bentham, Now First Collected: Under the Superintendence of His Executor, John Bowring* (Edinburgh, UK: W. Tait, 1842), 142.
22 James Madison, "Preliminary Draft of an Essay on Natural Order, [ca. November 10] 1791," *Founders Online*, National Archives, version of January 18, 2019, accessed June 15, 2018, https://founders.archives.gov/documents/Madison/01-14-02-0094.
23 Tench Coxe to James Madison, February 2, 1819 (James Madison Papers, Library of Congress, Washington, DC), in Hicks, *Madison's Approach*, 57.
24 C. F. Cato's *De Agri Cultura*, Varro's *Rerum Rusticarum*, Columella's *De Re Rustica*, and Hesiod's *The Works and Days*.
25 Bradford, "A Virginia Cato," 37.
26 Ibid., 39.
27 See Paris Amanda Spies-Gans, "James Madison," *Princeton & Slavery Project*, https://slavery.princeton.edu/stories/james-madison for Madison's conflicted and changing views on slavery.

Moraine Farm

Beverly, Massachusetts

Frederick Law Olmsted, 1880

0
300
600 ft

While landscape design is the best known of Frederick Law Olmsted's careers, he continually sought to improve American society and the living conditions of Americans through his wide-ranging expertise. Early work as a surveyor, businessman, merchant seaman, author and social commentator, farmer, and sanitary commissioner all influenced his park, neighborhood, and residential designs as healthy and civic places. However, no other endeavor influenced his practice as a landscape architect so much as his early experience as a scientific farmer, where he learned the fundamental relationship between plants and environment, research and practice, culture and cuisine. The cycles, time frames, and forms of farming, especially as practiced in scientific farming, would inform his landscape designs throughout his career. At Moraine Farm, "the most fully realized of Olmsted's early plans for a country estate,"[1] Olmsted integrated a working farm into an estate landscape, merging scientific farming and the *ferme ornée*. (Fig 5.1)

As a young man, Olmsted worked in several farming apprenticeships, first helping family members on their farms, then after meandering through several other careers, returning to farming with apprenticeships at his uncle David Brooks' farm in Cheshire, Connecticut, and at the farm of an acquaintance, Joseph Welton, in Hartford, Connecticut. Welton was the neighbor of Frederick Kingsbury, a classmate of Olmsted's brother at Yale and a close friend of both Olmsted brothers. He ran a farm and nursery in the maturing practice of scientific farming, agriculture based not on vernacular methods but on techniques informed by the rapidly growing scientific fields of botany, ecology, and soil science and tested on research farms. While scientific farming's eighteenth-century roots aimed towards a deeper understanding of the processes, relationships, and cycles of the natural world, by the second half of the nineteenth century scientific farmers were also concerned with addressing social and economic shifts. In the United States, commercial farms were gradually replacing small family farms; improvements in infrastructure gave east coast populations access to the livestock and grains from the rich agricultural lands of the Midwest. Northeastern farms had to specialize to compete; unable to match the efficiencies of scale of Midwestern farms, they had to focus on perishable goods such as produce and dairy, and that specialization required new knowledge. Welton read *The Cultivator* and he would certainly have introduced young Olmsted to the monthly journal, published by the New York State Agricultural Society, which provided a forum for farmers to exchange the results of their experiments. *The Cultivator* published house and farm plans, economic analyses of farms, and the results of experiments in livestock breeding, plant hybridization, fertilization, and crop rotation. (Fig 5.2)

In 1846, at age 24, Olmsted interned with gentleman farmer George Geddes at Fairmount, his 300-acre scientific farm in Camillus, New York. On his journey to Camillus, Olmsted stopped in Newburg, New York, at the offices of *The Cultivator*, hoping to meet with the editors. There, he met A. J. Downing, arbiter of American taste, author of *A Treatise on the Theory and Practice of Landscape Gardening, Adapted to North America*, and recently appointed editor

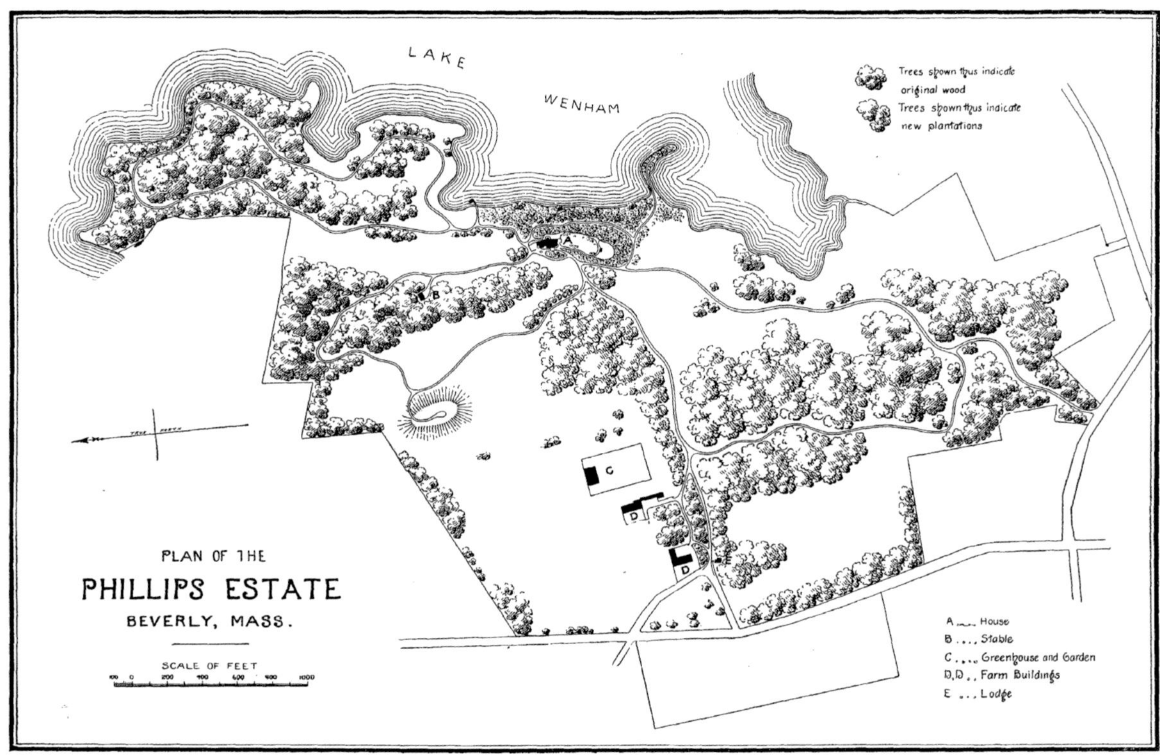

5.1
A 1892 plan of Moraine Farm shows the barn complex and fields in the northwest and forest in the northeast. Most of the central woods were new plantings to frame views from the roads.

of *The Horticulturalist*, where Olmsted would later publish his first writings. Downing's *Treatise*, published five years earlier, had extensive recommendations for rural landowners and landscape gardeners on the integration of beauty and utility in country estates. While Olmsted was primarily interested in the science of farming, he was familiar with Downing's writings on the *ferme ornée*, prescribing fields "divided and bounded by winding roads, bordered by hedges," the meandering roads arranged to "allow the owner or visitor to enjoy at the same time an agreeable circuit, and a glance at all the various crops and modes of culture."[2] Olmsted found this integration of productivity and pleasure at Geddes' farm, where he would learn the life of a gentleman farmer – deeply committed to scientific inquiry, but also to elegant beauty, refined civic life, and social improvement. This ideal would return throughout Olmsted's career in the country estates he designed for his clients.

In 1848, after a brief, unsuccessful attempt to farm a beautiful but rocky coastal farm in Connecticut, Olmsted purchased property on Staten Island that he would farm, off and on, for over seven years. Here he began his design praxis, integrating second and third nature, productive and aesthetic landscapes, as he improved the farming operations, moved outbuildings, and rerouted roads, transforming the property from a "dirty, disagreeable farmyard to a gentleman's house."[3] (Fig. 5.3) In addition to crops intended for sale in New York City – hay, corn, cabbage, turnips, and potatoes – Olmsted also planted a pear orchard and began a nursery, recogniz-

MERINO PRIZE SHEEP.

The Property of S. Jewett, Esq. Weybridge, Vermont.

See "The Cultivator," for 1846, page 56.

5.2
Merino Prize Sheep, from *The Cultivator*, 1846.

5.3
Olmsted's sketch of his Staten Island farm house, c. 1850.

5.4 (pages 64–65)
An 1879 topographic plan of Moraine Farm shows the glaciated ridge running north–south that Olmsted used to organize the roads.

ing that the profit margins for produce and hay were narrow and that tree fruit and nursery stock would provide a better return on investment.[4]

Two years after purchasing the Staten Island farm, the peripatetic Olmsted traveled to England, joining his brother who was traveling for his health. In an elaborately argued letter to his father, who would fund the trip, Olmsted described the trip as an agricultural education, to help him "carry out [his] ideas of husbandry and humanity successfully."[5] While in England, Olmsted visited at least one *ferme ornée*, although he did not visit Southcote's Woburn Farm, considered the originator of the integration of pleasure walks and agricultural fields.[6] But the focus of his trip was science, not aesthetics. He interviewed farmers, landscape gardeners, and nurserymen on the latest agricultural techniques and plant species, gathering information he would later use in the design of parks, neighborhoods, and private residences, and forming the basis of his first book, *Walks and Talks of an American Farmer in England.*

In his travel memoir, which he dedicated to George Geddes, Olmsted devotes several chapters to careful analysis of British agricultural practices. The book is sparsely illustrated, primarily with travel-scene images, except for illustrations of a plow, a clod crusher, and a harrow, indicating his intense focus on agricultural techniques. (He does note phlegmatically that the tools seem "very unnecessarily cumbrous and complicated," and deems American implements lighter, better, and cheaper.)[7] He finds some aspects of English farming worth replicating, especially the scientific methods advocated by the Royal Agricultural Society. Other aspects he finds wanting, calling British cider orchards "in every way miserably managed." Olmsted's chapters cover the arrangement of British farms, their tools and techniques, and their economics, showing him to be a keen observer and interviewer. He devotes chapters to the minutiae of growing various crops, raising livestock, producing dairy products, and improving and pruning fruit and cider orchards. And he details soil improvement techniques through drainage, amendments and crop rotation, and discusses the emerging field of soil science and matching crops to soils, techniques he would use in later design projects for his clients.

Throughout, Olmsted is skeptical of traditional, non-scientific methods. When discussing Cheshire cheese making, he refers to dairy "secrets," and laments the lack of "uniformity" and "exact rules." He says, "although the skill to *feel* when it is right is deemed highly important, it is almost never measured, even in the best dairies."[8] Instead, he values the scientific method applied to agriculture, as farmers seek efficiency, higher yields, and higher profits from their lands. Whether upholding tradition or challenging it, the scientific method provides Olmsted with quantifiable and transferable results. "This is experience" he says, "and science confirms it."[9]

Olmsted tested many of these ideas at Moraine Farm, in Beverly, Massachusetts. Here, he integrated short- and long-term soil improvements and economic production with an aesthetic ideal of a rustic gentleman's retreat. In 1879, John Charles Phillips, a Boston businessman, purchased a series of small farms and parcels on the shores of Wenham Lake, eventually amassing 275 acres,

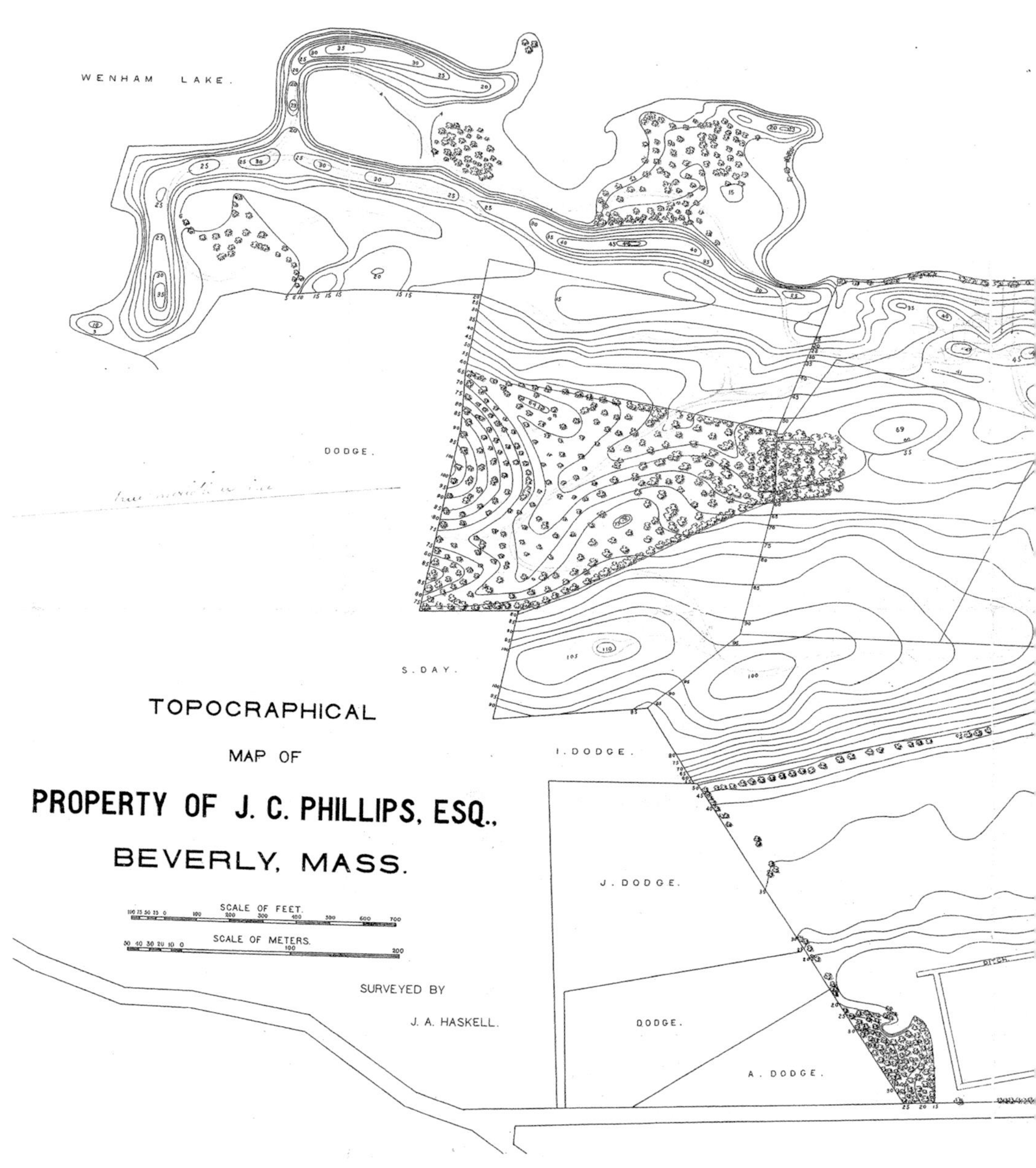

WENHAM LAKE.
DODGE.
S. DAY.
I. DODGE.
J. DODGE.
DODGE.
A. DODGE.
TOPOCRAPHICAL
MAP OF
PROPERTY OF J. C. PHILLIPS, ESQ.,
BEVERLY, MASS.
SCALE OF FEET.
SCALE OF METERS.
SURVEYED BY
J. A. HASKELL.

LAKE.
BATCHELDER.
L. WOODBURY.
PARSONS.
B. LORD.
DODGE ST.
L. SOUTHWICK.
C. LORD.
BROWN.
CEMETARY
WALLIS.
TOWN OF BEVERLY.
CONANT ST.
PERRY
HARRINGTON.
S. BROWN.
CABOT ST.
MASON.

and he asked Olmsted to design the site. The property, as the name implies, occupies a glacial moraine landscape – irregular rolling hills of soil and gravel deposited by the advance and retreat of glaciers – and includes a long ridge overlooking the lake. (Fig 5.4) Most of the property contained upland and swamp forests, or thin, poor glacial soils, and had been timbered, cultivated, and grazed to near infertility. Only forty low-lying, frequently flooded acres in the northwest were suited to crops. Using scientific farming principles like those developed by Madison and his peers, Olmsted matched agricultural practice to soil and slope, and like Madison at Montpelier, recommended trees as a principle crop. Overlaid on this productive landscape, he wove sinuous carriage roads in the *ferme ornée* manner, albeit with less dense planting than that installed at Woburn Farm. The border planting of trees and massed shrubs such as rhododendrons was composed to direct views across meadows and fields, visually incorporating the agricultural landscape into a cinematic aesthetic experience. (Fig. 5.5)

Phillips seems to have wavered in his ambitions for the property, sometimes desiring a "forest lodge,"[10] and at others seeking a "park-like place,"[11] or a farm. Olmsted designed Moraine Farm to integrate these two adjacent ideals of a rustic hunting lodge and a *ferme ornée*, each with its own crop suited to the landscape: forest and field. The two were considered as nearly independent aesthetic and agricultural ideas, with the lodge in the forest occupying the moraine ridge running north–south, and the ornamented farm occupying the flat landscape to the west. Phillips hired Boston architects Peabody and Stearns, who designed a "bold, rustic" house that Olmsted found "suited neither to a park nor a farm." He chided Phillips that the house would be "incongruous with the ideal of either – still more with an agglomeration of both."[12] Two entry roads highlight these two different attitudes towards the agricultural estate. Olmsted laid out a sinuous south entry road tracing a series of glacial hillocks through a newly planted forest, limning the edge of forest and meadow and climbing to the house overlooking the lake across lawns and perennial beds. (Fig 5.6) The design highlights the glacial terrain; the road traces the depositional slopes and leads to the house, where retaining walls containing the lawn and garden accentuate and exaggerate the existing topography. (Fig 5.7) A west entry road, meanwhile, passed farm buildings, a greenhouse, an orchard, and productive fields before climbing to the house, and a northern carriage loop provided clear views into the farm fields. (Fig. 5.8)

Recognizing that most of the soils at Moraine Farm were unsuited to crop or hay production, and no doubt remembering his own expensive trials in soil amendments on his farm in Connecticut, Olmsted proposed turning the bulk of the property to productive forestry for lumber, fuel, and soil rejuvenation. On the low-lying, fertile ground, Olmsted designed an underground drainage tile system, a technology he had learned in England, to prevent seasonal flooding and allow crop production, creating "one of the best and most productive fields in Massachusetts."[13] The editor of *Garden and Forest* noted that Moraine Farm "stands for what we hold as the fundamental principle underlying all successful agriculture – the adaptation of the crop to the soil. This principle is well understood

5.5
The south entry road was framed in clumps of shrubs and trees to stage views.

5.6
Sinuous carriage roads and paths around the main house were designed to include views of the farm and lake.

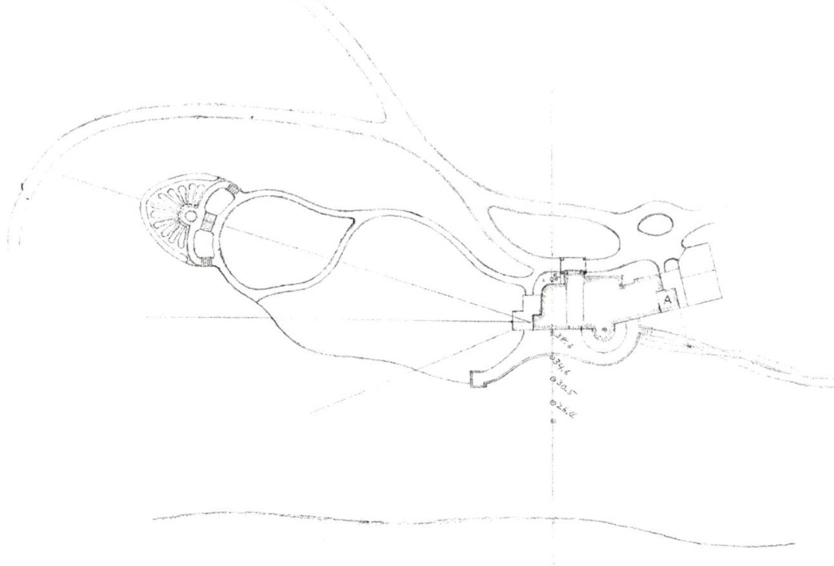

5.7
Retaining walls for the lawn and garden accentuate the form and material of the glacial terrain.

now in most European countries, but the neglect of it in this [country] has caused the unprofitable removal of millions of acres of valuable forests, but entirely unfit for permanent and profitable tillage."[14] Olmsted designed in several temporal scales simultaneously, and matched crop to site accordingly. More fertile soils were suited to semi-annual and annual crops, using crop rotation and manuring to maintain the soil's vitality. In areas of severely depleted or thin soils, Olmsted proposed crops with longer time frames – trees – to stabilize slopes, prevent further soil loss, deposit leaf duff to build the soil, and dig deep below the surface to extract minerals. While providing relatively quick profit (white pines would mature in fifteen to twenty years, with intermediate thinning crops every five to ten years), forests would supplement the primary agricultural activity by improving soils and reducing flooding. At the time, Moraine Farm was considered an "object-lesson of real public importance" as it showed a way to earn a profit on poor lands.[15] Then as now, farmers could rarely guarantee making a profit off their land.

For several generations, the farm was a summer home for the Phillips family, with farmers managing or leasing the agricultural acres, growing produce and hay for market. From 1928 to 1947, George Batchelder, Jr. purchased 180 acres of Moraine Farm, including the productive fields. On inheriting the property in

5.8
The north entry road includes long views across a wetland towards the barns and crop fields.

1977, George Batchelder III restored the Olmsted landscape and reinvigorated the Olmsted plans for agriculture and forestry, once again making the land profitable. Returning to Olmsted's multiple-timescale approach, the Batchelders leased the agricultural fields to farmers, while they grew Christmas trees and nursery stock, timber for firewood and lumber, and raised sheep for wool and meat.

Moraine Farm is located less than thirty miles north of Boston, and by the early 1990s, the Batchelders recognized that development pressures on the farm would only increase in the future. They placed the land under conservation easements to allow continued agriculture and forestry while restricting future subdivision and construction. Along with the Batchelder Trust, three non-profit agencies help to steward the farm: The Trustees of Reservations and the Essex County Greenbelt Association, two Massachusetts land trusts, and Friends of the Olmsted Landscape, which provides leadership and support for cultural landscape preservation. Under the management of The Trustees of Reservations, a community-supported agriculture (CSA) farm is operating on Olmsted's drained farm fields.

The twenty-nine-acre CSA offers weekly and alternate-week shares from May to October, as well as alternate-week fall and winter shares. The shares, which are sized for an individual or couple, are distributed at the farm, and about

15 percent of each share is pick-your-own crops, including herbs, beans, peas, and strawberries. The CSA is part of the land stewardship mission of The Trustees of Reservations, and CSA members are required to also be members of the conservation organization. Moraine Farm sells produce to local public schools in Salem and Beverly, with produce delivered the day it is picked, and also provides vegetables for local food pantries.[16]

Moraine Farm is a hybrid of two agricultural types: the picturesque *ferme ornée*, and a scientific farm rooted in close scientific analysis and knowledge of a site. Downing's "agreeable circuits," bordered by hedges and alternately screened and framed by trees, meander through the property, and a clear vantage point to the north provides a belvedere into the productive fields. Views from the roads and hilltop integrate the utility landscape of the farm into the pleasure landscape of the country seat. The views of the farm connect the owner and visitor to the work of producing food. But the diagram of meandering circuits, hedges, and long views into forests and agricultural fields, drawn from Southcote and Downing, was made specific by the details of the site. The loop roads follow and highlight the glacial topography and tree plantings are located to frame signal moments – the lake, the glacial valley, outcrops. The productive farm is carefully located on the best soils, which were improved using the most advanced technology of the day. Crops were matched both to the site and the market. Estates such as Moraine Farm were understood to be at least partially self-supporting, and farming was a necessary component in their productivity and profitability. The designed landscape of the house, gardens, and park-like forests, and the productive landscape of the farm are adjacent to and support each other.

Like many properties of this size and location, adjacent to a major city, Moraine Farm has faced development pressure. The desire for land to produce a profit hasn't disappeared; the mode has simply shifted from food, hay, and lumber to real estate. By placing the land under conservation easements, the Batchelders have protected the cultural, ecological, and productive landscapes by restricting future development. And by finding the right partners, the Batchelders have created a framework for continued agriculture into the next century.

Notes

1 Charles Capen McLaughlin and Charles E. Beveridge, eds., *The Papers of Frederick Law Olmsted: I. The Formative Years, 1822–1852* (Baltimore, MD: Johns Hopkins University Press, 1977), 491.

2 Andrew Jackson Downing, *A Treatise on the Theory and Practice of Landscape Gardening* (Little Compton, RI: Theophrastus Publishers, 1977), 74.

3 Frederick Law Olmsted, Jr. and Theodora Kimball, eds., *Frederick Law Olmsted, Landscape Architect, 1822–1903* (New York: G.P. Putnam's Sons, 1928), 86.

4 Witold Rybczynski, *A Clearing in the Distance: Frederick Law Olmsted and America in the 19th Century* (New York: Scribner, 2000), 81.

5 Charles E. Beveridge, Carolyn F. Hoffman, and Kenneth Hawkins, eds., *The Papers*

of Frederick Law Olmsted: VII. Parks, Politics, and Patronage 1874–1882 (Baltimore, MD: Johns Hopkins University Press, 2007), 337–341.

6 Frederick Law Olmsted, *Walks and Talks of an American Farmer in England* (New York: G. P. Putnam & Co., 1852), 108.

7 Ibid., 182.

8 Ibid., 126.

9 Ibid., 195.

10 Beveridge et al., *Parks, Politics, and Patronage*, 492.

11 Ibid., 549.

12 Ibid., 549.

13 "A Modern Massachusetts Farm," *Garden and Forest* 5, no. 214 (1892): 146.

14 Ibid., 145.

15 Ibid., 146.

16 Paul Leighton, "From local farms to local schools," *Salem News* (Salem, MA), Oct. 10, 2012.

Merchiston Farm

Morris County, New Jersey

Martha Brookes Hutcheson, 1911–1959

0
100
200 ft

At Martha Brookes Hutcheson's home, Merchiston Farm, the domestic and agricultural landscapes formed and informed each other over a period of fifty years in the first half of the twentieth century. Here, agriculture is the milieu and medium of the property while the gardens provide the formal armature, and the changing relationship between the two realms reveals a designer actively evolving her theory through agricultural practice. Hutcheson, one of the first female landscape architects in the United States, used axial, orthogonal forms in designing great estates throughout New England. Those same forms structure the pleasure gardens at Merchiston Farm and are echoed in the agricultural yards, providing a stable datum against which the seasonal activity of the farm can be read. Mediating between the architecturally defined gardens and the pastoral landscape of fields, meadows, and pastures is a water system designed to serve the aesthetic, recreational, agricultural, and conservation programs of the farm. An early example of ecological design, Merchiston Farm melds the "good principles in planning which have been handed down to us from the Old World"[1] with a layered planting structure and native plants, informed by the new science of ecology.

Martha Brookes Brown was born in 1871, in New York City. As a girl, she spent summers on her family farm, Fern Hill, near Burlington, Vermont.[2] There she learned the rhythms of agriculture and how the structures and forms of topography, water, and plants constitute the productive landscape. In 1893 she enrolled in the New York School of Applied Design for Women; the school focused on professional training in design for employment in illustration, textile and wallpaper design, interior design, and similar fields. After touring the gardens of England, France, and Italy, and after conversations with a family friend, the pioneering female landscape architect Beatrix Ferrand, Brown decided to enter Massachusetts Institute of Technology's new landscape architecture program, an optional course of study within the architecture program.[3] MIT was the only university offering a landscape architecture degree to women at the time, and Brown was one of a handful of women to take advantage of the opportunity to study landscape design, geology, surveying, horticulture, and sanitary and highway engineering with leading designers in the emerging profession. During her studies, she also attended a lecture series from Benjamin Watson at Harvard's Bussey Institution on horticulture, and studied at commercial nurseries, apparently dissatisfied with the horticulture courses MIT required each semester beginning in the second year of study.[4] In 1902, she began a successful practice in Boston, primarily designing private gardens and estates in New England, New York, and New Jersey.

After her marriage to William Anderson Hutcheson in 1910 and the birth of her only child in 1912, Hutcheson retired from practice. She continued to actively promote landscape architecture as a socially ameliorative practice, writing and lecturing on garden design and publishing in 1923 *The Spirit of the Garden*, a popular treatise on the topic. In a society where married women didn't typically own and manage professional firms, Hutcheson's home and farm was a site where she could continue to experiment and develop her concepts of landscape design, ecological design, and social improvement enacted through landscape architecture.

6.1
Merchiston Farm, seen here c. 1915, raised pigs, poultry, sheep, and dairy cows for market sale.

The farm was a fully functional economic industry, with a primary focus on family sustenance. Until his death in 1942, William Hutcheson was the principle manager of the farm, with Martha Hutcheson's involvement shifting over time, with greater involvement around World War I and after William's death. The Hutchesons grew domestic fruits and vegetables; cultivated field crops for their own use and for sale, including corn, wheat, rye, oats, and hay; raised pigs, poultry, sheep, and dairy cows; and sold pork, eggs, butter, milk, and apples to the local grocery.[5] (Fig 6.1)

The seasonal activities, mutable forms, ecological relationships, and physical labor of agriculture provided a testing ground for Hutcheson to develop an expanded theory and definition of garden design that she disseminated through her writings and lectures. Like Gertrude Jekyll before her, Hutcheson first hybridized the opposing nineteenth-century garden theories of the architectural and the wild garden to synthesize geometric and biomorphic geometries.[6] The choice, she said "lies with the architecture of the house, the lay of the land, and the taste of the owner."[7] Merchiston Farm incorporates both, in a tartan grid that extended the geometry of the buildings into the farm fields and meadows, and

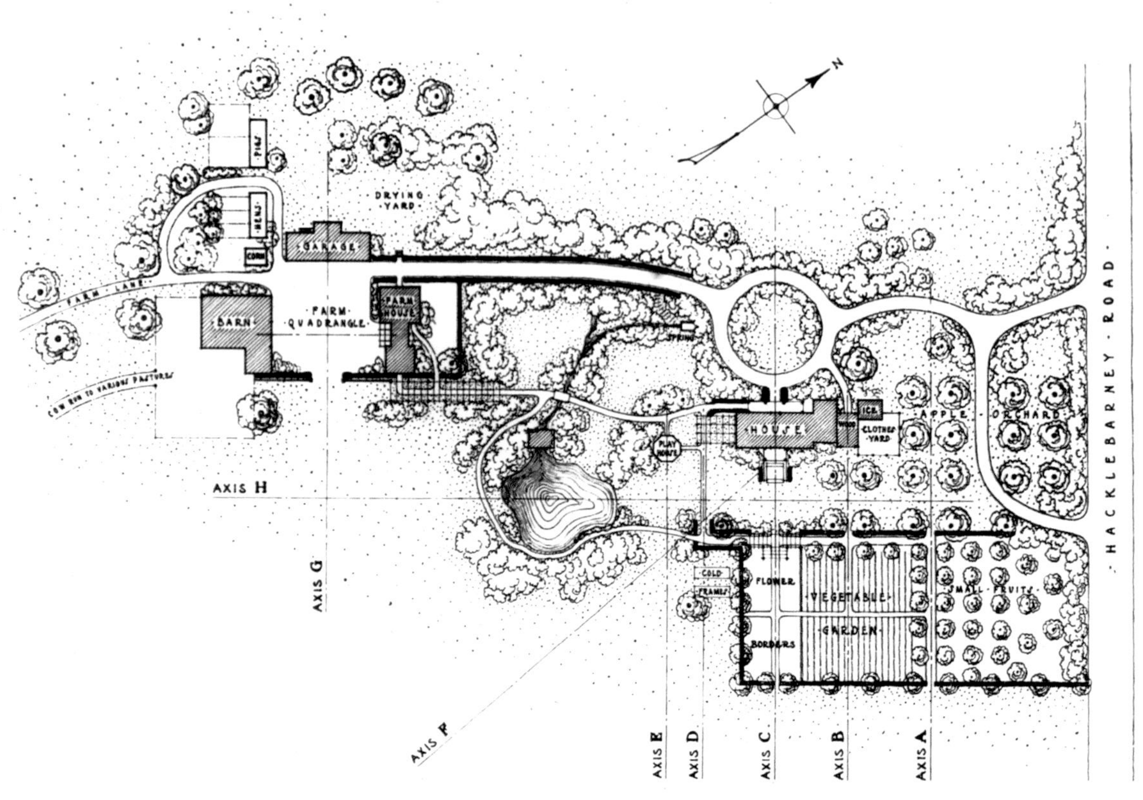

6.2
The "architectural" districts of the house and barnyard flank the "wild" district of the stream in this plan from *The Spirit of the Garden*, 1923.

drew the rhythms and materials of the farm into the garden. Two highly regulated, "architectural" realms – the house and gardens, and the farmyard – flank a water system which runs down a declivity between two hillsides. Organized on its own "wild" structure, the hydrologic system of the site is the central spine of the design.

In the five-acre core of the farm, the warp of architectural–wild–architectural is crossed by the weft of agricultural–domestic–agricultural. (Fig 6.2) The productive landscape was an extended domain of the house in which, "parts of the garden are essentially parts of the house, and there is no separating them if a successful scheme of the whole is to be realized."[8] From the house, three major axes and several minor ones extend into the agricultural landscape. Hutcheson used walls, paths, hedges, and allées to control and frame views from starting points, typically domestic, to scenic natural or town views. These "look-throughs" visually connect and compress the domestic landscape, productive landscape, and surrounding countryside as a single composition. (Fig 6.3) The plant palette is often calm; the "green elements" of boxwood, arborvitae, and similar trees and shrubs structure landscape rooms. In Hutcheson's view, over-emphasis on flowers led to "too solid a mass of color and too little well-planned green."[9]

Hutcheson incorporated the material aspects of farming into the garden, and aestheticized some aspects of the farm. The plants, rough wood, and watering ponds of the farm infused the gardens and blurred the line between aesthetic and productive. A grape arbor framed the view from the house to a flower bed, and cows in an oval pasture provided a foreground to the "Bow of the Woods," an attractive curve in Bamboo Brook viewed from the house through a frame of red cedars. (Fig 6.4) And a ha-ha and path used to guide cows from the barn to eastern meadows were both integrated into the garden with elegant stone retaining walls. (Fig 6.5)

As the farm evolved, so did the relationship between the agricultural and domestic realms. A 1912 plan shows an apple orchard, small fruit orchard, and vegetable garden incorporated into the orthogonal geometry of the gardens, and an irregular pool between house and barn that was used to water cattle and sheep. By 1927, the vegetable garden was gone, the apple orchard considerably reduced. The small fruit orchard was relocated to a more prominent location, displacing ornamental flower beds on the central axis of the house, and the livestock pond had been repurposed as a circular swimming pool. (Fig 6.6) The pond transformed over fifty years from a muddy, irregular pond, to a swimming pond edged in

6.3
Hutcheson designed the gardens, seen here in c. 1940, to include intimate moments and long views across the farm fields.

6.4
The pleasure gardens, seen here c. 1920, incorporated agricultural species such as grapes and red cedar.

6.5
Agricultural elements such as a ha-ha and cattle chute were incorporated into the gardens through stone retaining walls.

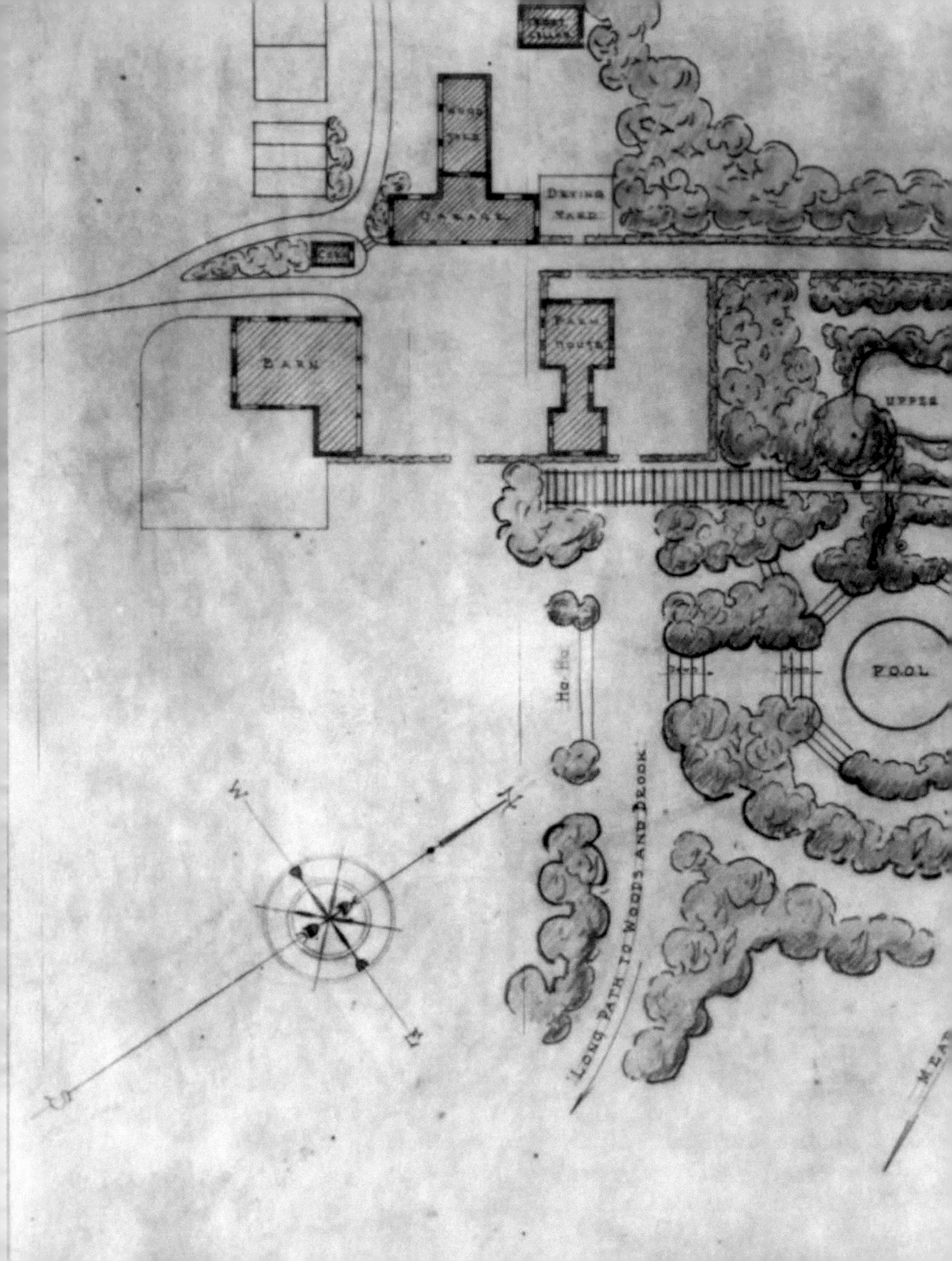
WOOD
DRYING
YARD
GARAGE
BARN
FARM
HOUSE
UPPER
POOL
HA-HA
LONG PATH TO WOODS AND BROOK
W
N
E
S

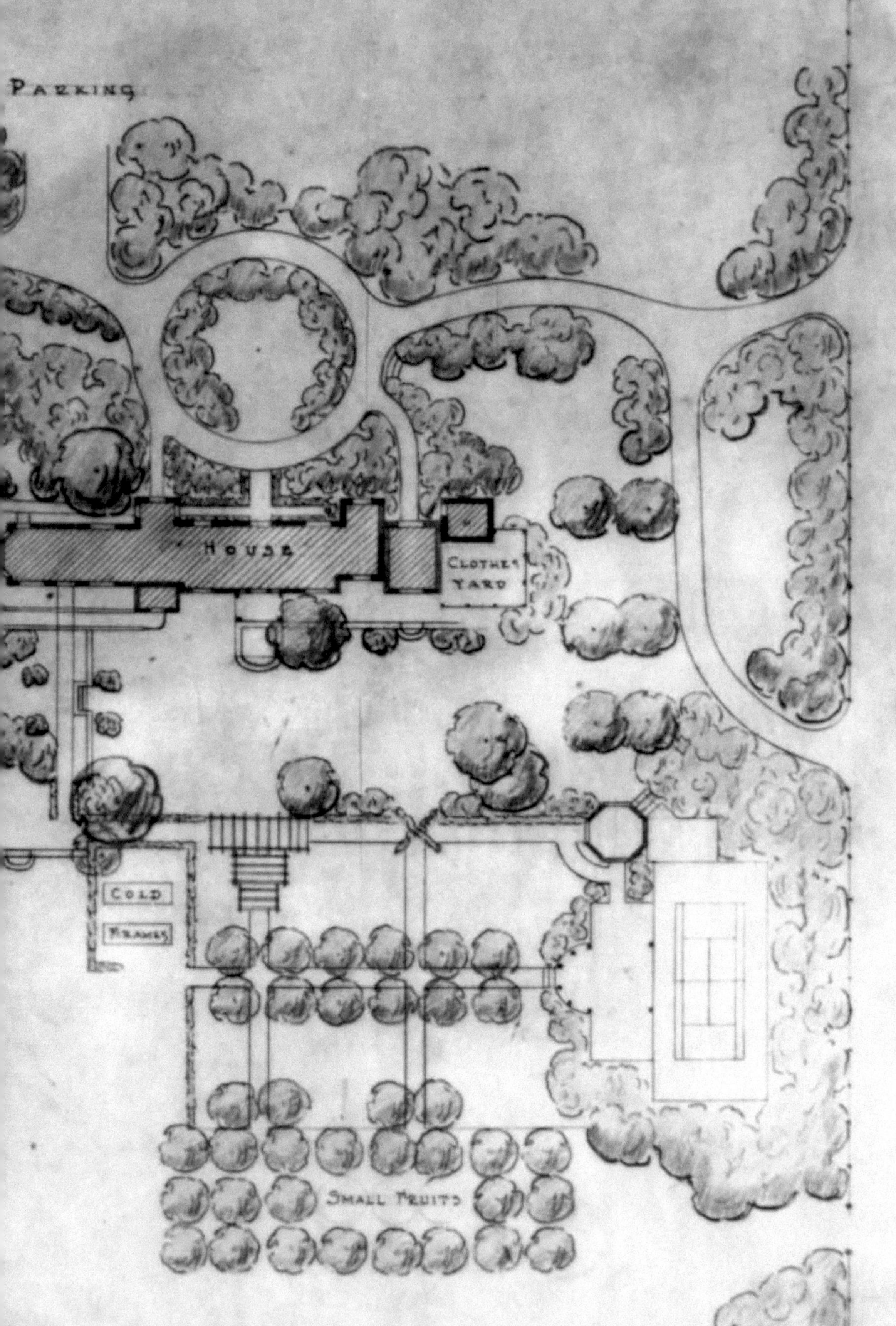
PARKING
HOUSE
CLOTHES YARD
COLD
FRAMES
SMALL FRUITS

wetland species of willow, clethra, iris, and spice bush, to a stone-edged circular swimming pool, as the planting design and geometry of the house slowly crept into the stream system. (Fig 6.7)

Later iterations of the farm design indicate Hutcheson's growing interest in ecology, seeking to understand the condition of agriculture situated within an ecosystem, and ecological thought as a guiding principle for design. Her work here prefigures the integration of agriculture, ecology, and design of the late twentieth century, seen in the later case studies of Green Gulch and Overlook. Hutcheson integrated native plant communities, implemented a soil conservation plan, restored animal habitat, and harvested water.

Hutcheson's designs were often based on classic Italian gardens but incorporated local, native plants. While she left no planting lists, some plants are distinguishable in photographs, and in her writings she advocated for greater use of "the embarrassment of riches" of "varied native vegetation tempered to the soil, the moisture and the climate of its environment."[10] In the introduction to *The Spirit of the Garden*, she described the need for ecological conservation and the value of native species, and in essays for the Garden Club of America, she advocated for the use of native plant species as both conservative of the nation's "native wealth of plant life"[11] and thrifty inasmuch as native species required less maintenance than exotic species.[12] And yet her descriptions of native plants always balance the practical with the poetic. She described the "great variety of both scientific and experimental knowledge which the landscape gardener must possess," needing to understand plant "habits, their hardiness, the soil they need, the winds they will not stand, the exposures they like, and whether you want an effect made by them which is going to be perfect in two years, in ten years, in fifty years, or in a hundred years."[13] But she also reminded her readers that "Our native growth ... calls to us through appealing grace and color. It flaunts blooms and berries ... and makes cover for the bird life it feeds. It ... carries with it unparalleled beauty of line for winter as well as summer."[14]

Her stance echoed that of her contemporaries: Wilhelm Miller's *The Prairie Spirit of Landscape Gardening* (1915), Frank Waugh's *The Natural Style in Landscape Gardening* (1917), and Edith Roberts and Elsa Rehmann's *American Plants for American Gardens* (1929) all addressed the question of a truly American style of landscape design based in understanding of and appreciation for native plant communities. These popular books advocated conservation and restoration of native ecosystems and their integration into landscape design at various scales. And the books drew on the emerging theory of plant ecology to propose designing with native species in clusters and communities that reflected and intensified native flora to establish regional specificity.[15] Hutcheson used this science of regional ecology to inform painterly and poetic compositions of wetland species, American sweetgum, sweetfern and iris, eastern red cedar, serviceberry, elderberry and arrowwood viburnum, most prominently around the water course, but also throughout the pleasure gardens.

6.6 (pages 80–81)
As Merchiston Farm evolved, the domestic and agricultural realms became more distinct, and the central stream became more complex, as seen in this c. 1940 plan.

6.7a–c
Hutcheson transformed the pond over time from a muddy spring, c. 1911, to a livestock pond edged in native plants, seen c. 1918, to a stone-edged pool, 2018.

Morris-Warren District
Hackettstown, New Jersey
****
Hutcheson, Mrs. Wm. M. M-Hr (25-16)2
Scale: 1" = 660' approx.

Field	Acres	Field	Acres	Field	Acres
1	4.0	5	8.0	9	16.0
2	13.0	6	12.0	Misc.	6.0
3	7.0	7	8.0		
4	3.0	8	25.0	Total	102.0

6.8
A 1944 USDA land use proposal for Merchiston Farm shows areas reserved for wildlife on the eastern border.

Beyond the efficiency of plants suited to their climate and region, and the poetry of a regionally specific plant palette, Hutcheson also explored the connections at the heart of ecological theory. A 1944 soil conservation plan notes the eastern edge of the property set aside as a wildlife corridor, and about half the property remained a woodland as a riparian buffer on Bamboo Brook, providing stream protection, habitat, and productive woodlot. (Fig 6.8) She advocated for designers to understand "the action of plants upon the soil, and the action of the different soils upon plants."[16] The soil conservation plan, intended to protect the vitality and fertility of the soils at Merchiston Farm, identifies four soil classes ranging from "suitable for cultivation with treatment" to "suited only for pasture or forest." The plan identifies amendments to improve soil health, primarily manure and lime; crop rotation to maintain nutrient balance in the soil; and soil protection practices to prevent erosion including contour cultivation, furrows, hedges, cover crops, buffer strips, and reforestation.

While soil conservation and habitat preservation formed a framework for the farm's vitality, Hutcheson expressed her ecological thinking in the water course at the center of the property. The system, fed by springs and harvested rainwater, connected the upland springs to Bamboo Brook through a series of pools, streams, dams, and falls. It begins in the Upper Water, an irregular pool with a dark bottom that creates a reflective surface for marginal plantings of forsythia, honeysuckle, and rhododendron. From there, water flows to a reservoir serving the house and farmyard and irrigating the gardens and greenhouses, then to a circular pool encompassed by octagonal steps and terraces. From the pool, the water joins a stream coursing over a series of small dams and spillways to flow beneath the Little House, a small garden structure where Hutcheson worked. Along the ingenious water harvesting and display system, water performed aesthetic, recreational, domestic, agricultural, and ecological functions, tying together the garden design ideas playing out across the farm.

While the farm was a site for synthesizing formal and scientific theories, Hutcheson primarily saw garden design as a progressive activity, an agent of cultural and civic improvement. *The Spirit of the Garden* was dedicated to "those with a *progressive spirit* in their concern for the fine art of garden making," and many of her lectures and writings for the Garden Club of America sought to shift the focus of that institution from a "mere social gathering and mutual admiration party" to a "political and civic force."[17] The farm too was a political landscape where Hutcheson, one of seven founding members of the Women's Land Army when it incorporated in 1918, employed "farmerettes" – a contraction of farmer and suffragette – to work the farm in 1918, one of thirty-two Women's Land Army units in New Jersey that summer.[18] (Fig 6.9) The WLA, in operation from 1917 to 1919, filled a gap in the US farm industry caused by World War I, and employed more than 15,000 women in forty states.[19] The WLA was a rapid response to the US entry into World War I and combined the political activism of the suffragette movement, the educational mission of the Women's National Farm & Garden Union, and the social influence of the

6.9
Hutcheson (center) with farmerettes during the 1918 harvest.

Garden Club of America, of which Hutcheson was an active and prominent member.[20]

Hutcheson described garden design as a combination of science and art and practiced it as an aesthetic, productive, and political praxis. Although her book, *The Spirit of the Garden*, intentionally does not focus on horticulture, planting schemes, or color palettes but instead on spatial composition, her essays describe a different practice, one reflected in her own farm, where the debate of architectural versus wild gardens was resolved through the temporal practice of farming, the spatial forms and material flows of ecology, and with the goal of carving out a place where women could productively contribute to society.

After Hutcheson's death in 1959, Merchiston Farm passed to her daughter, Martha Hutcheson Norton. She and her husband, Charles McKim Norton, donated the property to the Morris County Park Commission in 1972, and the farm now operates as Bamboo Brook Outdoor Education Center, offering horticultural and wildlife tours of the property. The house was restored in the 1990s and the gardens in 2004; the meadows, woods, and streams are networked with trails that link the property to over 1,000 acres of County parks.

Notes

1 Martha Brookes Hutcheson, *The Spirit of the Garden* (1923) (Amherst: University of Massachusetts Press, 2001), ix.

2 Rebecca Davidson, "Designing Woman: Martha Brookes Hutcheson," *Arnoldia* 61, no. 1 (2001): 23–24.
3 *Annual Catalogue 1902–03* (Cambridge, MA: Massachusetts Institute of Technology, 1901), 42.
4 Ibid., 45.
5 Farm records, Box 93.19, Martha Brookes Hutcheson Archives, Morris County Park Commission, Morris Township, NJ.
6 See William Robinson, *The Wild Garden* (1870) and Reginald Blomfeld, *Formal Gardens in England* (1892).
7 Hutcheson, *Spirit of the Garden*, 12.
8 Ibid., 50.
9 Ibid., 15.
10 Martha Brookes Hutcheson, "One of Our National Blights," *Garden Club of America Bulletin* (Nov. 1926): 31.
11 Martha Brookes Hutcheson, "Possible Inspiration through Garden Clubs toward Wiser and more Beautiful Plantings," *Garden Club of America Bulletin* (July 1931): 118.
12 Hutcheson, "One of Our National Blights," 30.
13 Martha Brookes Brown, "Landscape Gardening: A Conversation," *The Outlook* (July 24, 1909): 737.
14 Hutcheson, "One of Our National Blights," 31.
15 Roxi Thoren, "'Dreaming True'," Placesjournal.org, accessed January 15, 2019, https://placesjournal.org/article/martha-brookes-hutcheson-and-feminist-ecology/
16 Brown, "Landscape Gardening," 738.
17 Rebecca Warren Davidson, "Introduction to the Reprint Edition," in *The Spirit of the Garden*, Martha Brookes Hutcheson, 1923 (Amherst: University of Massachusetts Press, 2001), xxix.
18 Elaine F. Weiss, *Fruits of Victory: The Women's Land Army of America in the Great War* (Lincoln, NE: Potomac Books, 2008), 48, 175.
19 Ibid., 107.
20 Thoren, "Dreaming True."

Welwyn Garden City

Hertfordshire, England

Ebenezer Howard, Louis de Soissons, 1920

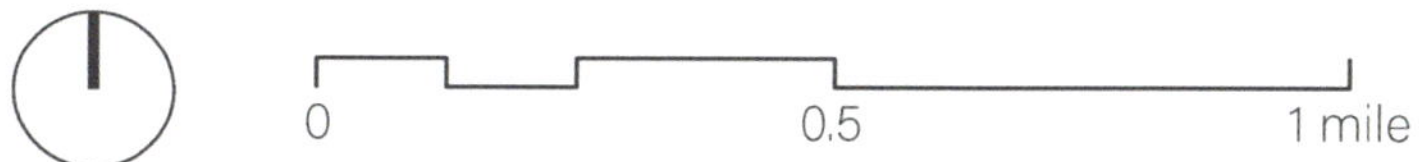
0
0.5
1 mile

Welwyn Garden City and the garden city movement that originated in England have frequently been discussed through planner Ebenezer Howard's frame of "a town designed for healthy living," combining the best aspects of city and rural life into a utopian hybrid community, with agriculture used as a buffering greenbelt around moderate-density towns. In studies of garden cities, agriculture is usually presented as one element within Howard's ameliorative view of nature that saw access to open space, clean air and water, and vegetation as physically, mentally, and spiritually restorative.

But agriculture was more than a green salve in the garden city idea; it was ideological, tied to both economy and ecology. In the garden city diagram, the comprehensive urban development of a small city provided for all the needs – social, economic, and physical – of a community. The garden city served as an early prototype for agricultural urbanism, one shift in twentieth-century agriculture from large-scale farms and estates to the granular integration of agriculture within urban development. Howard proposed two forms of agriculture in his diagram: a greenbelt surrounding the city that would provide ecosystem services, ensuring access to healthy food, recreational areas, clean air, and clean water; and allotment gardens that would provide opportunities for domestic self-sufficiency, a significant concern in the interwar period. Agriculture for Howard served multiple urban purposes. It was a critical element in protecting human health, it protected and improved regional soils, it provided citizens with a measure of self-sufficiency, and it provided economic resiliency at both the civic level, through land leases, and the individual level, through reducing a family's food budget.

Through the integration of agriculture into and around new cities, Howard intended to revitalize England's flagging agricultural industry by connecting farms directly to local markets and providing employment for urban dwellers.[1] He noted the loss of soil vitality as food produced in the rural landscape was brought to cities and waste was disposed in landfills or burned rather than being composted and returned to the soil. The garden city was designed as a closed-loop development that connected farm and market, reinvesting urban waste into soil regeneration.

In his writing, Howard proposed a diagram for urban development with circular, concentric rings of activities. The diagram proposed the cellular division of the landscape into a matrix of dense urban cores surrounded by agricultural greenbelts barring sprawl and protecting agricultural lands, and with closed-loop economic and ecological systems in each urban cell. But he recognized the need for local adaptation, and the cities that emerged, first Letchworth in 1903, followed by Welwyn in 1920, tested the capacity of the diagram to fit local circumstances.

In *Garden Cities for Tomorrow*, Howard identified benefits and problems of both city and countryside in late nineteenth-century England and proposed the garden city as an ameliorative marriage of the two. At that time, over 70 percent of the population of England and Wales lived in cities which provided economic and social opportunity but were crowded and unhealthy with smoke-filled air and pollution.[2] Rural towns offered the reverse, with healthy settings but few social or

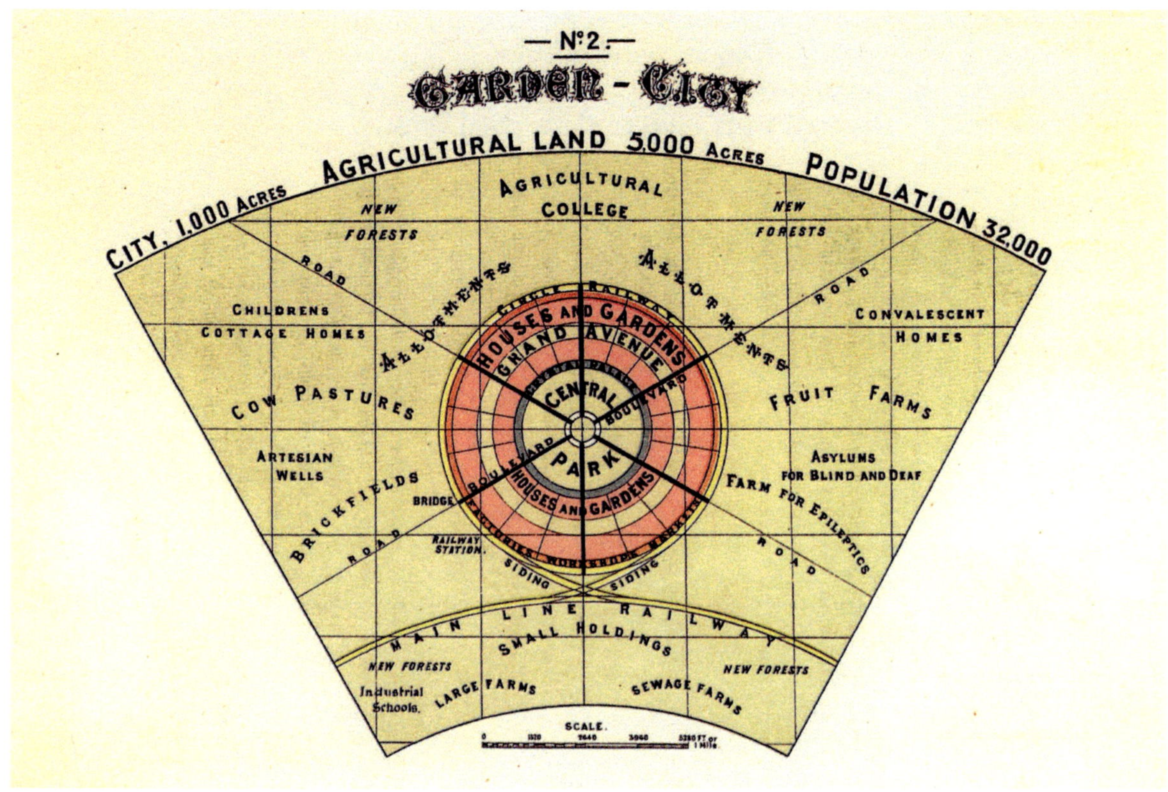

7.1
Howard's "Garden-City" diagram from *Garden Cities of To-morrow* shows the 1,000-acre city surrounded by 5,000 acres of agricultural land.

economic opportunities.[3] The garden city would combine the two, creating a new synthetic development with the best of both. At the same time, the garden city would solve two parallel problems: slum housing and rural depopulation.[4]

The garden city was a comprehensive urban development plan for a small city that would provide for all the social, economic, and physical needs of a community and would be part of a planned migration of workers from London to what was perceived as a healthy, rural setting. A form of utopian socialism, the towns would be self-contained, balanced, and compact urban centers, with 32,000 people living in a 1,000-acre town surrounded by a factory belt for employment, then ringed by a 5,000-acre greenbelt containing farms and institutions that would benefit from a rural context. (Fig 7.1)

Many of Howard's goals are tenets espoused in the twenty-first century as sustainable urban development. The greenbelt was necessary to maintain a healthy urban environment and to limit development to a walkable, high-density, compact center. The radially planned cities would be three-quarters of a mile from center to greenbelt, and were to be divided into six wards by radial boulevards, each 130 feet wide. The concentric city would center on a garden ringed by public institutions such as a library, town hall, and museum. Next was a broad ring of central parks, surrounded by covered shopping areas inspired by Joseph Paxton's Crystal Palace. These were surrounded by rings of residential development with a green boulevard at their core holding institutional buildings such as churches and schools. Finally, a narrow band of industry framed by a circular railroad provided sites of employment for the residents. (Fig 7.2) The garden cities would form a network across the countryside, connected by train lines and separated by protected greenbelts containing a wide range of agriculture, including large and small farms, fruit orchards, family allotments, dairy pastures, and forestry. (Fig 7.3) Within the greenbelt, Howard also located health institutions such as hospitals and sanitoria, providing access to nature for patients' recuperation.

The garden city was intended as a self-sustaining city, where citizens could live and work and where food for all would be produced locally. The schematic plan, clearly described as a "Diagram Only – Plan Cannot Be Drawn Until Site Selected," provided small-scale sustenance farming for families on allotment gardens, larger-scale commercial farming on fruit farms, dairy farms, and other large farms, and agricultural education.

Howard's approach to agriculture was influenced by time spent in the United States from age 21 to 28 (1872–1879). With two friends, he moved to Howard Co., Nebraska, where he purchased 160 acres, built a home, and planted crops including corn, potatoes, cucumbers, and watermelons. Like Olmsted before him, Howard was a better planner than farmer; the enterprise was a failure, and within months, he moved to Chicago where he was a shorthand court and press reporter for several years.[5] His years in Chicago doubtless influenced his garden city idea: Chicago, "the garden city," had burned in 1871 and was being rebuilt while Howard lived there, spurring urban design innovations and the construction of parks as healthful social amenities. Olmsted's 1869 design for Riverside, an innovative park-like suburb connected to Chicago by rail, was being built and likewise would have been noted by Howard. (Fig 7.4)

Howard's agricultural proposal was based in several ideas: access to rural land as a matter of social justice and utopian ideals; a closed-loop approach to soil vitality; and a sophisticated economic approach to agriculture. He believed that landownership was central to social justice, as land provided a source of sustenance and of wealth through development. He also felt that agricultural lands needed to be protected from the development imperatives of capitalism.[6] In the garden city diagram, Howard proposed agriculture as a private industry on leased, communally owned land. However, as the proposal developed through experiments at Letchworth and Welwyn, his ideas evolved and he increasingly saw zoning as the preferred tool for greenbelt preservation rather than common ownership of land.[7]

British agriculture was in crisis in the early twentieth century, with a shortage of farm labor as families moved to cities for industrial jobs, and a glut of cheap corn and wheat from overseas which had made those crops unprofitable in England.[8] Like Olmsted at Moraine Farm, Howard called for a shift away from grain production towards perishable foods such as dairy or market garden crops. His goal was to provide enough local food production to meet local needs, and by locating social and economic opportunities adjacent to agricultural

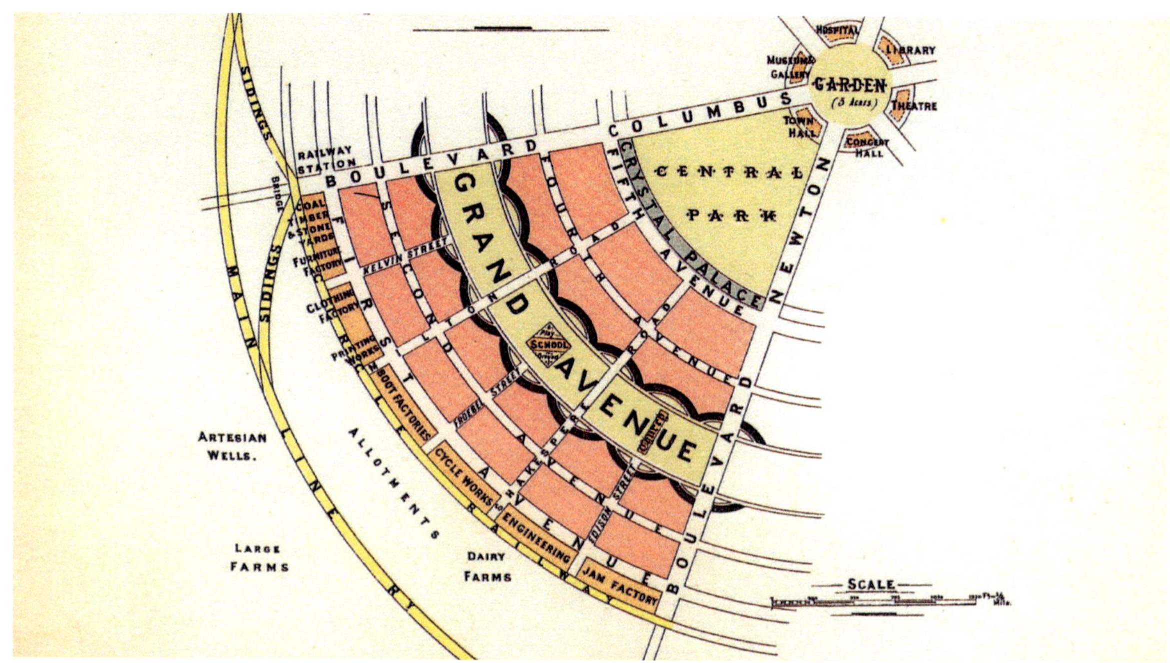

7.2
Howard's "Garden-City Ward and Centre" diagram shows his ideal organization with gardens and civic institutions at the center and industry ringing the city.

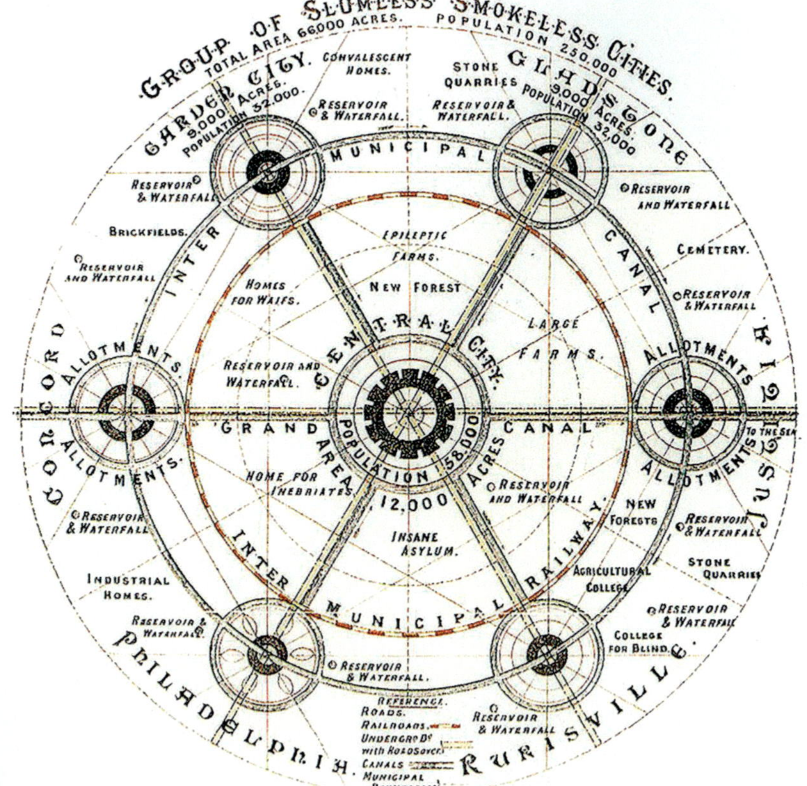

7.3
Howard's "Group of Slumless Smokeless Cities" diagram shows a green landscape of farms, forests, and sanitoria with a network of connected garden cities.

7.4
Olmsted, Vaux, & Co.'s 1869 design for Riverside included many of the garden city elements, such as rail connection, dense commercial districts, and protective vegetated zones.

lands, to provide an agricultural workforce to revitalize the British agricultural economy.[9]

In addition to a flooded market, British farmers had experienced several years of poor harvests, in part a result of weather but in part a result of declining soil productivity.[10] Howard proposed what is now termed a closed-loop system, reversing what Karl Marx described as a "metabolic rift" between country and city.[11] Marx observed that intensive agriculture in the country and food consumption in cities was depleting rural soils of nutrients, transferred through produce to the cities where they ended as waste, burned, or in landfills, accumulating as toxins and pollutants.[12] Marx called for co-locating agriculture and industry, for agricultural as well as political and economic purposes. It is unclear whether Howard intentionally drew on Marx, but he expressed the same ideas, calling to return nutrients to the soil with the "refuse of the town ... utilized on the agricultural portions of the estate."[13] He viewed household food waste and manure as a valuable nutrient resource, critical to improving local agricultural soils.[14]

Howard's plan was a hybrid socialist/capitalist approach, seeking to reconcile environmental and social needs.[15] Improved soil would provide improved crop yields, but also, Howard proposed, increased land value; soil fertility was proposed as a basis for economic growth. Investors' ability to finance the development of garden cities depended on inexpensive agricultural land values, a result of impoverished soils. The first income for the development would come through leasing the agricultural lands, and later compact development would generate revenue through land value, thereby subsidizing the social aspects of the community.[16]

The utopian ideals of the garden city were refined between the two world wars in an era of rapid social change. They were tested first in the development of Letchworth, designed by Raymond Unwin and Barry Parker, then at Welwyn. Howard instigated the development of Welwyn and located the site twenty miles north of London in an agricultural region, with good transportation infrastructure connecting it to the city. He also arranged financing and drafted the bylaws, selected directors, and located a chairman, engineer Theodore Chambers.[17]

Welwyn Garden City Company Ltd. incorporated in 1920, and hired planner C. M. Crickmer to draft a preliminary design showing a 1,500-acre town quartered by rail lines and ringed with an agricultural belt and parks. The plan was further developed by Louis de Soissons, showing little of the concentric city diagram developed by Howard. It included a broad 100-foot-wide parkway in the center of town, with sporting facilities such as tennis courts and a bowling green, and encircling open space that included woodlands, recreation, public works, and 900 acres of agricultural land.[18] The first homes were connected in twos and fours, with long, narrow lots intended to include residential kitchen gardens. (Fig 7.5)

Protected agricultural land was key to the marketing appeal of the town, with its "entire freedom from smoke pollution, its permanent open spaces … [which] ensured that pure air and sunshine, rural amenities and all they mean to health, would never be spoiled."[19] Agriculture was also key to the economic plan; prior to development, much of the land was leased for agriculture, which paid 3 percent above the capital costs of the corporation, allowing continued reinvestment in the development.[20]

The development corporation initially struggled to purchase land from reluctant landowners. The corporation purchased 1,458 acres at auction from Lord Desborough, and another 689 from Lord Salisbury; they sought to purchase an additional 250 acres from Desborough, who refused.[21] As a result, the designed agricultural belt is discontinuous, particularly to the east, and the plan included only about 600 acres of agricultural land out of about 2,400 acres, a far smaller percentage than Howard's original diagrams.[22]

As Welwyn was being developed, permitted, and constructed, the corporation leased the greenbelt land to dairy farmers to generate a steady income stream. The dairy industry at Welwyn shows the tight interconnection between agriculture, production, employment, and local consumption. In the 1920s, the New Town Trust, a Quaker cooperative, leased 650 acres of the agricultural belt for farming and raising dairy cattle, pigs, and chickens. They planted eighteen

7.5 (pages 98–99)
In Welwyn's Broadwater Road Estate, seen in 1928, many of the original residents planted kitchen gardens in their long lots.

acres of orchards, and sold bacon, currants, and mushrooms at the Welwyn Stores.[23] They produced "certified" milk, a proto-organic certification based on the cooperative's farming practices that allowed them to distribute unpasteurized milk. In line with Howard's vision of a healthy environment and quasi-socialist land management, the cooperative didn't use chemical fertilization and avoided commercial production, in a model similar to many of today's organic, community-supported agriculture farms. (Fig 7.6) Unfortunately, these practices drove up dairy prices for the cooperative beyond market rates, and the New Town Trust failed after a decade.[24] At the same time, the New Town Agricultural Guild converted a 320-year-old barn into a modern dairy, installing narrow gauge track to bring in feed and remove waste. (Fig 7.7) The dairy was surrounded by livestock pastures, and milk was distributed to the town by the Welwyn Stores. By 1927, the town had expanded to the dairy; the livestock were sold while the milk-processing facility remained, processing milk collected from local farms. The processing facility too eventually moved, in 1939, to the newly constructed Welwyn Department Store.[25]

By 1949, there were 471 acres reserved for agriculture, a significant reduction from the original 600 acres. Agriculture remained protected outside the urban perimeter, along with a golf course, woods, parks, gravel works, airfield, and hospital, but changing attitudes towards soil preservation and improvement could be seen in a note in the annual corporation report that the removal of the local Panshanger Airfield would open up 231 acres for agriculture and some reserve gravel or industrial areas might also be available.[26] Promoting these areas with poor, degraded, or even toxic soils as future agricultural sites indicates that agriculture was beginning to take a lower priority than industrial activities.

Within the developed town, there were thirty-five acres of family allotment gardens, most of which (thirty acres) were temporary, built in response to World War II food shortages, in areas planned as building sites. These were large contiguous areas with communal tool sheds and greenhouses. The city also included twenty-eight acres of smaller, privately owned gardens intermingled with the residential areas. (Fig 7.8)

Local agriculture remained popular through the 1960s. A 1957 report to the corporation showed a slight increase in productive acres to 511, although of those, 121 acres were ultimately intended for gravel extraction. In the post-war era, one in seven houses desired an allotment garden, but distributing them around town was problematic. In the older areas of town, there were thirty-five acres of gardens integrated into the fabric, but these were under-cultivated; older families had less interest in growing their own food. In newer areas with younger families, there was unmet demand for allotment gardens; these families relied instead on the large, sixty-five-acre central gardens. Following a period of disinterest from the 1970s to 1990s, resident interest in local gardening strengthened; in 2018, the Welwyn Hatfield Council managed twenty-six gardens in Welwyn with nearly 300 plots available ranging from 75 to 200 square meters. Although the town had opened six new gardens since 2010, there was still a wait list for the plots.

7.6
The model dairy at the Lower Handside Farm, c. 1930.

7.7
The electrical milking machines and narrow gauge rail system at the Lower Handside dairy farm were notable innovations.

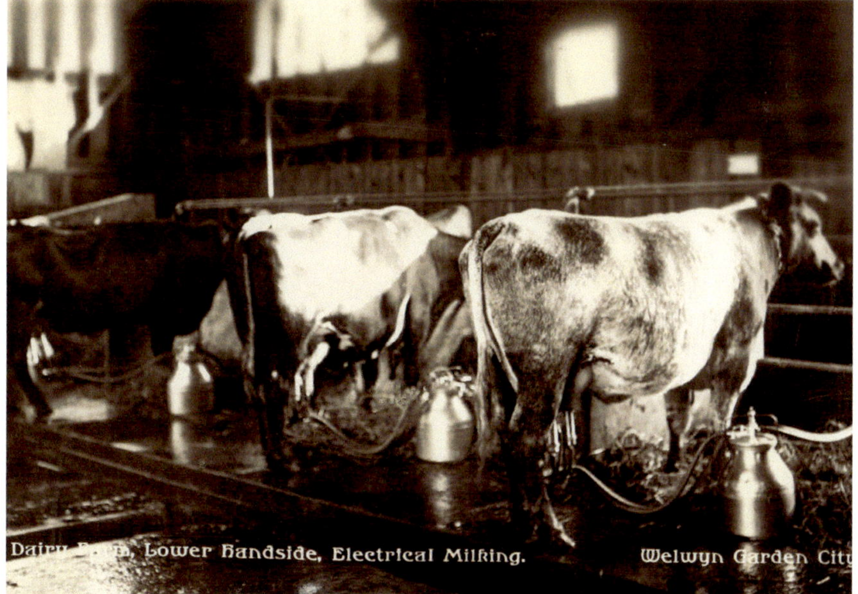

7.8
Many of the homes in the center of town originally had private kitchen gardens, visible in this 1935 photograph.

Howard was explicit that human society relies on nature: "All that we are and all that we have comes from it. Our bodies are formed of it; to it they return. We are fed by it, clothed by it, and by it we are warmed and sheltered … It is the source of all health, all wealth, all knowledge."[27] He saw the balance of city and nature as critical to our cultural and economic survival, as well as to our physical and mental health. Lewis Mumford saw Howard's garden city proposal as an ecological balance, displaying the "essential biological criteria of dynamic equilibrium and organic balance: balance as between city and country in a larger ecological pattern, and balance between the varied functions of the city."[28] At Welwyn Garden City prior to World War II, agriculture was closely tied to the economic development of the city, and to its attraction for urban residents seeking a healthy yet dynamic environment in which to live and work, with agriculture as a permanent, integral aspect of the city, as a barrier to sprawl, and a source of local self-sufficiency. After World War II, there was a brief period where local food production continued, but larger national and international forces made local agriculture increasingly unattractive at the family scale and difficult at the regional scale. Today, much of the greenbelt has been developed, or is in use as parks, school athletic fields, and golf courses, with some limited agriculture still extant to the north and east. While Welwyn succeeded as an agricultural town, it did so through land use policies, communal landownership, and individual dedication to food production.

Notes

1 Lewis Mumford, "An American Introduction to Sir Ebenezer Howard's 'Garden Cities of Tomorrow'," *Pencil Points,* March, 1945, 74.
2 Stanley Buder, *Visionaries and Planners: The Garden City Movement and the Modern Community* (Oxford: Oxford University Press, 1990), 68.
3 Ebenezer Howard, *Garden Cities of To-morrow* (1898) (Cambridge, MA: MIT Press, 1965), 47.
4 Ibid., 48.
5 Dugald Macfadyen, *Sir Ebenezer Howard and the Town Planning Movement* (Manchester: Manchester University Press, 1933), 10–11.
6 Frederic Osborn, *Greenbelt Cities: The British Contribution* (London: Faber and Faber, 1946), 20.
7 Ibid., 21–24.
8 Howard, *To-morrow*, 61.
9 Ibid., 64.
10 Brett Clark, "Ebenezer Howard and the Marriage of Town and Country: An Introduction to Howard's 'Garden Cities of To-morrow,'" *Organization & Environment* 16, no. 1 (2003): 90.
11 Ibid., 89.
12 Marx's work used agriculture as a metaphor for economic and political systems; his work was based on the German chemist Justus von Leibig's 1859 study of British agriculture. (Clark, "Ebenezer Howard," 89).
13 Howard, *To-morrow*, 55.
14 Ibid., 61.
15 Ibid., 65.
16 Ibid., 74.
17 Buder, *Visionaries and Planners*, 121.
18 R. L. Reiss, *The Town Planning Review* 8, no. 3/4 (1920): 180.
19 S. A. Sadler Forster, *Welwyn: Where Industry Prospers* (Welwyn Garden City, UK: Welwyn Garden City Ltd., 1939), 2.
20 Reiss, *Town Planning Review*, 180.
21 Maurice de Soissons, *Welwyn Garden City: A Town Designed for Healthy Living* (Cambridge: Publications for Companies, 1988), 35.
22 Ibid., 43.
23 Ibid., 53.
24 Buder, *Visionaries and Planners*, 124.
25 Robert Gill, "New Town Agricultural Guild," *Our Welwyn Garden City* (August 18, 2017), accessed October 15, 2018, www.ourwelwyngardencity.org.uk/content/topics/the_workplace/farming/new-town-agricultural-guild.
26 Louis de Soissons, *Report of the Welwyn Garden City Development Corporation* (Welwyn Garden City, UK: Welwyn Garden City Development Corp., 1949), 41.
27 Howard, *To-morrow*, 18.
28 Lewis Mumford, *The City in History: Its Origins, Its Transformations, and Its Prospects* (New York: Harcourt Brace & World, 1961), 516.

Ziebigk Siedlung

Dessau, Germany

Leberecht Migge and Leopold Fischer, 1926–1929

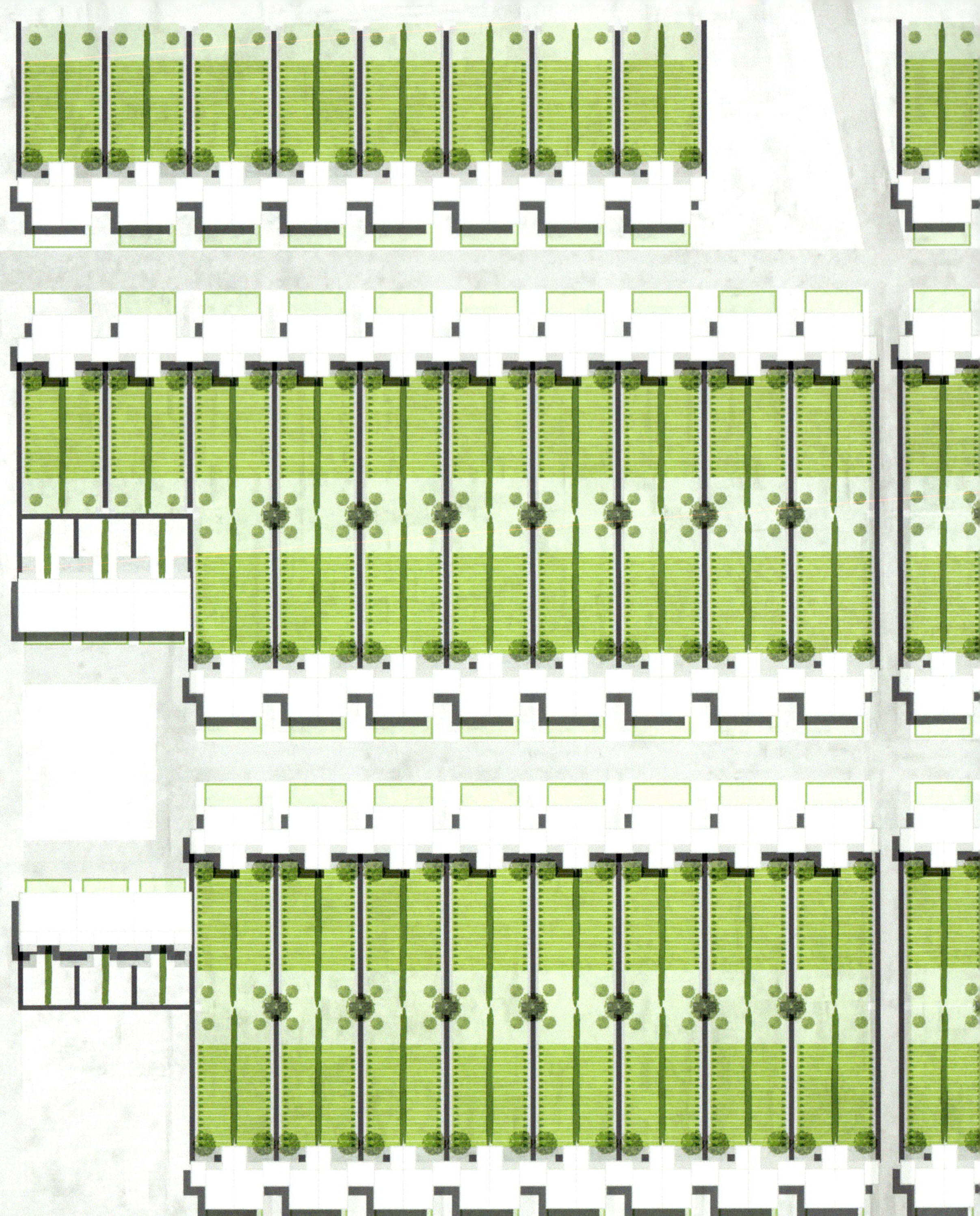

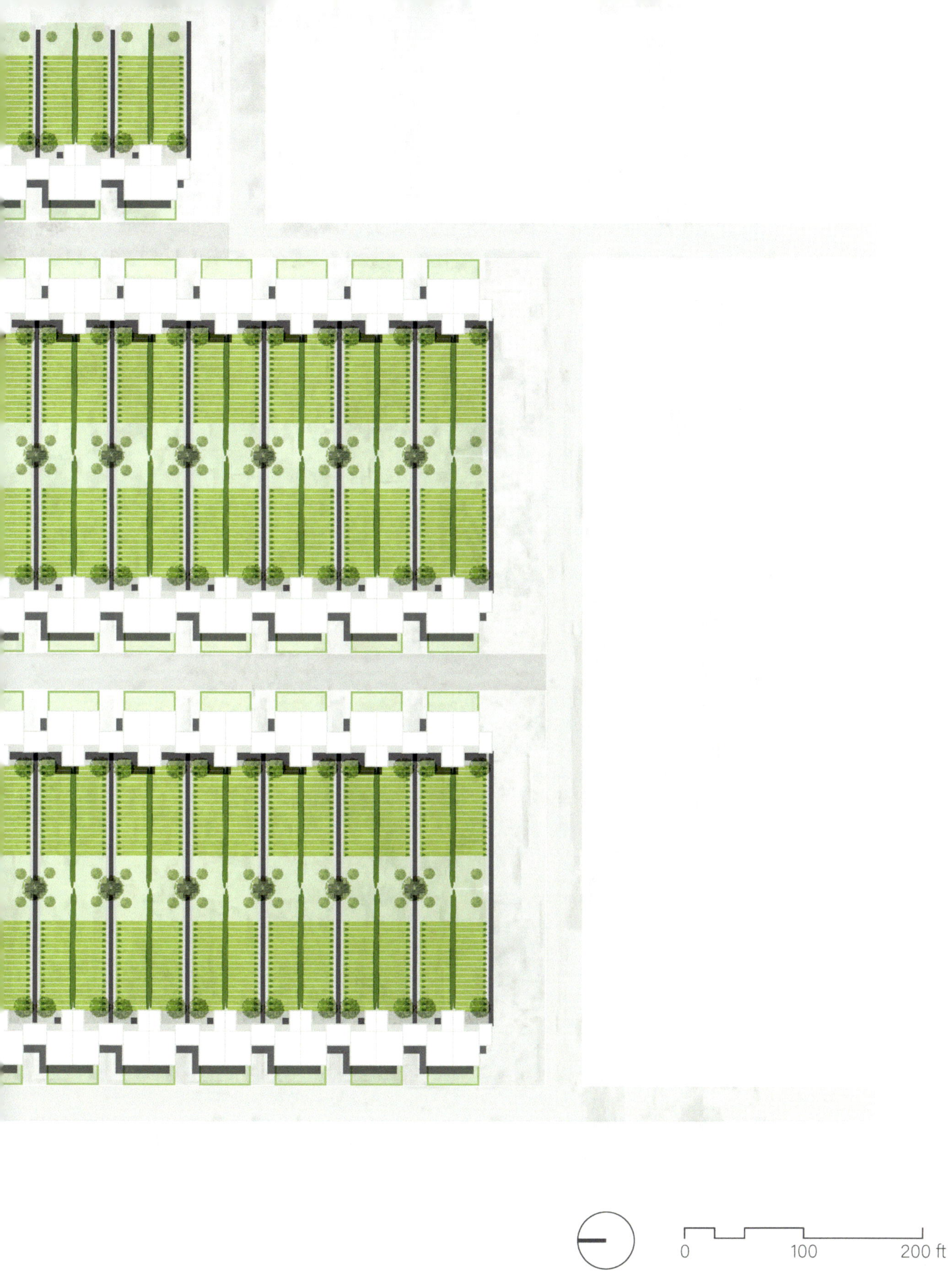

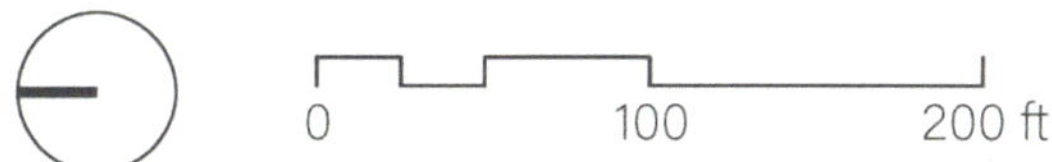
0
100
200 ft

In Ziebigk, a northwest suburb of Dessau, Germany, three-quarters of a mile from the famous Bauhaus school, garden designer Leberecht Migge and architect Leopold Fischer designed the clearest manifestation of Migge's theory of urbanism founded on domestic self-sufficiency and intensive agriculture. The neighborhood was one of many *siedlungen*, workers' estates, designed and built in the early twentieth century in Germany. It translates many Bauhaus design principles into garden design, while also incorporating a number of bio-technic principles not usually associated with functionalist design. In books and pamphlets, Migge had proposed urban development as an expression of his reform agenda, modern aesthetic, and civic ideology. He proposed urban agriculture as a form of "self-colonization" of the nation, which would allow Germans to become independent of capitalist material and monetary systems, with extensive gardens that provided food, healthy activity, and access to fresh air and sunshine. He conceived of the kitchen garden as the primary unit of urban development; at Ziebigk, Migge and Fischer tested his theories, thoroughly integrating the house and garden and using that module to define the block and neighborhood structure.

Migge was a frequent polemicist as well as an active designer, proposing new forms and agendas for garden design in the industrial age. His significant writings include *Garden Culture of the Twentieth Century* (1913), *Everyman Self-Sufficient!* (1918), *Green Manifesto* (1919), *German Domestic Colonization* (1926), and *Biological Principles for Growing Siedlung* (1932). The titles give a sense of Migge's reform agenda: defining a new agency for garden design to meet a changing society; solving a food supply concern through individual production; "colonizing" the nation itself as a source of food; and providing a biological approach to urban design. Migge originally published his *Green Manifesto* under the pen name "Spartacus in Green;" the pseudonym referenced both the gladiator who led a slave uprising against the oppressive oligarchy of the Roman empire and the Sparticists, a German communist movement, and also included one of the first uses of "green" as a political term.[1] While *Green Manifesto* was a political manifesto, proposing the small garden as a social and economic solution, many of his publications were prescriptive, especially *Everyman Self-Sufficient!*, which was effectively a handbook for urban homesteading that detailed tactics to ensure maximum food production on minimal land.

Migge saw garden design as the defining quality of twentieth-century urban life, "The old idea was called city. A new one lives, / The general idea of the 20th Century: Land!"[2] Writing in part in response to the food shortages of World War I and the devaluation of German currency in the years following,[3] Migge proposed creating, planting, and maintaining small gardens as a progressive social and economic tool that could also solve the problems of overcrowding that accompanied the rapid urban development of the era. He proposed growing food as a way to provide sustenance for all citizens, to curb the economic crisis in Germany, and to become independent from a capitalist economic system. In his writings, land reform and resettlement provided a "third way" between capitalism and communism, shifting production to the individual rather than the industrialist or the collective.[4]

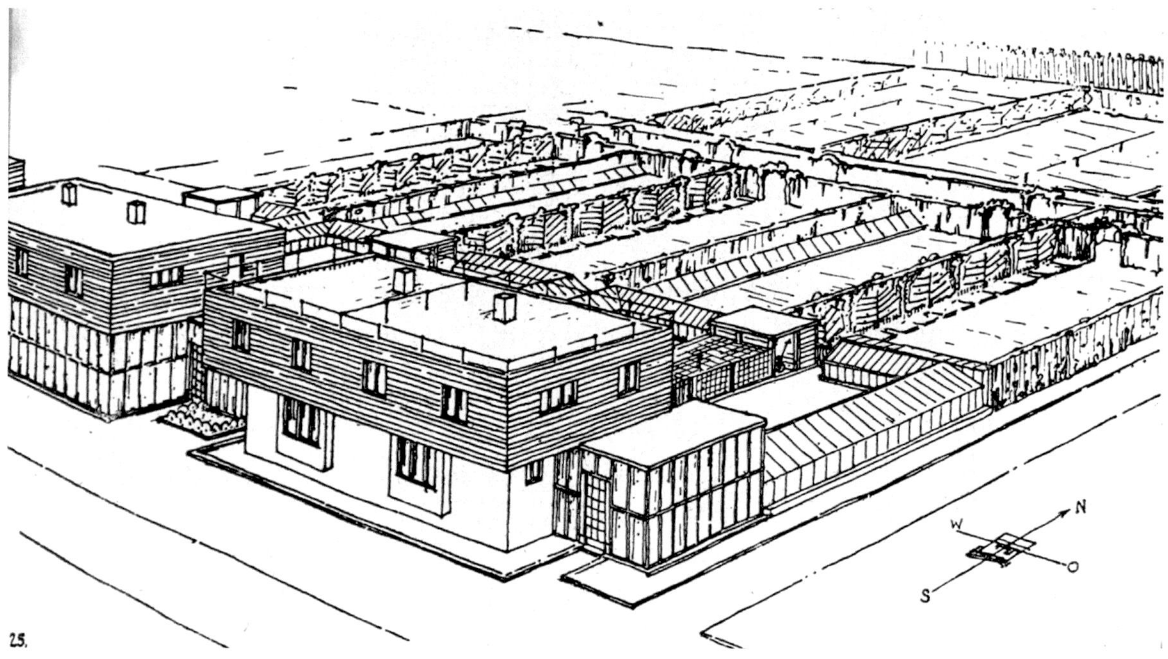

8.1
Migge's illustration of a *siedlung* shows the architecture of the duplex homes extending into the garden with greenhouses, outbuildings, cold frames, and espaliered fruit trees.

His was an active approach that required engaged citizens willing to work the land. "The land saves the city," he wrote, continuing, "One plants: public gardens – for the city-bound youth. / One plants: allotment gardens – for the city-bound dweller. / One plants: *Siedlungen* – for the city-bound worker. / And plants: model farms – for the needy. / One plants!"[5] Even at the time, there were critiques of this labor model, "not evening dilettantes, but work fanatics, not tired club members, but proud subscribers to success."[6] This labor-intensive way of life was neither a universal solution nor the sole solution to food shortages or provisioning the nation.

Migge's ideas of urban agriculture were informed by Ebenezer Howard's Garden City proposals but conceptually inverted Howard's idea. Where Howard described country-city, bringing dense development to a rural context and buffering the two realms with a greenbelt, Migge proposed *Stadt-Land,* bringing the rural, "the Green land of youth, of health and happiness. The fresh, virgin land,"[7] into the urban context and metaphorically re-colonizing or homesteading German cities. Migge viewed the garden as the primary unit of planning, able to scale up from the individual home to the city, region, and nation. He conceived of this both spatially as a series of nested vegetated places, as well as systemically as the regenerative cycles of the garden, especially composting, could form the basis of scaled networks for sanitation, water, and other services.[8] In his essays and books, Migge suggested the garden designer as the principal agent in urban design, with the forms and processes of gardening structuring urban dwelling from the individual house to the patterns of neighborhoods and cities.[9] (Fig 8.1) And like a garden, the city would grow and change over time as family compositions changed and residents altered their gardens to suit their evolving needs. (Fig. 8.2)

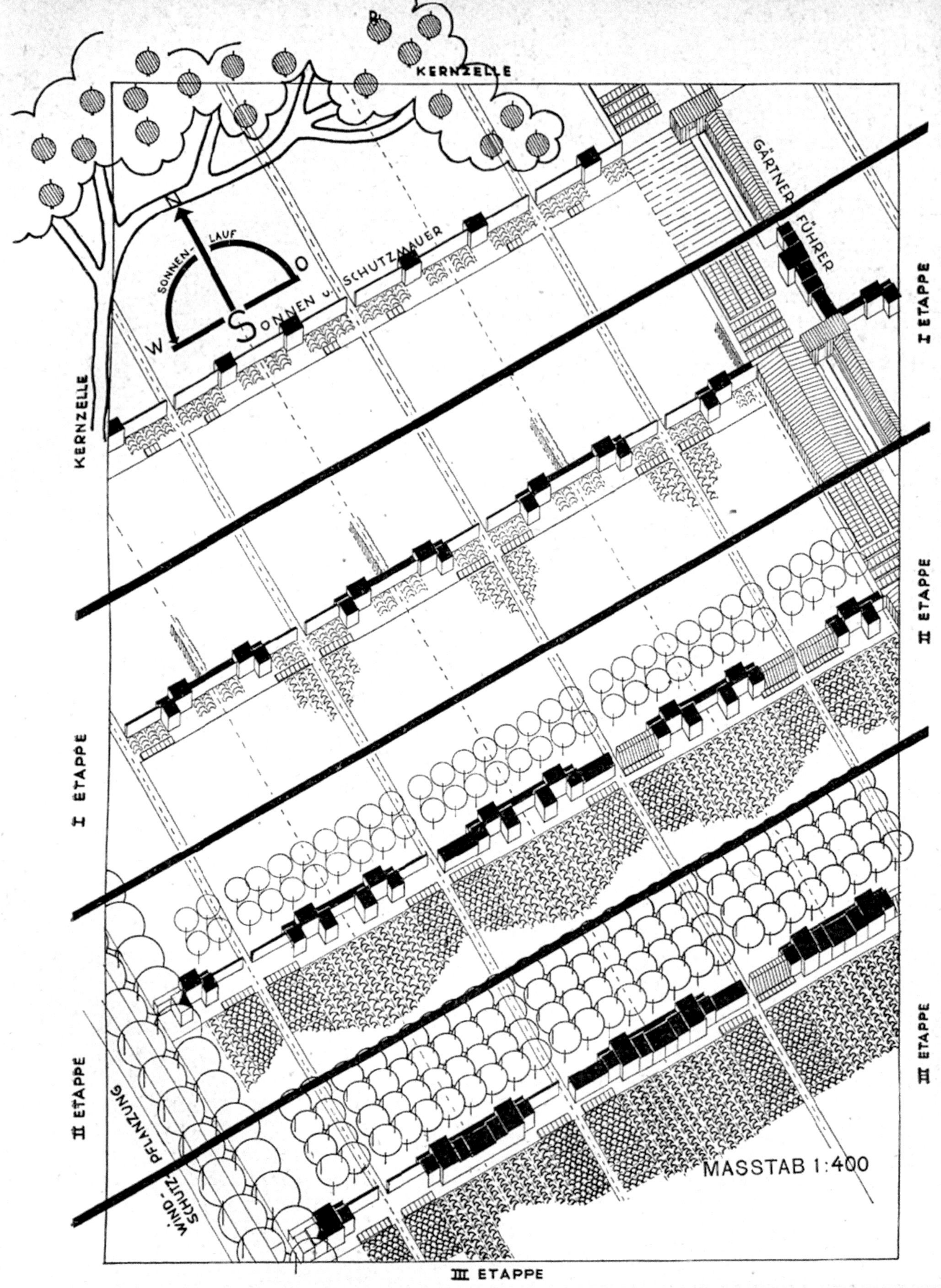
KERNZELLE
GÄRTNER
FÜHRER
SONNEN-
LAUF
N
W
S
O
SONNEN u. SCHUTZMAUER
KERNZELLE
I ETAPPE
II ETAPPE
III ETAPPE
I ETAPPE
II ETAPPE
WIND-SCHUTZ-PFLANZUNG
MASSTAB 1:400
III ETAPPE

8.2
Migge diagrammed three phases of urban growth, beginning with garden walls for privacy and solar collection.

This focus on the garden grew out of an existing garden culture in Germany. *Kleingärten* and *Schrebergärten* were small allotment gardens used for weekend activities that provided recreation and a source of nutrition. These were and remain extremely popular in Germany. Named after physician Moritz Schreber, who published dubious treatises on children's health and advocated for healthy exercise as central to well-being, *Schrebergärten* began as children's play yards and evolved into allotment gardens, the movement gathering popularity in the late nineteenth century.

While ideas for intensive urban agriculture were present prior to World War I, food shortages during the war highlighted the need for reform around provisioning the nation. Migge's *Everyman Self-Sufficient!* was a handbook for intensive agriculture, proposing food sufficiency as the basis for urban planning and form. The booklet described methods and proposed designs for families to provide their own food based on family size. In addition to individual lot designs, Migge proposed communal spaces and activities. Agriculture was divided into intensive gardening and extensive farming. The former included labor-intensive crops requiring smaller spaces, such as tomatoes, which would be grown by individual families; the latter included crops that required large spaces but less labor, such as turnips, which would be farmed collectively.[10] And the proposals included a community center, shared spaces for recreation, and productive landscape elements that would be maintained and harvested communally such as fruit trees used as street trees and hazelnut hedges.

The Ziebigk *seidlung* was a nearly full realization of Migge's ideas: an intensive garden system as the module of the neighborhood, a combination of family and communal spaces, and closed loops of consumption. The *siedlungen* were workers' housing projects, built throughout Germany to accommodate a population shift from rural to urban and the attendant lack of housing. They frequently included communal or private agricultural land, giving workers access to sun, air, exercise, and nutrition. Migge designed several *siedlungen* with prominent architects including Leopold Fischer, Ernst May, Bruno Taut, and Martin Wagner, and his landscape ideas were implemented by Adolf Loos as city architect for Vienna.[11] At Ziebigk, Migge and Fischer continued a collaboration begun the year before in the design of a model home for 1925 Home and Soil exhibition, organized by Taut.[12]

Migge's version of garden functionalism was a call to rethink societal relationships to land, food, waste, and even community. The urban garden should perform critical functions of food provisioning and urban exercise, and its form should be based not in a romantic view of nature, a desired aesthetic or views, but in the performance needs of its program: agriculture. Migge rejected an idea of style, saying, "The garden style of our time? We need not concern ourselves with it. It will present itself when the time is right."[13] He focused instead on functionality and a machinic approach of interchangeable parts. (Fig. 8.3) A good garden for the working class, "should be created especially for the occupation and relaxation of city-dwellers, just as their fans and radios are. So will the good garden be furnished and carried out in a well-calculated, industrial, and technical manner. If

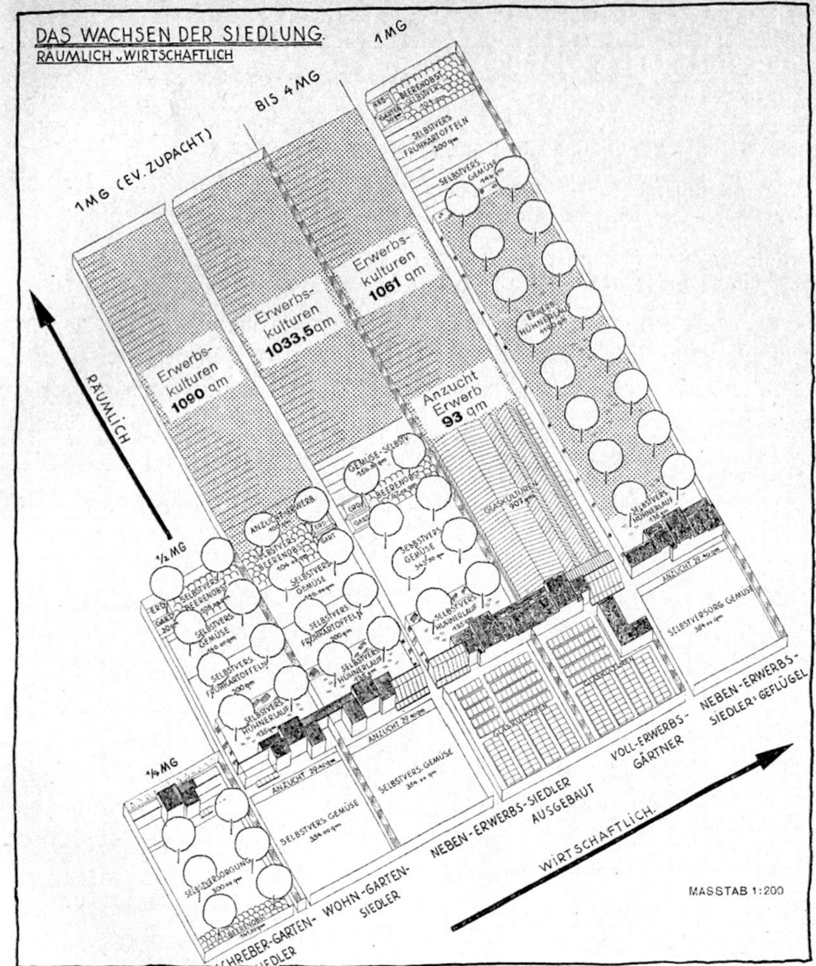

8.3
"The Growth of the Settlement" showing a variety of possible home and garden layouts, conceptually organized on axes of space and cost.

8.4
Plan of Siedlung Staaken with narrow garden lots divided by cane fruit and solar collection walls.

it is not, then it is not our garden. The contemporary, the technical, the modern garden–that is the good garden!"[14]

In 1926, it was extremely difficult to find an apartment in Dessau. Public housing was scarce; the city maintained a wait list for homes on which a five-year wait was not uncommon.[15] Homeownership was highly desirable, and the Ziebigk development similarly had a wait list of residents anxious to move in. The neighborhood design follows functionalist principles: the gardens laid out in narrow east–west lots for utility. The orthogonal lots are efficient and economical to lay out, install, and maintain, and are an efficient way to subdivide and plan the district. The neighborhood is divided into ten-by-fifty meter lots, each with a small front garden, a 250–500 square-meter house, depending on family size, and a 400 square-meter garden to provision a family of six to eight people, with the expectation that families would purchase bulk crops such as potatoes and turnips, and also purchase hay for domestic livestock.[16] (Fig 8.4)

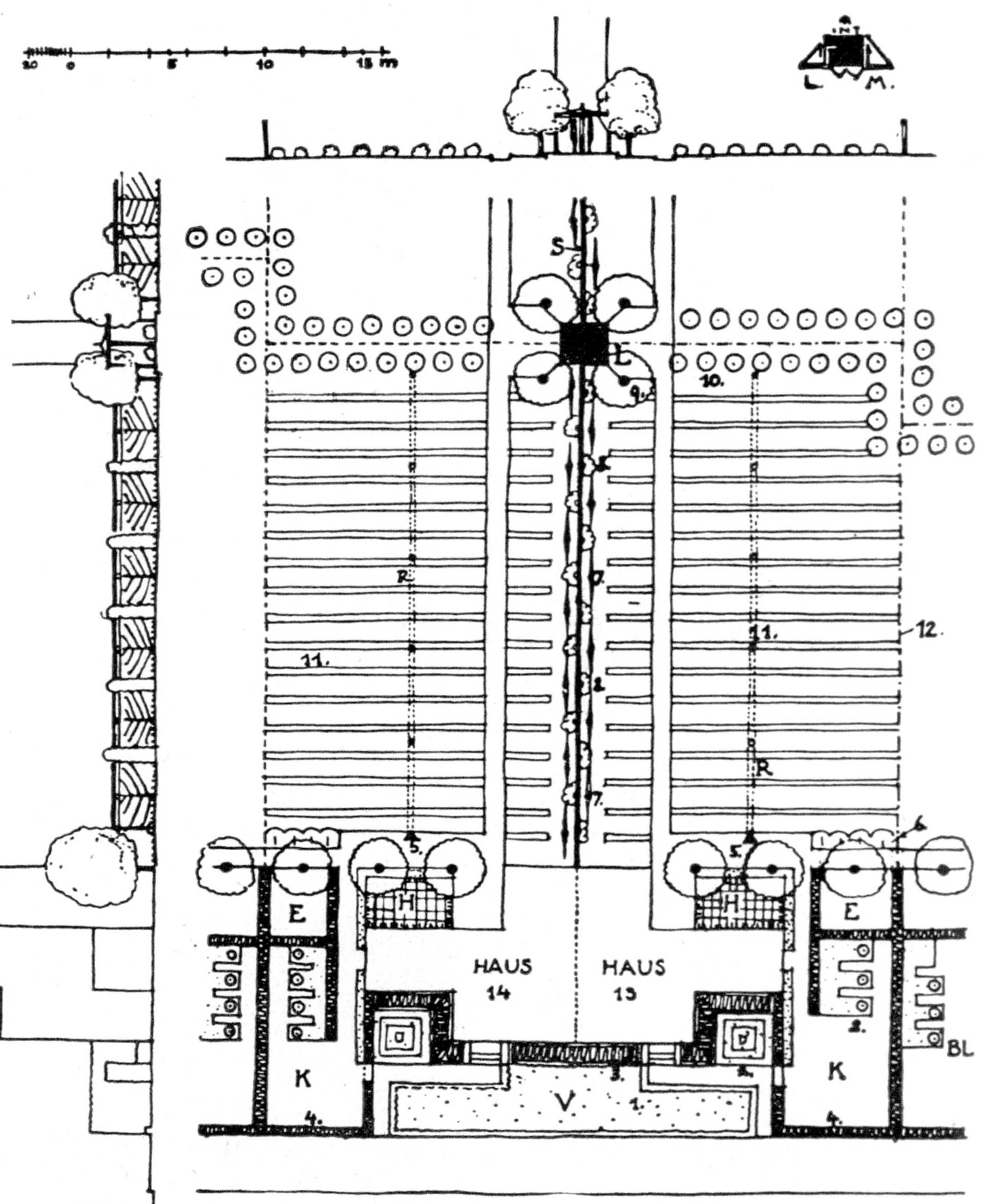

20 0 5 10 15 m
L W M.
S
L
9.
10.
R
11.
12.
7.
5.
6.
E
H
HAUS 14
HAUS 13
2.
BL
K
V
3.
1.
4.

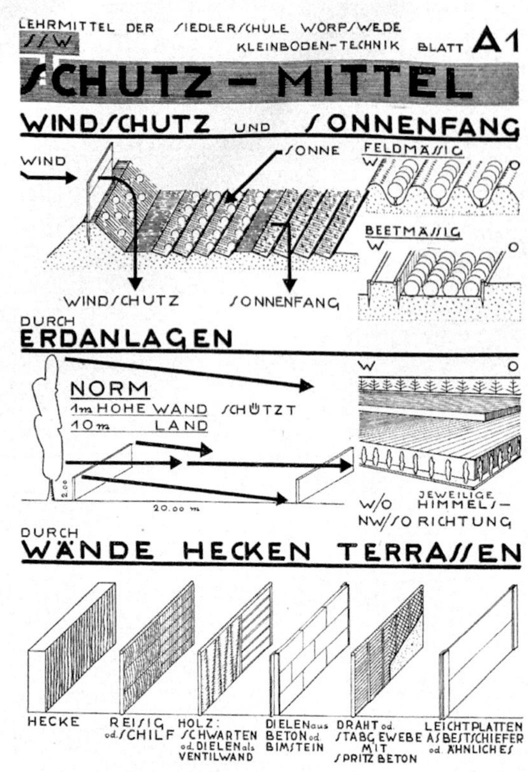

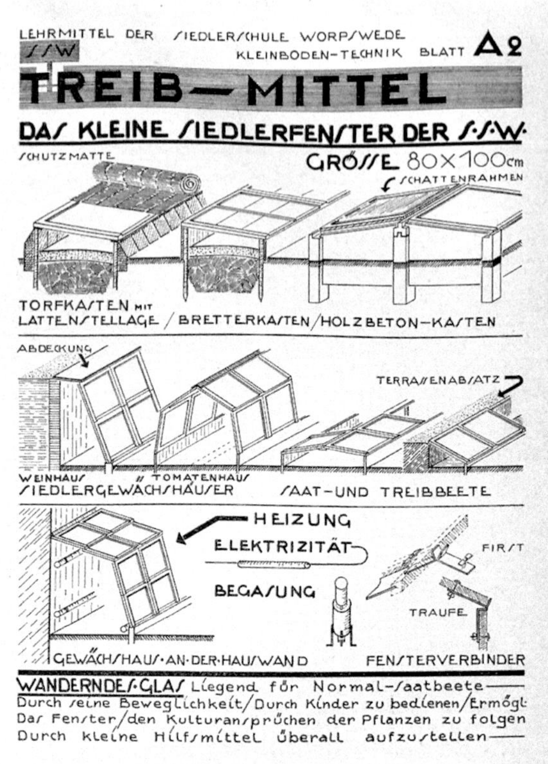

8.5
Migge proposed a variety of garden elements to block wind and collect sun.

A series of elements integrates the house and garden formally, materially, and climatically. Agricultural principles, including microclimate manipulation, changeable structures to extend the growing season, and crop cycling to extract multiple harvests in a single year, inform the mutable designs of the homes. (Figs 8.5, 8.6) A greenhouse, with removable glass wall panels, formed a microclimate zone that let sunlight into the house in the winter and transformed to a garden room in summer.[17] (Fig 8.7) A pergola provided a second open-air room, and a series of elements created climate buffers for the house: stables, sheds, and vine-covered walls. The line of the house extends into the garden to form a solar-collecting wall dividing every other garden; raspberry bushes divided the two gardens enclosed by walls. A pavilion was integrated into the garden walls, located at the corner connecting four gardens, joining four families in a shared social space shaded by birches.[18] The walls altered the microclimate of the garden, buffering from wind and gathering warmth. (Fig 8.8) Woody plants were both functional in the production of food, and also constructive, in the making of spaces.[19] In addition to vegetable beds, the gardens were planted with trellised fruit trees, cherry and plum trees, raspberry, currant and gooseberry bushes.[20]

Migge's gardens connected the house and garden through water and nutrient cycles as well as spatial forms. Garden products were used to sustain

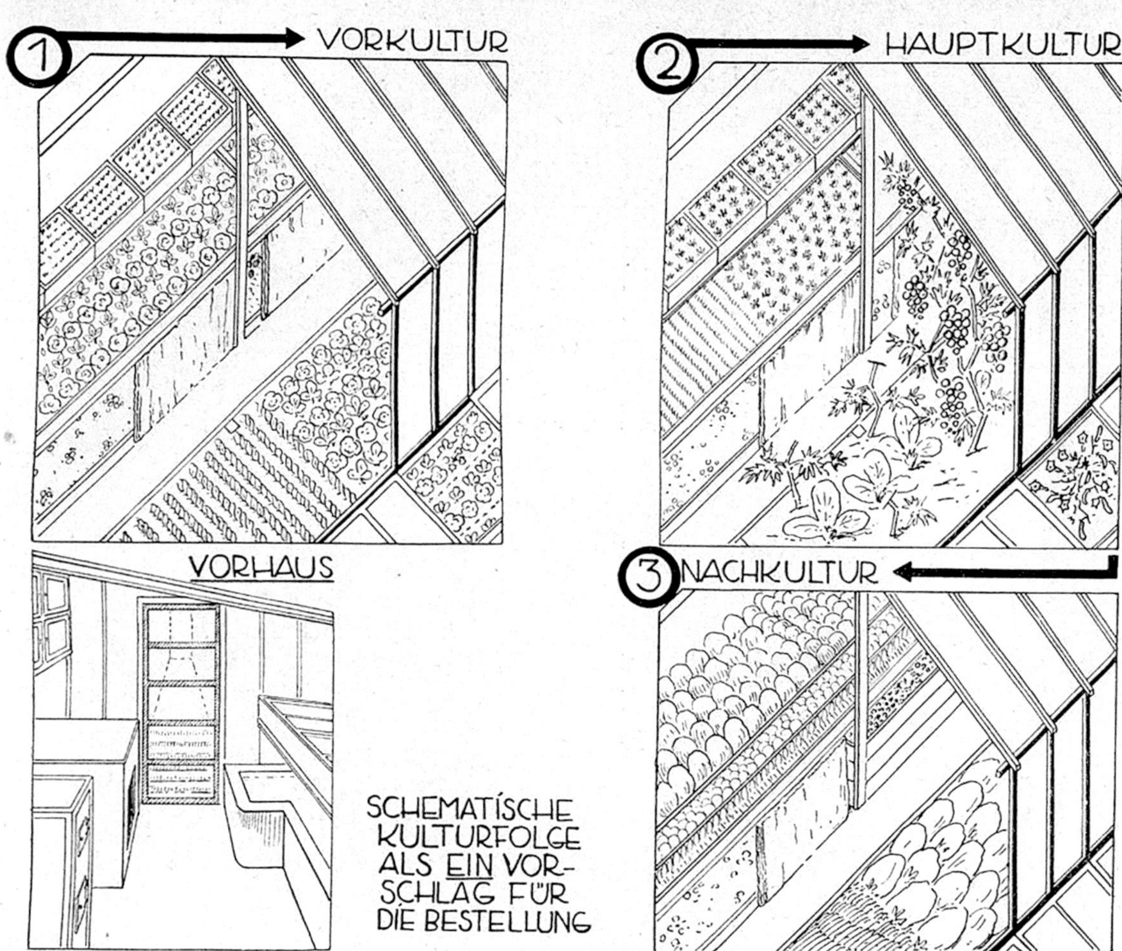

8.6
Suggested plantings for early, main, and late crops in *siedlung* greenhouses.

the household, and household products were used to sustain the garden. Migge advocated for a soil-based approach to garden productivity, using advanced technology to enhance biologic function in the garden. Like Howard, he viewed waste as a resource, but he took the idea to more complete and explicit realization than Howard, who focused more on nutrient waste as materials went to landfills. "The city must also give to the land ... All city waste to the land. Unify city and land. We should create our own 'earth.'"[21] Influenced by botanist and microbiologist Raoul Francé's *Life in the Soil* (1922), Migge saw house and garden connected through the cycles of elements, and saw the need to sustain the vitality of soil's microbiota. Francé saw artificial fertilizers as breaking these natural cycles. In *Everyman Self-Sufficient!*, Migge described the use of household waste in the garden, and

8.7
Migge illustrated the idea of a self-sustaining residence with this duplex with greenhouses to either side and garden outbuildings.

that system was implemented at Ziebigk. Believing that wet sewerage wastes water and creates a vector for sickness and pollution, Migge and Fischer specified dry composting toilets, the Metro-Clo, with waste mixed into a peat-based medium. Residents collected the material into a composting facility in the garden, and once fully composted, returned the compost to the soil as fertilizer.

Wastewater was similarly reused in the garden. Water from sinks and showers was collected in a settling tank mid-block, filtered to remove grease, then piped under the gardens for root irrigation and groundwater recharge.[22] Rainwater collected from the flat roofs was similarly channeled internally to distribution in the garden.[23] Although this was not the case at Ziebigk, Migge foresaw the possibility of scaling up this bio-technic approach to municipal and regional resource management systems, including waste, irrigation, and stormwater drainage.[24]

This bio-technic approach continued in the garden design and planting plans. The biological principles from the Wind, Warmth, and Water sections of *Everyman Self-Sufficient!* appear in the Ziebigk gardens. The lots are oriented east–west for maximum solar exposure, with protective walls to gather sunlight and block wind, and espaliered fruit trees against the walls. Weeping willows were planted to draw water away from building foundations, and Virginia creeper was planted to grow on building fronts to provide a thermal buffer for the house.[25]

At Ziebigk, Migge and Fischer designed a neighborhood as polemic. The gardens were conceived and designed as fully integrated with the house, and as the basis for formal, material, and climatic architectural and neighborhood structure. Gardens were seen as critical parts of the city's recreation infrastructure, providing each worker with a place to recuperate from industrial labors. Agriculture was viewed as central to a national character that was healthy and self-sufficient. (Fig 8.9)

This ideology was sometimes at odds with reality. The dry toilets were problematic, difficult to use, and could generate unpleasant odors; the toilets attracted rats and the composting silos in the garden attracted flies. The system was replaced with a water-based sewer system relatively early. During construction, workers dumped the excavated earth from foundations over the topsoil of the garden, leaving a thick, clay layer that had to be broken up and amended. The gardens were left fallow during construction, so by move-in in the fall, they looked "like a jungle." And most of the owners had grown up in the city and had neither tools nor training for gardening.[26] Over time, as the pressures of food shortages have lessened, most of the gardens have been turned to yards with a purely recreational program and the communal pavilions have been replaced with private

8.8
A solar collection wall for espaliered fruit trees with protective screens to extend the growing season.

8.9
Gardeners at work at the experimental garden at the Worpswede artists' colony, c. 1926.

storage buildings and cottages. Yet the idea of the garden as the primary unit of urban development is powerful, as is the desire for urban residents to retain some capacity for self-sufficiency. Although urban agriculture may not be ideal for everyman, it is a vital element in a diverse city.

Notes

1 David H. Haney, "Leberecht Migge's 'Green Manifesto': Envisioning a Revolution of Gardens," *Landscape Journal* 26, no. 2 (2007): 206.
2 Ibid., 203.
3 Corinne Jacquand, "Leberecht Migge et la colonie agricole évolutive selon les principes biologiques," *In Situ* 21 (2013): 5.
4 Haney, "Green Manifesto," 202.
5 Ibid., 205.
6 Ibid., 207.
7 Ibid., 204.
8 David Haney, "'No House Building without Garden Building!' ('Kein Hausbau ohne Landbau!'): The Modern Landscapes of Leberecht Migge," *Journal of Architectural Education* 54, no. 3 (2001): 150.

9 Haney, "Green Manifesto," 211.
10 Ibid., 207.
11 Ibid., 212.
12 Ibid., 213.
13 Leberecht Migge, "Der Kommende Garten," *Gartenschönheit: Illustriertes Gartenmagazin fur den Garten- und Blumenfreund* (1927): 64–65.
14 Haney, "No House Building," 152.
15 Fritz Becker, "Wohnen in der Knarrbergsiedlung," *Leopold Fischer – Architekt der Moderne: Planen und Bauen im Anhalt der Zwanziger Jahre*, Fritz Becker, Irena Below, et al. (Dessau: Funk Verlag, 2010), 42.
16 Frank Wolter, "Die Siedlung Knarrberg in Dessau," *Leopold Fischer – Architekt der Moderne: Planen und Bauen im Anhalt der Zwanziger Jahre*, Fritz Becker, Irena Below, et al. (Dessau: Funk Verlag, 2010), 34, 37.
17 Ibid., 33
18 Becker, "Wohnen," 45.
19 Dorothee Imbert, *Between Garden and City: Jean Canneel-Claes and Landscape Modernism* (Pittsburgh, PA: University of Pittsburgh Press, 2009), 10.
20 Becker, "Wohnen," 45; Wolter, "Knarrberg," 39.
21 Haney, "Green Manifesto," 204.
22 Wolter, "Knarrberg," 50.
23 Ibid., 32.
24 Haney, "Kein Hausbau," 155.
25 Wolter, "Knarrberg," 32.
26 Becker, "Wohnen," 45–46.

Nærum Allotment Gardens

Nærum, Denmark

C. Th. Sørensen, 1948–1952

0
100
200 ft

The tradition of allotment gardens integrates food production with city life, providing urban residents the opportunity to cultivate small plots of land. Although allotment gardens represent a form of urban agriculture largely disengaged from landscape architectural design, the Nærum Allotment Gardens in Denmark exemplify the value of the designer's hand. Carl Theodor Sørensen's *Runde Haver* represents a unique form of garden architecture that distinguishes itself from traditional Danish allotment gardens and orthogonal architectural conventions of early twentieth-century functionalism, as seen in Migge's designs.[1] A series of oval gardens, each surrounded by an elliptical hedge, organized in relation to the rolling topography of the site, offers apartment dwellers a measure of self-sufficiency and a place to unwind. Sørensen's garden provides a flexible framework that realizes not only its productive capacities, but its aesthetic and social potential as well.

The birth of the modern allotment garden movement in Denmark coincided with political developments related to industrialization and socialism in the second half of the nineteenth century. This was a time of growing concerns about the oppression of the working class and the emergence of the labor movement, which sought to establish better living and working conditions through the organization of workers. In the 1870s, newly formed trade unions and *Den Internationale Arbejderforening for Denmark* (The International Labor Association for Denmark) fought for social equality, higher wages, and the establishment of an eight-hour working day. Jorgen Berthelsen, Chairman of the *Arbejderforening af 1865* (Worker's Association of 1865) and an advocate for the rights of the working class, established the first Danish allotment garden in 1884 in the town of Aalborg, leasing from the municipality ten acres of marginal land south of the city and distributing eighty-five plots to workers for the cost of fourteen Danish kroner per plot. By 1904, there were already 20,000 allotment gardens in Denmark. As interest in allotment gardens grew, so did the need to protect the interests of the workers renting plots. In 1908, the first union of allotment gardens, *Kolonihave lejerforeningens Forbund* (Allotment Garden Tenants Association), was formed to represent gardeners in negotiations with government and private landowners. In 1916, the union became the *Kolonihaveforbundet for Denmark* (Allotment Garden Association of Denmark), a national association still active today. Organization provided gardeners with a mechanism to negotiate fair and uniform contracts and a way to counter the inherent vulnerability of allotments to land use change.

Allotment gardens were intended to empower the working class, providing equitable access to garden space for those who could not afford to purchase land. A refuge from the overcrowded conditions of dense city living, allotment gardens improved the quality of life and supported the independence of working people by providing city dwellers with the means to grow their own food. Tending the garden on Sunday provided both recreation and sustenance. Early photographs of allotments show proud families posing in abundant gardens. (Fig 9.1) Children ride tricycles or play while parents pose as chief gardeners, the master cultivators of the plot.

9.1
Allotment garden, Aalborg Denmark, c. 1900–1940.

The value of allotments, as critical sources of fresh food, ensured their growing popularity through the first half of the twentieth century. During World War II, the number of allotment gardens in Denmark swelled to more than 100,000 plots. German occupation forced a reorganization of Danish agricultural production for export to Germany,[2] resulting in food scarcity and rationing. From 1940 to 1942, Denmark provided Germany with 532,000 tons of meat and pork, 215,000 tons of fats, and 1.4 billion eggs. And with the withdrawal of German forces from other occupied territories in the last two years of the war, the pressure on Denmark to produce food only increased. From 1943 to 1945, 20 percent of all meat and one-third of all butter consumed in Germany came from Denmark.[3] With agricultural production thus occupied, citizens turned to allotment gardens as an alternative and vital source of food.

In post-war Denmark, allotment gardens faced increasing development pressures, and many were transformed into summer houses, as agricultural need was supplanted by the desire for a second home. When C. Th. Sørensen was asked by an allotment garden society to design a garden in Nærum, on the northern outskirts of Copenhagen, he proposed a surprising departure from the traditional pragmatic orthogonal layout of Danish allotments. In place of the functional forms of agricultural efficiency – rows, grids, rectangular plots – Sørensen's drawings for the garden show a geometric patterning of elliptical forms, a strangely beautiful motif of deceiving simplicity. (Fig 9.2) The productive garden is reimagined as a

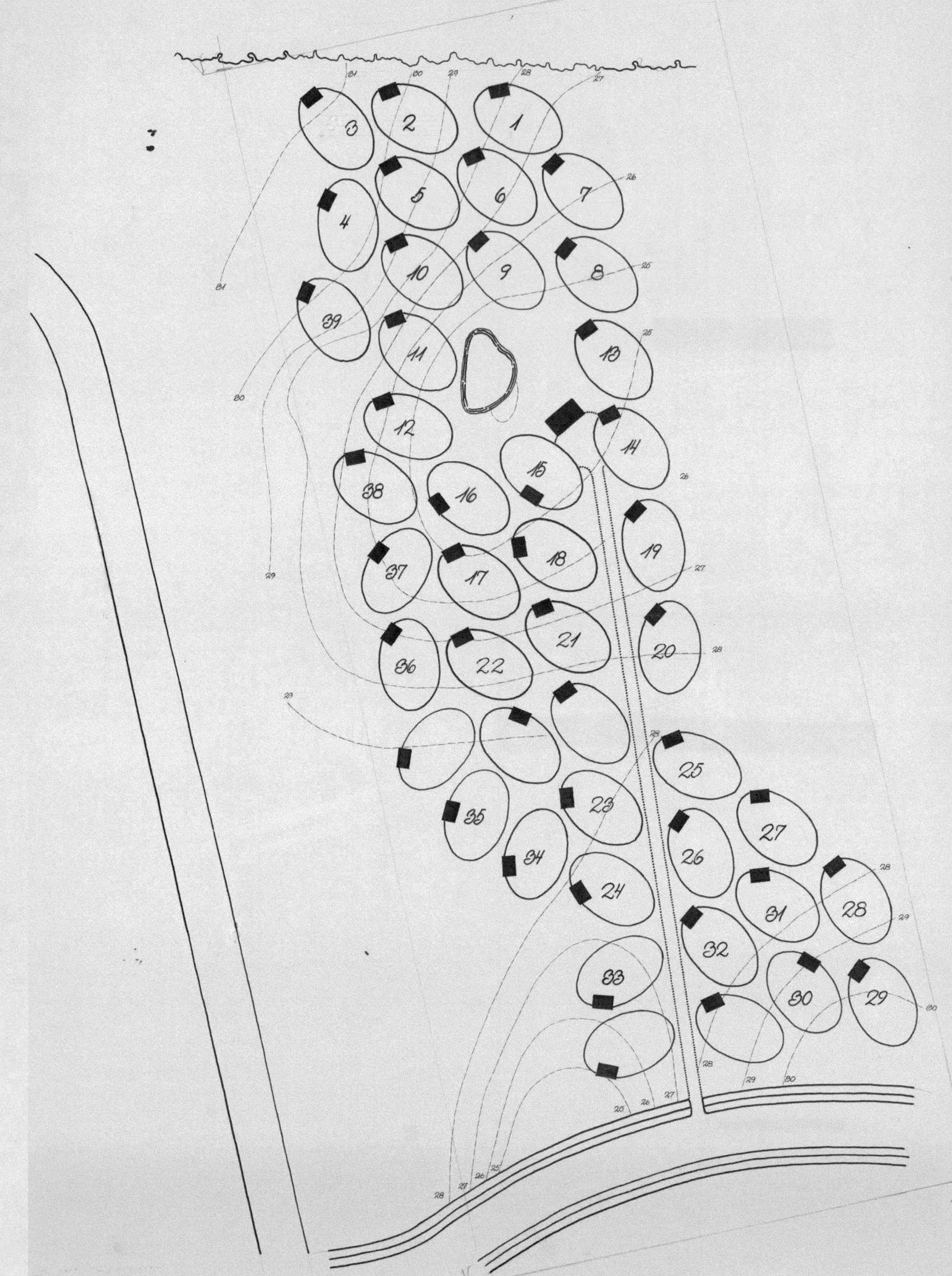

3
2
1
4
5
6
7
10
9
8
39
11
13
12
14
15
38
16
19
37
17
18
36
22
21
20
25
35
23
27
34
26
24
31
28
32
33
30
29

9.2
Site plan, C.Th. Sørensen, 1948.

9.3 (pages 128–129)
Garden house and shed situated within a pruned hedge.

work of art, expressing Sørensen's belief in the utility of beauty itself, an idea he described in his manifesto *The Origin of Garden Art* (1963):

> I grew up round the turn of the century in a remote part of the country among simple farmers. There was no actual want, life was hard and very austere, much was rejected because it was 'useless.' When I chose as my life's work a profession in which beauty plays a major role, I long had a bad conscience because I felt that it had no useful purpose; I produced nothing to ameliorate naked life. But then ... it was revealed to me that perhaps exactly the opposite was true: art is the essential, the eternal thing.[4]

With the single radical idea to use an elliptical hedge to enclose the garden plot, and to arrange the plots in response to the rolling topography of the site, Sørensen at once satisfied the functional requirements – subdivision, organization, enclosure, privacy – while attending to the power of the aesthetic. Forty-four elliptical hedges, oriented perpendicular to the contours of the land, enclose 400-square-meter gardens, each provided with a small house for daytime recreational use. Many of the gardens also contain a small shed for the storage of tools or other supplies. (Fig 9.3) A maximum of two structures are permitted within the garden. Their combined footprint may be no more than forty square meters, or 10 percent of the total garden area. In several of the gardens, however, a greenhouse has been added as a third structure to extend the gardening season. While the cultivation of fruits and vegetables is still commonplace, many gardeners view the colony as an affordable alternative to the summerhouse, a place to relax, to garden, and to enjoy the company of one's neighbors.

Despite the density of the gardens, gardeners enjoy a sense of privacy afforded by the physical and social boundary of the hedge. (Figs 9.4a-b) An open gate signals that visitors are welcome; a closed gate indicates "do not disturb." Through the use of separate hedges around each garden, Sørensen skillfully minimizes potential conflicts between neighbors, avoiding arguments over shared hedges. Community interaction is supported by the interstitial spaces between gardens, where children play and adults gather. Narrow, one-meter-wide, maze-like spaces bordered by tall hedges (Fig 9.5) give way to grassy open spaces. A community house, shaded by specimen birch trees, provides a place for dinner parties and community meetings. (Fig 9.6) The gardeners come together on two community work days per year, attending to projects like painting the common house or repairing the garden roads. They share jobs such as cleaning the toilets. An independent party is paid to trim the outer hedge.

Sørensen exhibited an admirable sensitivity to the needs of the gardeners, recognizing their role in shaping the ultimate form of the garden: "in order for the users to get the full potential of this particular plan, and for it to be a genuine success, give a good result, it demands the consideration and understanding on the part of the gardeners."[5] Aware that his vision for the garden depended upon the gardeners' maintenance of the hedges and cultivation of their own plots,

Sørensen provided a seven-page guide, including four alternative designs for the individual gardens. (Fig 9.7) Hedges of hawthorn, sweetbriar, crab apple, hazel, or lilac could be sheared or natural, maintained at a minimum height of two meters. Of the four proposals, three show the house incorporated into an unclipped hedge. And yet, at the time of this publication, there is only one garden configured in this manner. It would seem that the residents preferred instead to site the house fully within the privacy of the garden, to clip their hedges, and to design the interior not according to Sørensen's plan, but to suit their own needs.

And yet, despite the fact that the gardens have been altered and adapted by the gardeners themselves, the strength of Sørensen's plan remains. With the

9.4a-b
Garden hedges and gates afford a measure of privacy.

9.5
The interstitial space between hedges is a space of light and shadow, changing in dimension as one moves along the outer perimeters of the gardens.

9.6
The community house provides a place for gatherings and meetings.

exception of six additional oddly shaped gardens squeezed in amongst the original forty-four, the essential framework of Sørensen's design has been retained, along with the intent that the gardens provide space for apartment residents to grow their own food. Row crops (onions, potatoes, beets, asparagus, rhubarb, zucchini, tomatoes, strawberries, herbs), fruiting shrubs (blackberries and raspberries), and fruit trees (apples and cherries) are grown amongst flowering shrubs and perennials. (Fig 9.8) One garden has devoted space to keeping bees. (Fig 9.9) Many gardeners exhibit a preference for espaliered apples, using the form as an architectural element that maximizes production within the constraints of the small garden. (Fig 9.10)

Sørensen's four proposed designs for the gardens all conform to the same basic diagram. The house, integrated into the hedge or placed just inside, sits within a living space, defined by a gravel or tile forecourt. This space of leisure looks out on the chef's garden, rows of crops organized in different configurations. In all cases, the living space is separated from the productive garden by a hedge of fruiting shrubs – currant, blackcurrant, or gooseberries – or flowering shrubs – lilac, forsythia, jasmine. (Fig 9.11) In its spatial organization, the garden distinguishes between work and play, between the productive and the ornamental. From the living space, one gazes at the fruits of one's labor, the cultivated garden laid out as a thing of beauty, an object of pleasure and satisfaction.

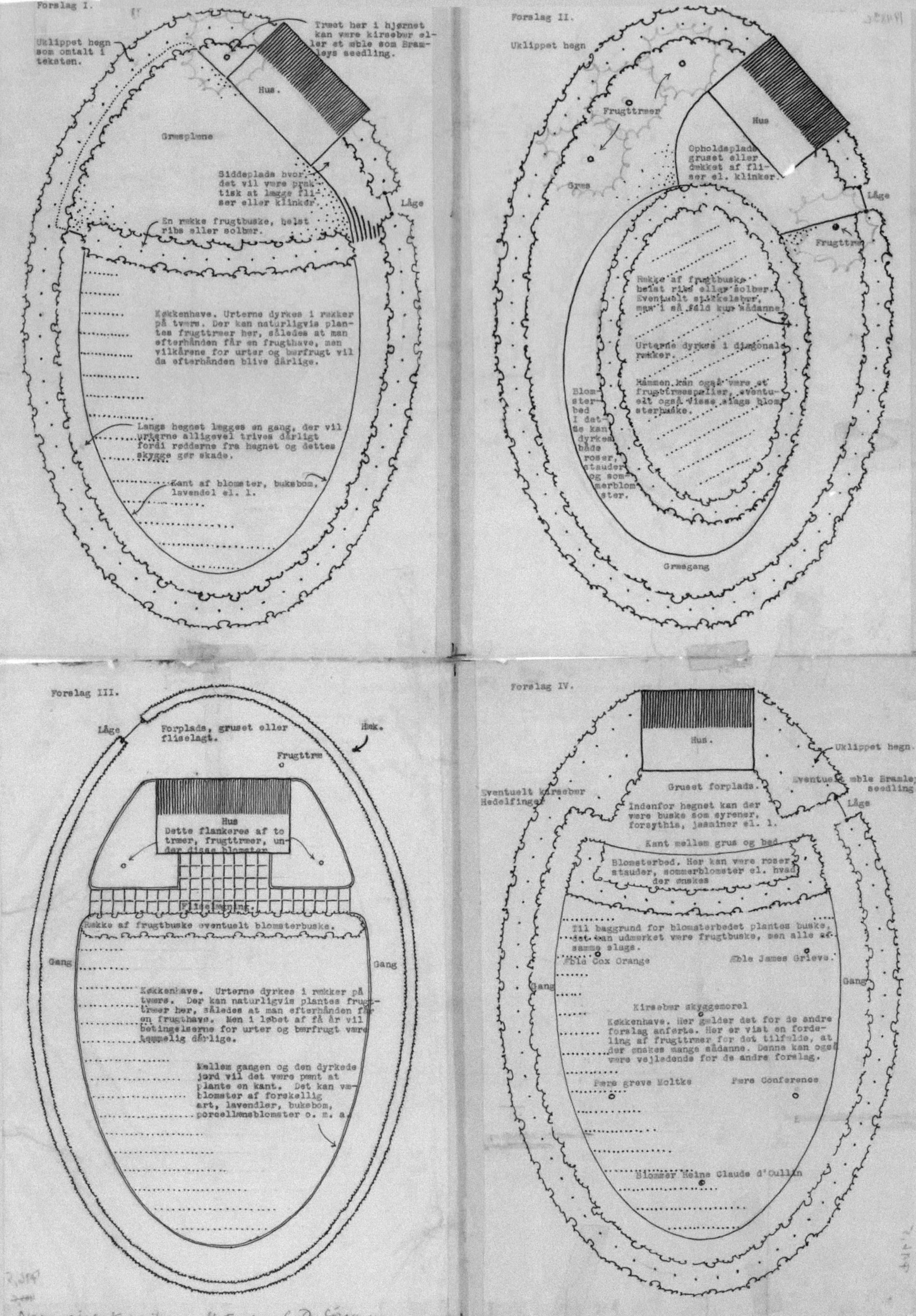
Forslag I.
Uklippet hegn som omtalt i teksten.
Træet her i hjørnet kan være kirsebær eller et æble som Bramleys seedling.
Hus.
Græsplæne
Siddeplads hvor det vil være praktisk at lægge fliser eller klinker
Låge
En række frugtbuske, helst ribs eller solbær.
Køkkenhave. Urterne dyrkes i rækker på tværs. Der kan naturligvis plantes frugttræer her, således at man efterhånden får en frugthave, men vilkårene for urter og bærfrugt vil da efterhånden blive dårlige.
Langs hegnet lægges en gang, der vil urterne alligevel trives dårligt fordi rødderne fra hegnet og dettes skygge gør skade.
Kant af blomster, buksbom, lavendel el. l.
Forslag II.
Uklippet hegn
Frugttræer
Hus
Opholdsplads gruset eller dækket af fliser el. klinker.
Græs
Låge
Frugttræ
Række af frugtbuske helst ribs eller solbær. Eventuelt stikkelsbær, men i så fald kun sådanne.
Urterne dyrkes i diagonale rækker.
Rammen kan også være et frugttræespalier, eventuelt også visse slags blomsterbuske.
Blomsterbed I dette kan dyrkes både roser, stauder og sommerblomster.
Græsgang
Forslag III.
Låge
Forplads, gruset eller fliselagt.
Hæk.
Frugttræ
Hus
Dette flankeres af to træer, frugttræer, under disse blomster
Flisebelægning
Række af frugtbuske eventuelt blomsterbuske.
Gang
Gang
Køkkenhave. Urterne dyrkes i rækker på tværs. Der kan naturligvis plantes frugttræer her, således at man efterhånden får en frugthave. Men i løbet af få år vil betingelserne for urter og bærfrugt være temmelig dårlige.
Mellem gangen og den dyrkede jord vil det være pænt at plante en kant. Det kan være blomster af forskellig art, lavendler, buksbom, porcellænsblomster o. m. a.
Forslag IV.
Hus.
Uklippet hegn.
Gruset forplads.
Eventuelt æble Bramleys seedling.
Eventuelt kirsebær Hedelfinger
Låge
Indenfor hegnet kan der være buske som syrener, forsythia, jasminer el. l.
Kant mellem grus og bed
Blomsterbed. Her kan være roser, stauder, sommerblomster el. hvad der ønskes
Til baggrund for blomsterbedet plantes buske, det kan udmærket være frugtbuske, men alle af samme slags.
Æble Cox Orange
Æble James Grieve.
Gang
Gang
Kirsebær skyggemorel
Køkkenhave. Her gælder det for de andre forslag anførte. Her er vist en fordeling af frugttræer for det tilfælde, at der ønskes mange sådanne. Denne kan også være vejledende for de andre forslag.
Pære greve Moltke
Pære Conference
Blommer Reine Claude d'Oullin

9.7
C. Th. Sørensen's four draft plans for the design of individual allotments, 1948.

9.8
Row crops and flowering perennials neatly laid out within the space of the garden.

In this respect, Sørensen indicates a deep understanding of the complexities of allotment gardening, neither wholly agricultural nor purely ornamental, but an integration of both. There *is* a difference between work, the work of cultivating the soil, producing food for the table, and leisure. And yet, the allotment garden itself is a space of refuge from the realities of the home and the workplace, and a different kind of work takes place here. The cultivation of a plot of land feeds a physical need and one much deeper, the need to cultivate beauty, to feed the soul through prolonged intimate interaction with the soil. No richer knowledge of place, no deeper relationship with the soil beneath one's feet, is formed than that which is created through the act of cultivating the land, feeding the body through the fruits of one's labors, feeding the intellect and the soul through the making of a place of beauty.

In a time of relative security and food abundance, many allotment gardens across Europe have lost their original agricultural identity. In some cases, gardeners have abandoned the cultivation of fruits and vegetables in favor of purely ornamental gardens or areas of lawn intended to maximize non-gardening leisure activity. While gardeners at the Nærum Allotments acknowledge the increasing importance of the gardens as recreational space,[6] they continue to use them to grow food. The desire to cultivate crops and fruit trees remains strong, even amongst the gardeners who lack the time to maintain a fully productive space.

For the majority of gardeners, there is little distinction between recreational and agricultural activity; in cultivating the garden for food, one finds recreation and sustenance simultaneously.

Amidst ever increasing urbanization and development pressures in cities worldwide, allotment gardens face an uncertain future. Even in Denmark, where the *Kolonihaveforbundet for Denmark* actively works to protect the rights of gardeners, and where Danish law protects gardens granted "permanent" status by the Ministry of the Environment, allotments have proved vulnerable to development. When allotments are conceived as purely recreational amenities, their contribution to food security is easily dismissed. And when allotments are understood

9.9
Bee keeping in the garden.

9.10
Espaliered fruit trees maximize production in a small space.

9.11
A low unpruned hedge of fruiting shrubs separates the living area at the house from the space of the garden.

to be merely productive plots, their connection to communities and the way they are intertwined with the social and cultural life of a place is often overlooked. In times of food shortage, allotment gardens are popular out of necessity, but in times of relative affluence, allotments lacking a recognized cultural value, in a unique and identifiable shape and form, tend to disappear. Because of its significance as a cultural artifact, the beloved *Runde Haver* has been listed by the Danish Agency for Culture on the National Register of Cultural Heritage. Ultimately, it is Sørensen's masterful capacity to discover the potential for beauty in agricultural and social systems, realizing through design a unique form for the allotment, which ensures the garden's future preservation.

Notes

1 Andersson, Sven-Ingvar, and Steen Høyer. *C. Th. Sørensen: Landscape Modernist* (Copenhagen: Danish Architectural Press, 2001), 136.
2 Nissen, Mogens R. "From War Profits to Post-War Investments: How the German Occupation Improved Investments in Danish Agriculture in the Post-War Years," in *War, Agriculture, and Food: Rural Europe from the 1930s to the 1950s*, eds. Brassley, Paul, Yves Segers, and Leen Molle (New York, NY: Routledge, 2012).
3 Lund, Joachim, "The Wages of Collaboration: The German Food Crisis 1939–1945 and the Supplies from Denmark," *Scandinavian Journal of History* 38, no. 4 (2013): 480–501.
4 Sørensen, C Th. *The Origin of Garden Art = Havenkunstens Oprindelse* (København: Danish Architectural Press, 1963), 38.
5 Andersson and Høyer, *C. Th. Sørensen*, 138.
6 *Runde Haver* gardeners, Interview with author (Phoebe Lickwar), Naerum, Denmark, June 8, 2015.

Village Homes

Davis, California

Michael Corbett Town Planners, designed 1973–1975, constructed 1975–1982

0
100
200 ft

Amidst the turbulence and idealism of the early 1970s counterculture movement, a new kind of suburb was developed. Aimed at addressing rising concerns about agricultural and ecological vulnerability, the design linked food production, community cohesion, and water and energy stewardship, while blurring the boundaries between private and public land. Village Homes, a neighborhood of 244 housing units sited on sixty acres of California farmland, is celebrated for its groundbreaking innovations in energy efficiency, stormwater management, and edible landscaping. In the integrated design, every element performs multiple functions: for example, play areas store rainwater, and shade trees and hedges provide food. A product of its time and an early precursor to twenty-first-century agriculture-centered housing developments,[1] Village Homes demonstrates an innovative approach to integrating agriculture for maximum social and ecological benefit.

The Johnson–Nixon years, a time of war, environmental crisis, and mistrust of petrochemical-based industrial agribusiness, saw the simultaneous rise of the environmental movement and organic farming. The dangers of the military–industrial–agribusiness complex and its dependence on "elixirs of death,"[2] DDT, napalm, and other defoliants and pesticides, were brought to public consciousness most famously by environmentalist Rachel Carson. Economist E. F Schumacher[3] and agrarian Wendell Berry railed against the devastating environmental and cultural consequences of large-scale agribusiness, drawing connections between "the disintegration of the culture and the communities of farming – and the consequent disintegration of the structures of urban life."[4] Berry described the disintegration of small-scale rural farming communities and the simultaneous disappearance of agriculture from urban centers as an ecological crisis with severe impacts to ecosystem and community health. In *The Unsettling of America*, published in 1977, Berry chronicles the consequences of equating agricultural productivity with economic productivity at the expense of fertile soils, clean water, and strong communities.

In the context of this growing environmental consciousness, designers Michael and Judy Corbett sought safer and more sustainable alternatives to mainstream ways of life. Critical of normative development, Michael Corbett argued the need for a more sustainable design of communities:

> In urban areas, we have landscaped our homes and towns with unproductive plants because we thought we had plenty of land to grow food elsewhere, plenty of water to irrigate it, plenty of energy for machine cultivation and long-distance hauling, and the ability to maintain ecologically unsound mechanized farming with large quantities of ecologically unsound pesticides and artificial fertilizers.[5]

The Corbetts set out to design a planned community that would challenge the status quo, reduce food miles, and improve local natural resources. Inspired by Ebenezer Howard's garden city ideals, Village Homes borrows principles of

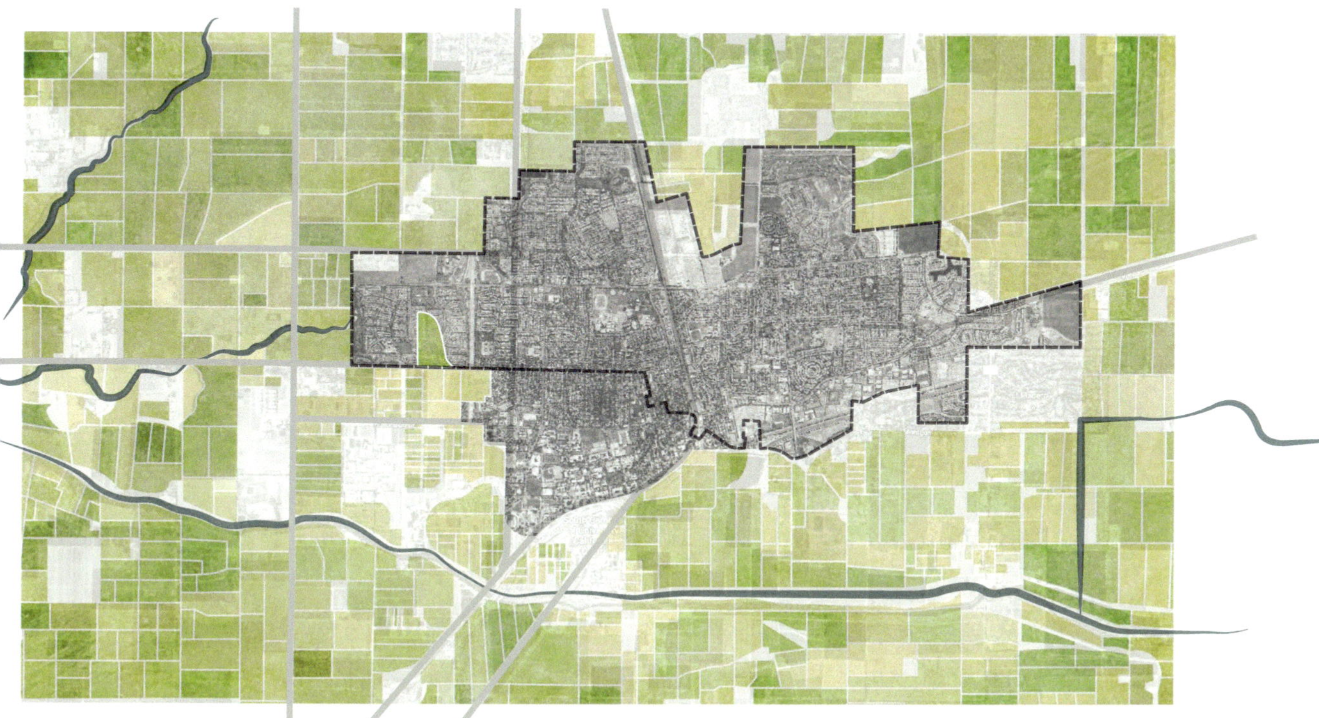

10.1
Village Homes blurs the boundary between agriculture and the city, synthesizing food production with urban life.

the garden city model, including a balance of land uses, separation of vehicular and pedestrian circulation, communal green space, the use of greenbelts, and the incorporation of agricultural land. To these strategies, the designers added an ecological overlay, employing solar energy, organic agriculture, and surface drainage to achieve a sustainable "garden village."[6] Village Homes was designed in recognition of the limits to those resources, as a model of locally regenerative design.

Village Homes was built on existing farmland in Davis, a small city in California's central valley possessing some of the most fertile and productive soils in the world. The former use of the land for crop production, primarily tomatoes in rotation with other annual vegetable crops, presented the opportunity to retain the productive capacity of the land even as it was transformed into a housing development for a largely non-farming population of roughly eight hundred individuals. Twelve acres of agricultural land provide a variety of food-producing landscapes, including orchards, vineyards, community gardens, and household commons. Unlike Migge's *siedlungen*, Village Homes invites, rather than requires, residents to participate in food production. Residents are surrounded by an incredible abundance, trees heavy with fruit, grapes ripening on the vine, orchards of almonds, apricots, and persimmons, and gardens of different shapes and sizes displaying all manner of fruits and vegetables.

The small-scale agriculture of Village Homes supports the social ecology of the place. Neighbors develop relationships as they work the land together, making

decisions collectively to shape their gardens and divide the harvest. Agricultural production takes place at three scales, each facilitating different types of social interaction. At the individual scale, residents cultivate their own plots in the community garden, working side by side with neighbors to grow their own food. At the household scale, groups of eight households share the responsibility for design and maintenance of a common productive garden, benefitting from pooled labor, the capacity to plant a greater variety of species with varying ripening dates, and neighbors to share the bounty. And at the neighborhood scale, the entire community comes together to manage and harvest the orchards and vineyards.

10.2a-b
Fruit trees at the edges of patio gardens shade outdoor living spaces.

The farmed landscape at Village Homes is designed to do more than simply produce food. In addition to supplying a substantial proportion of food to the community,[7] household and neighborhood agriculture also provides the same benefits as purely ornamental landscaping, supporting community, ecology, and culture at once. Food production is dispersed across the neighborhood rather than being relegated to the circumferential edge. The farm-like setting, visible at every turn, is a powerful symbol of residents' commitment to small-scale localized production

of food; it also supports the sustainability goals of the development and strengthens social networks. As noted by Mark Francis in his comprehensive case study *Village Homes: A Community by Design*, the design of the edible landscape, as an integral aspect of social and environmental systems, "demonstrates that there is a value to zoning agricultural uses within existing cities, rather than the current thinking that farms must exist apart from where people live."[8] (Fig 10.1)

The productive household commons, providing food for neighbors and a shared space for gathering and child's play, are also an integral aspect of the development's passive solar design. In *A Better Place to Live*, Michael Corbett prescribes the use of apple, filbert, fig, and apricot trees for shading small outdoor spaces, plums, cherries, and pears for protection from the afternoon summer sun, walnuts and pecans for large-scale shade, citrus trees as year-round windbreaks, and grapevines for summer shading of south-facing windows.[9] At Village Homes, grapevines and fruit trees are utilized as part of the passive solar strategy, facilitating winter heating and summer cooling of indoor and outdoor spaces. South-facing windows reduce heating costs in the winter but require shading in the

10.3a-b
Productive gardens and drainage swales run parallel to pedestrian pathways.

extreme heat of summer. Grapevines, trained on vertical and overhead trellises, leaf out at precisely the right time, providing dense shade in the hottest months while also supplying families with fresh fruit for juice or wine. Fruit trees shade outdoor spaces, planted at the edges of patios and along the pathways connecting the commons. (Fig 10.2a–b) Persimmons, pomegranates, and other fruiting trees form the bones of the shared gardens and entice residents to walk or bike rather than drive.

Unlike the New Urbanist developments of the 1980s and 1990s, intended to create socially cohesive, walkable neighborhoods by re-envisioning the public realm of the street, Village Homes builds community through shared productive landscapes which provide the added benefit of supplying food.[10] The streets of Village Homes are designed to function purely as vehicular space. They lack sidewalks and are lined with carports and fenced private courtyards. Street widths are minimized to reduce stormwater runoff and maximize available land for agricultural production. It is the shared area between the backsides of houses, not the streets, that are privileged as outdoor community space. Accessed on foot or by bike, these household commons are occupied, cultivated, and maintained communally. Productive gardens and fruit trees are arranged along pedestrian pathways and surface drainage swales that run the length of the commons. (Fig 10.3a–b) The topography of the lots directs rainwater towards the swales, used to hold water on site or direct it to larger channels for recharge of the groundwater aquifer. The surface drainage system supports the productive commons by directing water back into the soil, reducing irrigation needs and creating cooling microclimates. (Fig 10.4a–c)

At Village Homes today, the strong interdependence between growing food, strengthening community, and enhancing ecological function remains. However, there is growing evidence that the collective spirit has eroded somewhat over the decades. Joint decision-making has proven difficult through the years and today residents desire a greater degree of autonomy over their cultivated land.

10.4a–c (pages 145–147)
Drainage areas support the edible landscape by directing water back into the soil.

10.5
The productive commons replaced with ornamental planting.

10.6
The thriving community gardens indicate that individual plots are more popular than areas farmed collaboratively.

Several decades after construction, the Village Homes Board instituted a policy that homeowners are responsible for their own properties up to the sidewalk, effectively eliminating the idea of a commonly designed and maintained area between households. (Fig 10.5) However, some owners are still maintaining their common areas together, placing extra funds in their homeowner's dues so they have money to maintain common areas jointly. The community gardens, where individuals maintain control and ownership over the cultivation of their own plots, are wildly successful, requiring a waitlist for new applications. (Fig 10.6) Residents desire a sense of community, it seems, without the required collaboration and coordination of a group project.

There is also diminished enthusiasm for the community harvesting of the almond orchard and grape vineyards. Because so many of the houses employ grapevines for shade, there is an overabundance of grapes. Residents invest time and effort into harvesting and processing their own grapes into juice or wine. Consequently, the grapes in the community vineyard are often left to rot on the vine. (Fig 10.7) Serving a largely aesthetic purpose, the vineyards may prove vulnerable to future development. The almond orchard is similarly time-consuming to harvest. In the early days, the almonds were harvested using a mechanized process, but in recent years insurance has been difficult to obtain, and now residents harvest by hand. The diminished production means there is not enough to sell at the farmer's market, further discouraging participation. When asked what she thought might happen to these community spaces, Judy Corbett cited the critical importance for homeowners to own the land being farmed: "My guestimate is that someday the farming will drop out and they will just put more houses on it."[11]

Added to changes in community participation are changes resulting from a shifting climate. California recently experienced a major drought, setting a record for the driest consecutive years from 2013 to 2016. The drought state of emergency was lifted in April 2017, but climate scientists predict ongoing future

10.7
Unharvested grapes at the community vineyard.

drought, and the City of Davis has maintained mandatory water use restrictions. Amidst ever-increasing water concerns, residents are questioning the long-term viability of raising water-intensive crops.

The current dry spell may have failed to discourage the cultivation of crops in the thriving community garden, but it has had a pronounced effect on the health of the thirstier species, causing concern for the longevity of plantings across the neighborhood and the need to reconsider water use in the future. Citrus and avocado trees and annual vegetable and fruit crops require significant supplemental irrigation. The central common, planted with turf grass and lacking an agricultural value, is notorious for its high water consumption. Species that have never required irrigation, the fig trees for example, are showing signs of stress. Fruit trees have suffered damage, as branches laden with fruit grow heavy and crack in dry conditions. The orchards, formerly a point of pride, are in decline. All of these factors may lead to future changes in the overall composition of the edible landscape, with an increase in drought-tolerant species. (Fig 10.8)

10.8
A native California garden intentionally planted by a homeowner to replace water-thirsty edible landscaping.

Michael and Judy Corbett were well aware of water-scarcity issues and the need for water conservation at the time of project conception. They predicted that the community of Davis would begin to encounter problems associated with a reduced groundwater table by 2010.[12] The surface drainage system of vegetated swales and retention areas puts stormwater back into the ground, recharging precious groundwater relied upon for the irrigation of crops. But effective aquifer recharge requires the precise locations of groundwater basins, information that is still unavailable at the time of this writing. In the meantime, residents are exploring the use of drought-tolerant plantings, including a substitute for turf grass in the central green, in order to limit the amount of water drawn from the neighborhood well.

The future sustainability of Village Homes will depend upon adaptations that strengthen mutually beneficial relationships between agriculture and environmental function. Only by aligning the goal of producing food with the goal of water conservation will the neighborhood continue to thrive. While the community evolves, agriculture can continue to provide a guiding framework for strengthening social bonds. Through the planting and cultivation of productive lands, this community will continue to realize the designers' original intent, to integrate community, ecology, and agriculture, bringing citizens together to gain a measure of self-sufficiency and a healthier relationship with the land. Village Homes remains a seminal example for future agriculture-centered developments, demonstrating the tangible benefits and challenges of community farming in the twenty-first century.

Notes

1 According to the Urban Land Institute, agriculture-centered developments, or "Agrihoods" are the twenty-first-century alternative to the golf course development, offering similar added value, with the added benefits of a sustainable environment and access to healthy food. See Bendix Anderson, "Food Adds Flavor (and Value) to Real Estate: 'Agrihoods' and Other Food-Based Concepts," *UrbanLand*, June 28, 2016, https://urbanland.uli.org/sustainability/food-adds-flavor-value-real-estate-agrihoods-food-halls-food-based-concepts/.
2 Rachel Carson, *Silent Spring* (Boston: Houghton Mifflin, 1962), 15.
3 See E. F. Schumacher, *Small is Beautiful: Economics as if People Mattered* (New York: Harper & Row, 1973).
4 Wendell Berry, *The Unsettling of America: Culture & Agriculture* (San Francisco: Sierra Club Books, 1977), 45.
5 Michael N. Corbett, Judy Corbett, and John Klein, *A Better Place to Live: New Designs for Tomorrow's Communities* (Emmaus, PA: Rodale Press, 1981), 92.
6 Judy Corbett and Michael N. Corbett, *Designing Sustainable Communities: Learning from Village Homes* (Washington, DC: Island Press, 2000).
7 A study by Thomas Lenz in 1990 found that 25 percent of residents' fruit and vegetable consumption is provided by the edible landscaping. See Thomas Lenz, "A Post-Occupancy Evaluation of Village Homes, Davis, California" (Master's Thesis, Technical University of Munich, 1990).
8 Mark Francis, *Village Homes: A Community by Design* (Washington, DC: Island Press, 2003), 70.
9 Corbett et al., *A Better Place to Live*, 95–96.
10 Ibid.
11 Judy Corbett, Interview with Phoebe Lickwar, Davis, California, October 20, 2015.
12 Ibid.

Winslow Farms Conservancy

Winslow, NJ

Martha Schwartz Partners, 1996

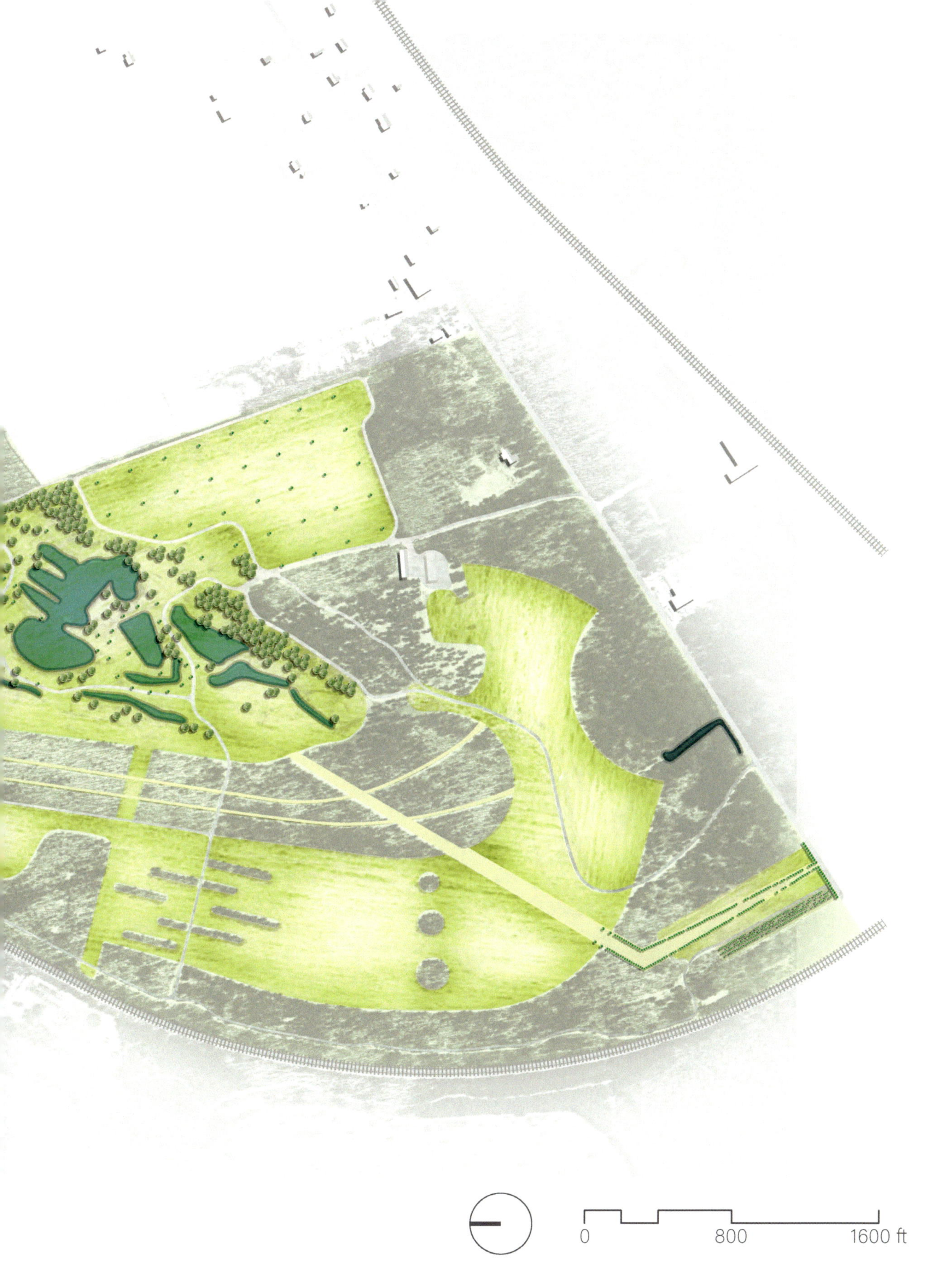
0
800
1600 ft

Twenty-two miles southeast of Philadelphia, in the New Jersey Pine Barrens, six hundred acres of land have been radically transformed by a conservationist and a landscape architect. What began as a search for a country retreat evolved into a project to create the largest certified organic farm east of the Mississippi. In the late 1980s, Hank McNeil, a conservationist and minimalist art collector living in Philadelphia, began looking for an escape from the city where he could train his Labrador retrievers for field trial competitions. When a large parcel of land in Winslow, New Jersey, came up for sale, McNeil relished the opportunity to save it from development as a housing subdivision. The price was heavily discounted, but the sale was a bargain for a reason: this was land no one wanted. An abandoned seventy-five-acre clay quarry was being used as a dump. People were getting killed, dealing drugs, discarding bottles, tires, and cars. Where others saw a liability, McNeil saw an opportunity. Together with landscape architect Martha Schwartz, McNeil embraced the challenge to remediate the industrial wasteland and recover the site's value as productive land. The design of Winslow Farms Conservancy marries the productive and post-industrial landscapes to reclaim depleted and vulnerable land at both the scale of the farm and the scale of the region.

11.1
Clearings for hayfields carved from the forested land.

11.2
View of the remediated quarry landscape with the agricultural fields in the far distance.

11.3
An installation of clipped cedar trees represents the seven hundred houses that might have been built had the site been developed.

Winslow Farms Conservancy's history tells a familiar story, but its future expands the territory of agriculture in the twenty-first century, providing a replicable model for over 240,000 acres of abandoned quarries across the state of New Jersey alone. Like much of the New Jersey Pine Barrens, this land was cultivated for small-scale farming until a clay quarry was established in the 1860s to mine material for the bricks that built Philadelphia. For close to one hundred years, farming and quarrying operations coexisted, a diversified economic operation employing productive and extractive strategies as parallel enterprises. When quarrying operations ceased in the mid-1900s, the soils had been so severely compacted by machinery and contaminated by toxic sludge from the clay-firing kilns that they could no longer sustain plant life. The farm surrounding the quarry was abandoned around the same time and the fallow fields slowly reforested. By the time McNeil purchased the site, an abundance of invasive species had populated the former farm while the abandoned clay quarry had been adopted as an illegal dump, a motocross track, and a meeting place for gangs.

Martha Schwartz worked closely with McNeil to envision a way to remediate the clay quarry while restoring the farm, developing a plan to reshape these two degraded landscapes simultaneously. The design includes clearings for agriculture (Fig 11.1), a quarry landscape remediated for wildlife habitat and the training of hunting dogs (Fig 11.2), and an installation of clipped cedar trees distributed to represent the seven hundred houses that might have been built had the land been developed. (Fig 11.3) Corridors through the forested landscape connect these large-scale spaces, providing miles of walking trails and a measure of anticipation as one moves from dense forest to open territory of agricultural fields, ponds, and wet meadows. (Fig 11.4)

The influence of Baroque garden design is unmistakable in the long axial corridors carved through field and forest, the juxtaposition of the hori-

11.4
Straight corridors through the forest provide miles of walking trails.

11.5a–d (pages 160–161)
Clipped topiary used as an organizational device and a measure of human scale.

zontal plane of fields against the vertical plane of forest edges, the use of reflective water to create unity between landscape and sky, and the use of clipped topiary as a sculptural element defining points along lines and grids and providing human scale to vast open spaces. (Fig 11.5a–d) The serpentine geometries of curving paths, rolling topography, and irregularly shaped ponds are set against the forms of the flat plane, straight lines, circles, and grids, which unify the landscape as an overall composition. Schwartz's contemporary interpretation composes the productive and the post-industrial landscapes

as reciprocal gardens set within a larger context, each a clearing in the forest. (Fig 11.6)

11.6
Agricultural fields (foreground) and remediated quarry (background) composed as reciprocal gardens.

These two landscapes, the farm and the quarry, are further interrelated through the material process of their construction. Clearings carved from 120 acres of pine and oak forests reclaim the former farmland to produce organic hay while at the same time providing material for remediation of the former quarry. Trees thinned from the site's agricultural areas were mulched and incorporated with lime into the sterile quarry "moon dirt," transforming highly acidic, compacted clay furnace waste into a planting medium capable of supporting new life. A single strategy, the thinning of trees, at once carves out space for the agricultural fields and provides the material for the quarry's new living soil medium. The remediation of the quarry is made possible by the rejuvenation of the farm, through a material transfer that connects these two landscapes symbiotically.

Over 300,000 cubic tons of remediated soil were shaped to form the quarry's gently rolling landscape of ponds and open fields, graded to minimize erosion of the vulnerable new slopes. A series of twelve basins situated in a low meadow dotted with cedar and pine trees provides the perfect terrain for field trials for McNeil's champion Labrador retrievers. (Fig 11.7) Ground cover species growing a maximum height of twelve inches were planted to provide

11.7
The rolling terrain of the former clay quarry provides ideal conditions for field trial competitions.

a future seed bank and food source for wildlife while eliminating the need for mowing.

Wherever possible, McNeil looked for sources of recycled materials to minimize both cost and material inputs. Crushed concrete from a New Jersey highway improvement project was used to construct roadways. A telephone company provided discarded telephone poles for the property's boundary fence. Leaves collected from residents of the county are delivered for free and composted on the farm.

If Winslow Farm Conservancy was to serve as an economically feasible model for remediating the 240,000 acres of clay, sand, and gravel quarries in New Jersey, it needed to operate as a profitable farm. Though McNeil had no previous experience in farming, he recognized that future sustainability depended upon successful agricultural production. Through trial and error, McNeil discovered the critical importance of identifying a viable existing market prior to growing crops. Early attempts at marketing echinacea and bayberry as agricultural products along with vegetable crops failed due to the absence of a robust market. What McNeil found was not a demand for food or the products of native plants, but a demand for replenished beaches, a market that presented the opportunity to contribute to site remediation at a larger scale.

11.8
Beachgrass fields northeast of the quarry landscape.

A series of storms had left New Jersey beaches battered and in need of restoration. The demand was high for beach grass, a plant used to rebuild coastlines along the Atlantic seaboard. Fields northeast of the quarry landscape were put into production, in an opportunistic move responding to an extraordinary need for beach grass seedlings. (Fig 11.8) The sandy soils in this location are ideal for the cultivation of beach grass and the renewable harvesting method, whereby one plant is put back in the field for every twenty-five plants harvested, results in a profitable and sustainable high yield. Within a few years, Winslow Farm Conservancy became a major supplier of beach grass for government purchase in the state of New Jersey. (Fig 11.9)

American beach grass, *Ammophila breviligulata*, is a perennial grass native to sand dunes along the Atlantic coast from Newfoundland to North Carolina. Both

11.9
Beachgrass production.

its form and structure adapt in response to the coastal landform system shaped by forces of water and wind. When windblown sand builds up around the grass, it sends up a vertical rhizome in response, producing a new stem. Conversely, buried stems have the capacity to become roots. The plant's rhizome mat extends horizontally to form an interlocking and stabilizing structure that can extend vertically to a depth of twenty feet. Beach grass stabilizes the dune in a way that other plants cannot, adapting in concert with the dune's changing form both horizontally and vertically.

The cultivation of beach grass has a long history as a tested method of sand stabilization in the United States. As early as 1712, colonists were planting beach grass to stabilize sand on Cape Cod. In the early republic, widespread deforestation caused sandstorms that buried coastal towns and threatened harbors. Between 1826 and 1839, Congress appropriated $28,000 for the planting of beach grass to protect the harbor of Provincetown.[1] The practice spread south along the Atlantic coast when a group of concerned duck hunters from Massachusetts began stabilizing the North Carolina Outer Banks with beach grass in 1904. Their successful efforts were formalized and repeated in the 1930s, with a federal and state sponsored conservation program that planted more than 2,965 acres.

In recent decades, Atlantic coastal communities have scrambled to rebuild and stabilize the most potent defense against severe storms, the primary coastal dune. Coastal dunes are critical barriers to storm surges and flooding, dissipating storm wave energy. During the storm, sand transported by wave action forms offshore sandbars which typically migrate and slowly return to the beach over time. Beach sand is eventually blown back to the dunes, over years, provided another storm doesn't interrupt the process. In this way, the rebuilding of coastal dunes can happen naturally, but the process can take years.

In the face of ever-increasing storm events due to climate change, communities are using beach grass stabilization to hasten the natural dune rebuilding process. But the demand for plant material is so high that the nursery trade can supply only a fraction of east coast dune restoration projects each year. In its second season of beach grass cultivation, Winslow Farms Conservancy tripled production and still couldn't meet the demand. By 2012, in the wake of hurricane Sandy, beach grass continued to be in short supply. The Cape May Plant Materials Center of the USDA National Resource Conservation Service reported one request alone for 1.5 million plants at a time when the center only had 325,000 plants on hand, and this small number was designated for projects in five states.[2] At the time of this publication, the demand for beach grass still exceeds Winslow Farm's ability to produce it; the need for an expanded production remains high.[3]

It is easy to envision a future where degraded properties across the New Jersey Pine Barrens like Winslow Farms are transformed to fulfill the region's need for coastal restoration planting. As research informs the development of new strategies, we may witness a diversification of species grown for this purpose. Beach grass is effective only if coastal dunes are actively accreting sand. Once the sand has been stabilized, typically after three to six years, beach grass declines and dies off, giving way to the natural succession of other species. The Cape May Plant Materials Center recommends interplanting additional species of grasses such as coastal panicgrass, switchgrass, and saltmeadow cordgrass and forbs such as seaside goldenrod, beach pea, and trailing wild bean, on the backside of frontal dunes to provide a future seed source as beach grass declines over time.[4] New studies on the efficacy of a biodiverse planting for long-term success may create a market for diversifying the plants grown at Winslow Farms, and open an even wider market for new farms within the New Jersey Pine Barrens.

Winslow Farms Conservancy represents a potential new model of the networked farm, synthesizing remediation and restoration through agriculture to address the impacts of climate change. Through design, the agricultural and remediated landscapes are interconnected and interdependent, linked not only through the process of transforming the property, but also through the ongoing cycles of harvest and restoration that extend beyond property boundaries. Farming in this case is an act of restoration, for this site, and sites beyond. And so, Winslow Farms Conservancy makes it clear that the farm is a landscape networked to other landscapes outside its boundaries, with the capacity to provide resources to restore not only local site ecology, but devastated landscapes far beyond.

Notes

1 Charles Louis Flint and Manly Miles, *American Farming and Stock Raising: With Useful Facts for the Household, Devoted to Farming in All Its Departments, Volume 1* (New York: Casselberry, 1901), 158.
2 Scott Gale, "Beach-Grass Shortage Slows Sandy Recovery Efforts," *Crain's New York Business*, July 12, 2013.
3 Hank McNeil, Interview with Phoebe Lickwar, September 14, 2018.
4 Louise Wootton, Jon Miller, Christopher Miller, Michael Peek, Amy Williams, and Peter Rowe, *New Jersey Sea Grant Consortium Dune Manual*, 2016, retrieved from njseagrant.org/dunemanual, accessed May 25, 2018.

Shenyang Architectural University

Shenyang City, China

Turenscape + Peking University Graduate School of Landscape Architecture, 2004

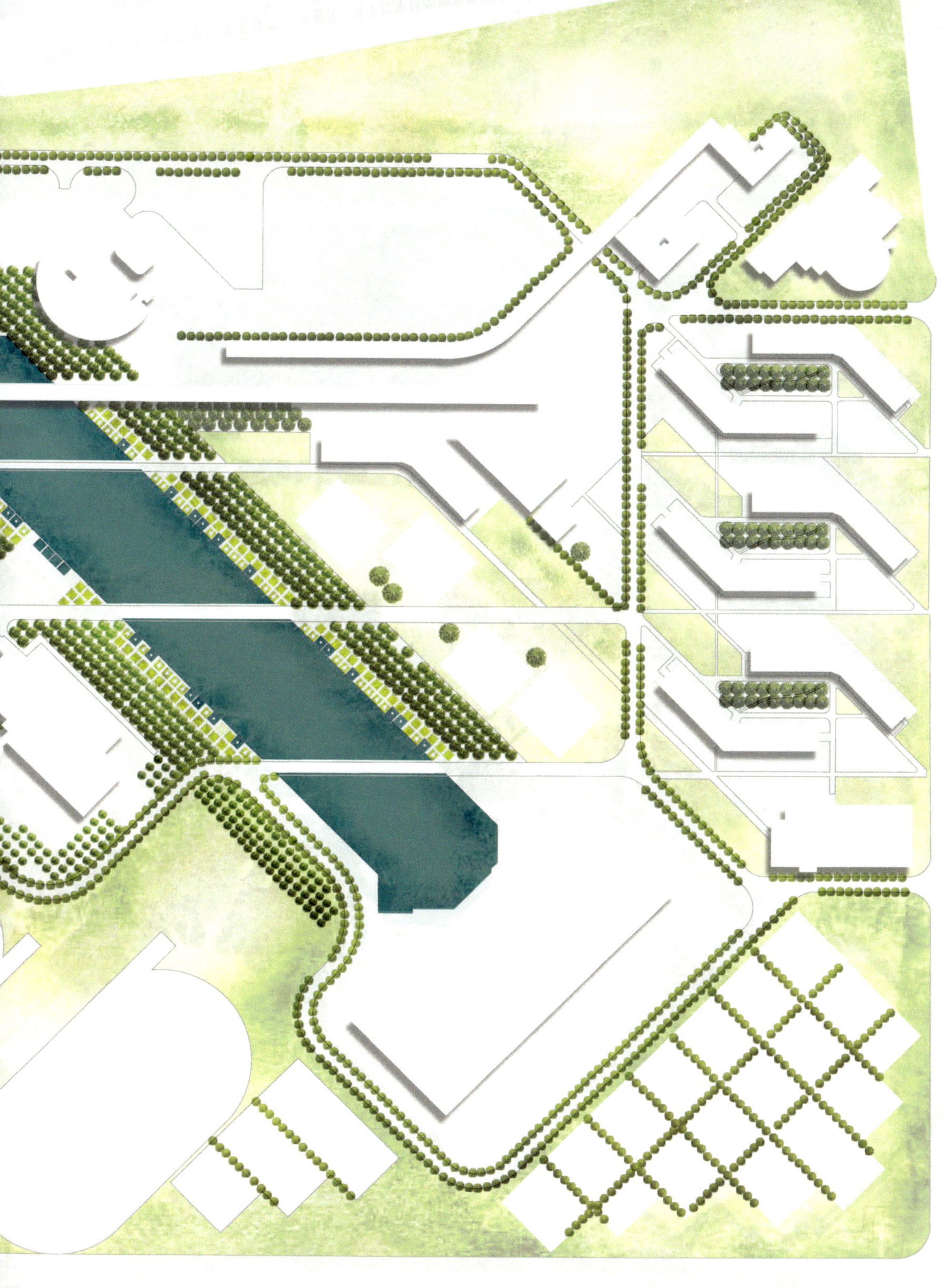
0
150
300 ft

The city of Shenyang lies in a rice-producing region of Northwest China where farmland is currently threatened by rapid, peri-urban development. Like many cities across China, Shenyang has experienced explosive growth resulting in the loss of agricultural land at the urban fringe, where the impacts of expanding development and industrial pollution are typically most extreme. However, the design of Shenyang Architectural University demonstrates that the expansion of the city need not displace agriculture altogether. A new campus, designed by Turenscape and the Peking University Graduate School of Landscape Architecture, retains the agricultural use of the land, integrating crop production with university life. Seven acres of cultivated fields, punctuated by outdoor classroom platforms and outlined by the strong geometry of pedestrian pathways, produce the region's famous Northeast Rice. Overlapping programs, one academic, one agricultural, occupy the same space, their seasonal cycles alternately inflecting the learning environment, providing a highly visible opportunity for education in cultural heritage.

The campus landscape seeks to reconcile contemporary urbanity with rural agricultural traditions and productivity, "rebuilding the connection between the land and people – especially the younger generation who have been estranged from the land due to urbanization" and "raising the awareness of the current food crisis and land ethic."[1] At a pivotal moment in China's history, when rapid urbanization and the loss of agricultural land threaten national food security in the country, this campus models a way of combining urban development and food production, and educates students and visitors about the critical importance of traditional husbandry methods as a foundation for new models of sustainable farming integrated into urban life. In recent years, the suburban area surrounding the campus has been transformed to accommodate a dense fabric of residential towers. What was once a horizontal rural landscape of rice paddies is now a vertical urban landscape inhabited by a burgeoning population. To urban and rural students alike, the campus rice fields are a strange experiment: agriculture retained in the unlikeliest of places.

The temporal overlapping of education and agriculture is designed to maximize learning opportunities and create reciprocal seasonal cycles that facilitate community participation. Formerly cultivated as rice fields, the site of Shenyang Architectural University's new campus is particularly well suited to the production of high-quality japonica rice, a variety with a longer growing season than the rice varieties grown in southern China. The design keeps fertile land in production while adapting the forms and systems of agriculture to serve the university's educational mission. Northeast rice is an ideal agricultural crop in this hybrid landscape, as its planting and harvest dates overlap with the academic calendar of the university. Students and faculty are on campus and able to participate in spring planting and fall harvest. Across the academic year, there exists a reciprocal relationship between academic activity and the cultivation of rice; the fallow season for one is the fecund season for the other.

Visible from campus classrooms, the bold geometry of the cultivated grounds below signals a decidedly urban space. (Fig 12.1) A system of pathways

12.1
View of rice fields designed as a campus landscape.

12.2
Students studying in the rice fields.

and platforms is overlaid across sunken parcels where rice and buckwheat are cultivated. Wide granite walks form a gridded field that relates orthogonally to the campus. Definitive diagonal desire lines crisscross the paddies, providing direct connections to buildings. Narrow concrete paths penetrate the rice fields, leading to platforms where students can gather. (Fig 12.2) The stark lines of paving play against the changing color of the fields, the dark rich soil awaiting planting, the mirrored surfaces of flooded paddies, the lush brightness of green seedlings, and the brilliant gold of the harvest. (Fig 12.3a–b) The seasonal rhythms of rice cultivation sit side by side with the cycles of the academic year, overlapping at the beginning and end of each cycle. Two systems, the agricultural and the academic, share space, each measured against the other.

12.3a–b
The rice landscape changes dramatically over the course of the academic year.

The cultivation of rice connects the university community to a regional heritage at risk, providing a cultural education about local agricultural traditions. The life of the campus hovers above the rice landscape; students pass through the fields on raised walkways or watch from desks several floors up. (Fig 12.4) Looking down or passing through, students notice the change of seasons, the growth of

crops, and the cultivation of the fields by local farmers. The academic community is invited to experience the beauty of the cultivated landscape, to learn about the agricultural traditions it represents. But only on two occasions throughout the year do students and faculty get their hands dirty. On the first Saturday after mid-May, Rice Planting Day, the campus community plants rice seedlings (Fig 12.5) and on the last Saturday in October, Rice Harvesting Day, they harvest the rice. (Fig 12.6) Even though this opportunity to work the land is brief, students and faculty remain connected to the rice landscape. The pragmatic and sensual aspects of cultivating rice are inseparable from the life of the campus, observed on a daily basis. Walking through the fields and watching them from high above is an education in itself. The rice fields are always available, a constant reminder of the cultural heritage and agricultural traditions of the region that are threatened by development.

Traditional rice agriculture in China has been a way to steward the land, maximizing benefits to humans and non-humans alike by connecting agriculture to ecology. The presence of a demonstration farm has given this school a unique identity as a place where students can learn about agricultural practices and discover the many environmental benefits of the rice ecosystem. Classified as human-made wetlands by the Ramsar Convention, rice paddies can play a significant role in improving air and water quality while providing important biodiverse habitat for fish, birds, frogs, crabs, snails, and insects. Rice fields increase the storage capacity of river basins, lower peak flow of rivers, increase groundwater recharge, and moderate air temperatures in peri-urban conditions. Rice production can also

12.4
Visible from classrooms, the rice landscape is a constant reminder of the region's agricultural heritage.

12.5
Rice Planting Day.

12.6
Rice Harvesting Day.

12.7 (pages 178–179)
The rice ecosystem in summer.

improve soil fertility, fixing nitrogen and increasing the availability of phosphorus, iron, and zinc.

However, commercial rice agriculture in China largely fails to provide these benefits and has been associated with significant environmental impacts. The need to feed a rapidly growing population with limited arable land has placed enormous pressure on farmers to increase yields. China owns only 10 percent of the world's arable land, but must feed 22 percent of the world's population. Projected population growth rates of 13 million people per year will require a 20 percent increase in rice production by 2030. While rice production has doubled in northern China from 1995 to 2009, development pressures have reduced the amount of land in rice production nearly two and a half million acres.[2] All the while, preference for higher quality japonica rice, lower in yield than other varieties, continues to rise, while increasing global temperatures shorten rice life cycles and reduce yields.

In response to rising demand, commercial growers in China have increased their use of fertilizers, pesticides, and herbicides. Overuse of these inputs has polluted waterways, degraded soils, and diminished overall biodiversity. In 2002, the average nitrogen application rate in China was 75 percent higher than the world average, even though only 20–30 percent of the typical application is taken up by the rice plants. Added to this misuse of fertilizer, an average 40 percent overuse of pesticides has severely impacted the rice ecosystem, resulting in unintended pest outbreaks from the reduction of beneficial insect populations.[3] While commercial practices initially brought significant yield increases, they have failed to realize higher and higher yields in recent years.[4] With rising consumer demand and less arable land, new methods of intensive production are needed. Furthermore, if China is to feed its population and remain food independent, growing rice on its own soil without continued environmental degradation, then alternatives to current commercial rice production must be found.

For over two thousand years rice-fish farming was practiced in China, until the rise of commercial rice production, when the widespread use of fertilizers and pesticides toxic to fish and other aquatic creatures brought about its decline.[5] The practice has seen a resurgence in China, where public support led to a doubling of land farmed for integrated rice-fish farming between 1994 and 2001.[6] The campus rice fields play a part in the movement to reclaim traditional rice-fish farming by demonstrating what a healthy integrated rice ecosystem looks like.

Using traditional local farming practices, the campus rice fields are free of pesticides and herbicides, ensuring a robust ecology that can support integrated aquaculture and agriculture. Fish, freshwater crabs, and frogs can thrive in the flooded fields; the frogs and crabs have been harvested for special meals. The omnivorous muddy loach (*Misgurnus mizolepis*) effectively controls mosquito populations and other pests while contributing nutrient-rich droppings that are taken up by the rice crop, obviating the need for commercial fertilizers. These sensitive species are highly adapted to the temporary conditions of the fields. They benefit the production of the rice crop by controlling weed and pest species and increasing yields.

12.8
Vegetated pathways, scaled to the human body, provide shade in the heat of summer.

Students and faculty at the university observe the creatures that inhabit the rice fields and come to know the productive landscape as a place that resonates with life. (Fig 12.7) Pulsing with the sound of frogs, birds, and insects, the rice ecosystem is a constant reminder that agriculture is not only about the production of food, but also about our interdependence with the non-human world as we seek to cultivate a life-supporting environment for ourselves and others.

The thriving rice ecosystem teaches the university community about the contemporary relevance of farming methods passed down for generations, where land stewardship and agriculture are addressed simultaneously. Mao Zedong's Great Leap Forward (1958–1961) dismissed the critical importance of local traditions that produced food while stewarding the land, a costly mistake that contributed to the starvation of over 45 million people. Subsequent food security challenges, as the nation struggled to feed a rapidly growing population, similarly devalued traditional agriculture in favor of the green revolution, with mechanized, input-heavy crop production. As landscape architect Kongjian Yu acknowledges, an idealization of rural village life will not provide solutions to food security in twenty-first century China,[7] but traditional models of thriving, productive ecosystems may well form the foundation for new approaches.

Such models may prove particularly useful in urban environments, where space constraints require multifunctional landscapes. Vernacular agricultural

12.9
Agricultural fields are a living laboratory for the campus.

traditions such as rice-fish farming maximize the productive capacity of the land, but even more importantly, such methods of cultivation provide environmental benefits that create healthy spaces for urban populations. Kongjian Yu's campus design offers an optimistic proposal, that agriculture can be adapted to meet the constraints of the urban environment. Farming in the urban context requires new spatial and temporal efficiencies, developed through multifunctional strategies that address scarcity of land and resources. Stormwater is collected and stored in a central pond, providing an irrigation source as well as a stunning reflecting pool for the campus. The main pedestrian pathways, divided by a strip of groundcover planting, are scaled to the human body as well as farming equipment, providing passage and inhabitation as well as access for tending. (Fig 12.8) Crops and frogs are harvested for campus dining halls, contributing to delicious meals no longer solely sourced from distant farms.

These new hybrid systems are designed to be legible and understood as urban landscape, thereby challenging the notion that agriculture is necessarily rural. The aesthetic of the project adapts farming forms to the contemporary context of the university campus. Sensory pleasure and knowledge together connect a non-farming campus to this new form of rice agriculture. The plantings of rice and buckwheat are beautiful to observe. They provide a harvest that delights the palette. The intimacy that develops over time between the academic community and the agricultural fields has cultural value as a daily reminder of the community's dependence on agriculture. (Fig 12.9) By seeing how the rice is grown, and participating in the ritualized planting and harvest, students and faculty come to understand the space, time, and labor embedded in rice cultivation. As future designers of the built environment, students of engineering and architecture are potential contributors to addressing China's food security issues. The rice campus is their laboratory, a hybrid landscape that demonstrates the role design plays in adapting agriculture to new development, preserving the productivity of the land in an increasingly urban society.

Notes

1 Kongjian Yu, "The Good Earth Recovered," in *Wiederkehr der Landschaft / Return of Landscape*, ed. Donata Valentien (Berlin: Jovis Publishers, 2010), 233.
2 GRiSP (Global Rice Science Partnership), *Rice Almanac, 4th edition* (Los Baños, Philippines: International Rice Research Institute, 2013), 106–107.
3 Ibid., 108.
4 Michael Frei and Klaus Becker, "Integrated Rice-Fish Culture: Coupled Production Saves Resources," *Natural Resources Forum* 29, no. 2 (2005): 135.
5 C. H. Fernando, "Rice Field Ecology and Fish Culture – An Overview," *Hydrobiologia* 259, no. 2 (1993): 109.
6 Frei and Becker, "Integrated Rice-Fish Culture," 141.
7 See Kongjian Yu and Mary Padua, *The Art of Survival: Recovering Landscape Architecture* (Mulgrave, Victoria: Images Publishing Group, 2006). Yu argues that contemporary landscape architecture must recreate a new "Land of Peach Blossoms," where land productivity and stewardship together form the basis for a new art of survival.

Green Gulch Farm Zen Center

Muir Beach, California

San Francisco Zen Center, 1972–present

Mithun, Long-term Vision Plan, 2008

Prunuske and Chatham, Inc., Creek Restoration, 2014–2015

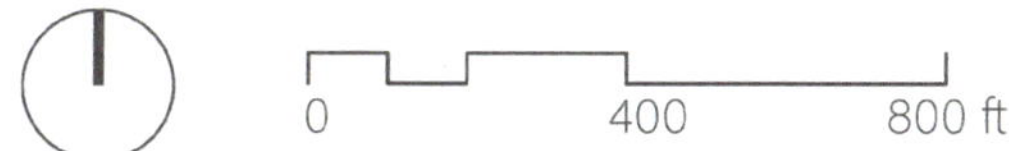
0
400
800 ft

One might infer from the fences and gates that mark the physical extents of Green Gulch Farm that a fixed boundary exists between cultivated and wild landscapes, but the demarcation is surprisingly immaterial. Since its acquisition in 1972 of 115 acres in a northern California valley, the San Francisco Zen Center has sought to connect their farm and community to the wider landscape in which the farm is situated, to realize the interdependence of the farm with the species and plants that inhabit its watershed, and to feed and educate local communities beyond the farm's gates. Slowly, and with deliberate intent, the Green Gulch community is working to integrate farming and ecological conservation, transforming the land in a way that respects the interdependence of the cultivated and the wild.

The long-term adaptation of the landscape from a formerly degraded cattle ranch to a healthy agroecosystem demonstrates an intentional shift from an agricultural model of depletion and extraction to one of regeneration. The Zen Buddhist community that resides and works at Green Gulch Farm has demonstrated commitment to stewardship and cultivation of the land for the benefit of all beings. Farming is understood as a mode of Buddhist spiritual practice, a means to connect to the inner self and to the wider world. This framework requires balancing ecological restoration and agricultural production, a challenging undertaking in a water-scarce climate.

Green Gulch Farm Zen Center is nestled in a valley draining to the Pacific Ocean, ten miles from San Francisco. (Fig 13.1) To the north is Muir Woods National Monument and to the south is the Golden Gate National Recreation Area, both expansive tracts of ecologically significant preserves. Green Gulch was originally worked as a dairy ranch by Portuguese settlers brought to develop the area by William Richardson, who had gained a Mexican land grant in 1838 to establish Rancho Sausalito. Horse trainer Ray Button later modified the ranch and created trails for raising horses, which still mark the hills today. A hay barn built in 1910, the main house, and the ranch house were all sited near the confluence of two creeks, Spring Valley Creek and Green Gulch Creek, important tributaries of Redwood Creek for which the watershed is named.

George Wheelwright, co-founder of Polaroid, and his wife Hope Wheelwright, bought the ranch in 1946, a total of 800 acres. After researching cattle ranching methods, Wheelwright began significant alterations to the landscape to accommodate farming operations. With the aid of the Army Corps of Engineers, he began to reshape the valley's hydrologic systems. He moved Green Gulch Creek and Spring Valley Creek from their historic creek beds, and straightened, channelized, and dammed them to create a series of reservoirs for storage and irrigation. Native scrub was cleared from the hills, and in its place exotic grasses were planted, species identified by Wheelwright in his travels to New Zealand as suitable to the Marin County climate and providing good pasture for cattle. (Fig 13.2, 13.3)

The Wheelwrights lived off the land until the 1960s when Hope became ill with cancer. Her husband built her a sanctuary, Hope Cottage, high on a ridge overlooking the Pacific Ocean, which served as a refuge until her death in 1967.

13.1
View of Green Gulch Valley, looking southwest towards the Pacific Ocean.

George Wheelwright wished to transfer the land to the National Park Service, but surely could not bear the stipulation that all structures would be demolished, particularly his beloved cottage. To preserve the memory of his wife and their working farm, Wheelwright partnered with the Nature Conservancy, saving the land from suburban development. In 1972, the San Francisco Zen Center was invited to purchase 115 acres, including Hope Cottage, the main barn, and outlying buildings. In return, the new residents agreed that Green Gulch would "forever be held for scientific, educational, esthetic, religious, or agricultural purposes"[1] and to permit public access and connection to the adjacent Golden Gate National Recreation Area trails.

While the existing buildings provided the new community with spaces that could be adapted for the Center's use, these structures were sited poorly and required improvements. The hay barn became the meditation hall, or *zendo*, but the space, located in the former creek bed, was often damp and cold, and was vulnerable to flooding. The thin structure proved inadequate for the seismic activity of northern California and required renovation in the aftermath of the 1989 Loma Prieta earthquake.[2]

Wheelwright's transformation of Green Gulch as a working cattle ranch presented additional difficulties for the Zen Center's farming efforts. The pastures

13.2
Green Gulch Valley, adapted for ranching, c. 1972.

13.3
Green Gulch Creek, straightened and channelized.

required significant remediation to produce crops where Wheelwright had grazed cattle, and in general, the farm needed to be restored from an extractive, single-use model of agriculture based in grazing to a regenerative, multi-species model of farming that improves the soil, based in the understanding of the soil itself as a living ecosystem. The heavily compacted soil was aerated by hand with pickaxes. A new productive landscape began to emerge, underpinned by Buddhist principles of interdependence and mindfulness and undoubtedly informed by the teachings of Zen Center founder Shunryu Suzuki, who died just one year prior to the Zen Center's acquisition of Green Gulch. Suzuki characterized farming as a form of stewardship: "The Buddha's teaching is not about the food itself but about how it is grown, and how to take care of it."[3]

Several advisors guided the Zen Center's incremental adaptation of the land in the early years. Alan Chadwick, a horticulturist, Shakespearean actor, garden designer, and leader in the biodynamic and organic farming movement, arrived at Green Gulch in 1973. He stayed only one season, establishing a temporary garden at the site of a former horse corral with the aid of his own apprentices and several Zen students. Later, in 1979, Chadwick returned to Green Gulch for the last six months of his life, transferring his knowledge of biodynamic farming to a group of dedicated students. Developing his own technique derived from the French Intensive approach and Rudolf Steiner's biodynamic principles, Chadwick emphasized crop-specific soil preparation, incorporation of moderate amounts of compost, companion planting, and planting according to phases of the moon. With these methods, Chadwick attained yields four times greater, with half as much water, than could be produced in the same area through commercial agricultural means.[4] But efficiency of agricultural production was, according to Chadwick, more the result and less the intent of his efforts. Chadwick railed against the violence of the industrial machine, preferring to trade efficiency at all costs for labor-intensive methods whose success was derived from a personal knowledge

13.4
The herb circle in the garden designed by Zen Center students. The garden incorporates edible and ornamental species and is situated between the zendo and farm fields.

of interconnected natural systems. He taught his students how to engage the garden as an ecosystem of interrelated beings and to use that knowledge as the basis for understanding the self, asserting that, "it is not the gardener who makes the garden, but the garden that makes the gardener."[5]

Chadwick's teachings are prominent in the practices of subsequent Zen Center farming advisors. Together with botanist and native plant expert Harry Roberts, Chadwick is looked upon as one of the early caretakers of Green Gulch, contributing to the Zen Center's evolving body of farming knowledge specific to this valley and the species that inhabit it. Today, this farming lineage links the current community to the history of stewardship in this valley, to a tradition that places farming in the context of caring for the land.[6]

After Chadwick's death, his students designed and built a 1.75-acre garden as a tribute to his gift of teaching. The garden mediates between the farm fields and the zendo, an eclectic mix of edible and ornamental species organized in a series of rooms. The garden is a distillation of the farm, a hybrid space designed for both agricultural production and spiritual practice, intended to bring the user into harmony with the world through both labor and meditation. A space for experimentation in horticultural practices, the garden includes beds of flowering perennials, culinary and medicinal herbs, rows of lavender, native shrubs, and fruit and nut trees. A rectilinear perimeter yew hedge and four rose arbors mark the boundary of a garden known as the herb circle, whose form is defined by low boxwood hedges, shrubs, roses, herbs, and a single Japanese snowbell tree at the center. (Fig 13.4) Across a central path, espaliered fruit trees define an edible garden planted in rows. (Fig 13.5) The adjacent contemplative garden provides a quiet protected space planted with bamboo, Mugo pine, and cherry trees, species that symbolize strength, flexibility, and transient beauty (*sho-chiku-bai*) in the Zen tradition. (Fig 13.6)

At Green Gulch, working the land is understood as a form of work-practice, a gateway to mindfulness and intention through work. The hyphenation is intentional: work and practice arise at the same time. Norman Fischer, abbot of Green Gulch from 1995 to 1999, distinguishes between "work as meditation" and "work as offering,"[7] the former a mode of raising consciousness, the latter a mode of

13.5
Espaliered fruit trees and herbs in the garden. Hope Cottage is visible in the upper left corner.

13.6
Planting reflecting the Zen tradition in the garden.

13.7 (pages 194–195)
Windbreaks form the edges of agricultural fields, protecting crops from winds.

contributing to the community. Farming is both. Simple repetitive tasks offer the opportunity to develop mindfulness of the physical performance of the work, the efficient movement of hands, feet, and breath. Other tasks are understood in terms of providing benefit to the human and more-than-human world, building healthy soil, maintaining healthy air and water quality, providing habitat to insects and mammals, feeding people.

Wendy Johnson, one of Chadwick's students and a founder of the organic Farm and Garden Program at Green Gulch, describes the cultivation of the garden as a cultivation of awareness, a way of "extending the field of meditation into engagement with the life of the world."[8] This begins with looking at and noticing the complex set of relationships between interdependent beings, materials, and phenomenon. In building a living soil, the dynamic interplay between microbes, roots, sun, air, water, fungi, and bacteria can be observed and understood. Pestiferous arthropods come and go, in turn attracted by sacrificial patches of preferred plants and managed by beneficial insects who flock to borders of Queen Anne's lace, borage, wild radish, vetch, and buckwheat. Mounds of compost reveal the cycle

of life into death into life, as the pile decays and ripens, then returns to the soil to feed plants, insects, animals, and humans.

Farming follows the seasonal rhythms of the valley's coastal northern California climate, mirrored by the Zen Center's meditation schedule. A six-month growing season, from mid-April to mid-October, is followed by a six-month practice period. Saturated with runoff from the surrounding hills, the fields rest during the rainy winter months under a planting of soil-building cover crops. With fewer work hours devoted to the farm, attention turns towards a period of intensive meditation practice. During the growing season, practitioners return their focus to farming, and they are solely responsible for managing all farm operations, including greenhouse production, planting, irrigation, composting, harvesting, tractor work, and market deliveries.

Aimed at undermining the notion of a separate self, farming as work-practice offers a means for Zen students to realize connection not only with the farm's internal, biological communities, but also with surrounding human communities. Produce is distributed to local farmer's markets, local restaurants, grocery stores, and the Zen Center kitchens in San Francisco and at Green Gulch. Fields are gleaned for Marin County food banks and the farm donates plant starts to schools. Green Gulch has partnered with Marin Organic as a participant in the Farm Field Studies Program, which brings children and young adults to the farm to learn about connections between environment, agriculture, and food. Every year, between eight hundred and one thousand school children come to the farm to learn about living soil, compost, bugs, plants, and food.

As the Zen Center continues to engage communities and individuals through farming and environmental education, it has also reached out to the non-human world through its conservation efforts. Seven acres of cultivated farm fields, divided by windbreaks of majestic Monterey cypress and Monterey pine, extend from the gardens westward toward the sea. The striking borders of tall evergreens define the edges of agricultural space and provide a place for insects and birds to inhabit, supporting crucial members of the intricate ecosystem of the garden and farm. (Fig 13.7) Protected from winter storms, the farm fields are habitat for humans and non-humans alike, a co-mingling of practitioner-farmers, pollinators and other insects, microscopic organisms, birds, crops, and the occasional deer, raccoon, river otter, and other mammals who transgress the farm boundary.

While the highly altered and controlled creeks provided the farm with a source of water for irrigation, the loss of habitat on the property and degradation of ecosystem health within the watershed concerned many. Originally grounded in the post-Vietnam counterculture of the early 1970s, the Zen Center community long desired a relationship with the land aligned with the environmentalist ethic of the times. Early pilot projects included wind power, composting toilets, and organic farming. Concern for endangered species and the degraded condition of the creek ecosystem have prompted a series of stream restoration projects that have reshaped the farm. Part of a long-term vision plan designed by the firm Mithun, the redesign of the Zen Center property will release the creeks from

13.8
Rendering of Mithun's long-term vision plan.

controls imposed by Wheelwright over fifty years ago. Some of the buildings will need to be relocated as a result, and farm fields, roads, and pathways will be reconfigured. Balancing cultivation and conservation, the Zen Center is committed to a process that may take fifty to one hundred years to be realized. (Fig 13.8)

The establishment of healthy creek ecosystems in the watershed began in earnest in 2005, when the Zen Center partnered with the National Park Service to restore Redwood Creek. The Zen Center gave up fifteen acres of cultivated land for a restoration easement intended to repair a dysfunctional hydrological system and provide habitat for endangered or threatened species, including Coho salmon, steelhead trout, and California red-legged frogs. Coho salmon, listed as a federally endangered species in 2005, were observed the same year in Green Gulch Creek, adjacent to farm fields. A wildlife biologist confirmed the presence of one thousand Coho fry in 2006; the confirmed sighting of Coho on the Zen Center land galvanized the community's support for creek restoration efforts.

The first phase of the Green Gulch Creek restoration, completed in 2014, required sacrificing one of the lower farm fields for critical Coho spawning habitat. Environmental restoration firm Prunuske Chatham transformed what was a narrow, straight channel to a meandering creek including 1.5 acres of floodplain

13.9
Green Gulch creek restoration in construction.

13.10
Green Gulch creek restoration one year after construction.

13.11
Spring Valley Creek, daylighted through the garden.

wetland and riparian habitat. (Fig 13.9, 13.10) Four thousand native plants were installed to help improve water quality and maintain the cool temperatures critical for Coho salmon and steelhead trout spawning, along with willow wattles for bank stabilization and woody debris necessary as refugia for the fish. The second phase of the project, completed in 2015, daylighted a portion of Spring Valley Creek through the garden, bypassing the zendo pond with a direct connection to Green Gulch Creek. (Fig 13.11) Sediment critical for fish spawning is no longer dumped into the zendo pond, carried instead to Green Gulch Creek downstream. But diverting water before it reaches the zendo pond, which serves as the farm's irrigation reservoir, raises concerns given California's recent years of drought. Will there be enough water to irrigate the fields? And how much water can the farm take without impacting the creek ecosystem? A grant from the California Wildlife Conservation Board is funding a water use analysis and alternative storage plan to determine the feasibility of storing water off-channel while still permitting the creek to flow year-round.

The Zen Center grapples with these questions in its ongoing transformation of Green Gulch, ever mindful of the need to balance cultivation and conservation. The integration of Buddhist practice guides future development, supported by decades of observation and the accrual of knowledge about the species and systems upon which farming depends. As the community continues to engage conservation and agriculture as mutually beneficial uses of the land, it serves as a model of farming for a sustainable future.

Notes

1 Property Deed dated November 28, 1973, from Nature Conservancy to Chief Priest of Zen Center, Marin County, California, book 2744, page 657.
2 For personal recollections about the use of the barn as Zendo, as well as firsthand history about farming and stewardship at Green Gulch, see Mick Sopko, "A History of Green Gulch Farm," accessed May 12, 2015, www.cuke.com/zc-stories/gg-history.htm.
3 Shunryu Suzuki and Edward Espe Brown, *Not Always So: Practicing the True Spirit of Zen* (New York: Harper Collins, 2002), 48.
4 John C. Jeavons, "Biointensive Sustainable Mini-Farming: II. Perspective, Principles, Techniques and History," *Journal of Sustainable Agriculture* 19, no. 2 (2001): 70.
5 Tom Cuthbertson, *Alan Chadwick's Enchanted Garden* (New York: E. P. Dutton, 1978), xiii.
6 Sara Tashker, Interview with Phoebe Lickwar, May 4, 2015.
7 Norman Fischer, "Zen Work," in *Dharma Rain: Sources of Buddhist Environmentalism*, ed. Stephanie Kaza and Kenneth Kraft (Boston, MA: Shambhala Publications, 2000), 248.
8 Wendy Johnson, *Gardening at the Dragon's Gate: At Work in the Wild and Cultivated World* (New York: Bantam Books, 2008), 49.

Babylonstoren

Franschhoek, South Africa

Patrice Taravella, 2010

0
400
800 ft

The Franschhoek Valley, in the Western Cape province of South Africa, is an agricultural region known for its vineyards, orchards, and fields of grain. At the foot of the Simonsberg mountain, between the cities of Paarl and Franschhoek, lies Babylonstoren, a five-hundred-acre farm with a four-hundred-year legacy capitalizing on the rich agricultural history of the valley. Notable for its integration of agriculture and botanical collection, the farm includes a designed productive garden that offers a sensual and educational experience of the edible landscape. The garden's collection of indigenous and exotic species, highly ordered and formally displayed, contrasts with the farm's natural reserves, areas preserving biodiversity within a broader context of orchard and vineyard monocultures.

Babylonstoren is named after the conical hill, or *koppie*, overlooking the farm and thought to resemble the Tower of Babel. First called Babilonische Tooren, later Babilonstoring and Babylonstoren, the farm was associated through its name with the biblical tale explaining the origin of cultural difference. In the Tower of Babel, God creates linguistic diversity so that the population, previously sharing a common language and unified in building a tower and a city, is dispersed across the earth. Though the story is often interpreted as a tale of hubris and punishment, contemporary biblical scholars have identified an alternate reading of the text as a legitimization of pluralism and diversity, an explanation of cultural difference as God's intention for the world.[1] The Tower of Babel is a fitting reference for the seventeenth-century Franschhoek Valley, a place of great linguistic and cultural variation including a mix of Dutch, French, German, Khoi, and San populations with inflections of Asian culture and language introduced by the spice trade, and it remains a fitting descriptor for a farm that continues to combine plants from around the world adapted to the local climate.

Today, Babylonstoren retains strong ties to the origins of its name, translating cultural diversity through plants. Located in the midst of wine country monocultures, the farm seamlessly blends agricultural production with botanical collection, integrating a dizzying variety of native and adapted plants. Fields of grain, vineyards, and orchards of citrus and plums surround an eight-acre geometric fruit and vegetable garden designed by architect Patrice Taravella. Natural areas, including the *koppie* and a riparian corridor bisecting the property, are preserved and stewarded as critical ecological resources. (Fig 14.1) The garden, agricultural fields, and natural areas are linked through design to ensure economic and ecological viability, supporting the production of agricultural goods for export as well as a robust program of agritourism.

At the heart of the farm is the geometric garden inspired by the seventeenth-century Vereenigde Oost-Indische Compagnie (VOC) Kompanjiestuin, or Company's Garden. (Fig 14.2) The VOC garden, located in Cape Town on the slopes of Table Mountain, provided sustenance for early settlers and sailing ships of the Dutch East India Company. Organized as a grid of rectangular plots surrounded by hedges providing protection from winds, the garden included food plants and seeds sourced from ships arriving from Asia, Europe, and the Americas. As a

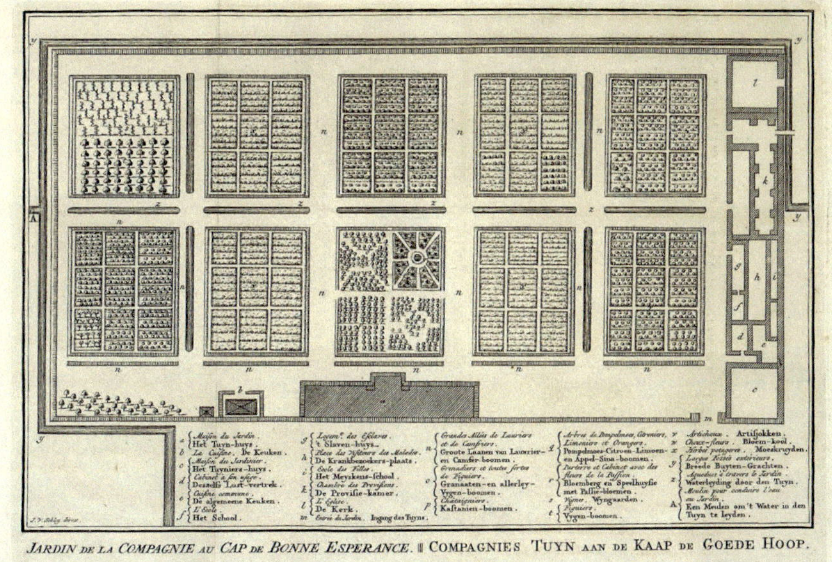

14.1
View of Babylonstoren, showing left to right, the *koppie*, farm fields, "Tigris" stream corridor, and formal garden.

14.2
Company's Garden at the Cape of Good Hope, c. 1753.

14.3
The garden *leiwater* delivers water to the garden from the "Tigris" stream.

14.4
The main North–South axis, planted with mature guava trees, frames a view of the *koppie*.

point of world trade, the garden included an unusual diversity of species and plant uses including fruit trees, herbs, medicinals, vines, and pines and oaks grown to increase the supply of wood.

In 1680, under Governor Simon van der Stel, a series of canals and channels were constructed to irrigate the VOC garden with water from the Fresh River. Twelve years later, van der Stel granted the land thirty miles northeast of Capetown that would become Babylonstoren to free burgher Pieter van der Byl. Free citizen farmers like van der Byl were provided with land to aid in producing food for the new settlement. As these farmers started to make significant contributions of vegetables and fruit for the community, the need for the VOC garden to grow food was less critical, and the garden slowly shifted towards botanical collection. Under Governor Jan Andries Auge, arriving at the Cape in 1747, many native trees and plants were added, greatly expanding the role and purpose of the garden to serve new educational and recreational functions.

The garden at Babylonstoren borrows formal qualities from the VOC garden while also drawing upon the model of hybridity, maximizing the potential for biodiversity by combining productivity and botanical collection. While the garden is primarily used as a kitchen garden, additional educational and agritourism programs are woven seamlessly into the fabric of the design. Using a similar layout of orthogonal plots subdivided by pathways and water courses, the garden's design facilitates the functional necessities of agriculture – planting, harvesting, rotation, irrigation – while also creating an organizational strategy for the display of plantings as collections.

The orientation of the garden, derived from the historic *werf*, or farmyard, responds to existing buildings, walls, and gates, rendering the historic and natural features of the property powerfully legible. Restored and repurposed buildings in the Cape Dutch style, with whitewashed walls, ornate gables, and thatched roofs, define the northern and eastern boundaries and are orientated to the "Tigris" stream along the southern edge, an important source of water supporting agriculture at Babylonstoren for hundreds of years. Thirteen new guest cottages stand on the footprints of the original laborers' cottages. The former cow shed houses Babel, a farm-to-fork restaurant welcoming visitors at the garden entry.

The garden's two main axes reinforce the lines of the *werf* and the connection to significant natural features. A raised channel, or *leiwater*, runs the length of the main East–West axis, separating guest cottages from the garden and delivering life-sustaining water from the "Tigris" stream. (Fig 14.3) The main North–South axis, a formal avenue planted with mature guava trees, provides a physical and symbolic connection to the Babylonstoren *koppie* south of the historic *werf*. Extending from the farm's restaurant across the geometric garden to the boundary at the "Tigris" stream, the avenue frames the primary view of the *koppie*, connecting distinct but interdependent elements of the farm – restaurant, garden, riparian corridor, vineyards, and ecological reserves. (Fig 14.4)

The layout of the garden is defined by a 3.75-meter grid, a subdivision of the total measurement between two existing farmyard gates along the main North–South axis (Fig 14.5). An abundance of plant and animal life is organized within this rational framework facilitating function and categorization. Hedges and walls reinforce the grid, enclosing plantings and providing vertical definition of the different garden areas. Hedges are composed of edible, medicinal, fragrant, and pollinator plant species, including bay, buddleia, pomegranate, myrtle, quince, carissa, tecomaria, kumquat, searsia, and diospyros. Walls are made from stones collected on site and whitewashed with lime. Walkways shaded by trees, planted pergolas, and rose towers terminate in focal points like gateposts, fountains, and benches. Species lining the walks include carobs, olives, figs, and citrus underplanted with edible and medicinal herbs such as thyme, cotton lavender, and wild garlic.

14.5
Geometric garden plan, showing 3.75 meter layout grid.

14.6 (pages 212–213)
Returning from the garden with the daily harvest. Visible in the foreground are the fishponds planted with edible aquatic plants.

14.7
Irrigation system delivering water from the "Tigris" stream to the garden. Unused water is returned to the stream.

Entering the garden, guests are greeted by a fragrant labyrinth, the word Babylonstoren carved as a pathway through beds of lavender and thyme. Three rectangular raised fishponds planted with edible aquatic plants form the western boundary of the entry area. (Fig 14.6) Featured within the ponds is *waterblommetjies*, a native aquatic plant first used by the Khoi people and later by Dutch settlers in preparation of *waterblommerjiebredie*, or water flower stew. Unified through exacting geometry, the elements of the entry area set the stage for a sensory experience rich in scent, sound, sight, and taste.

South of the entry area lies an expanse of gardens of incredible diversity, including fruit and vegetable crops, native and medicinal plants, and animals. These include an olive and citrus orchard, vegetable beds lined with espaliered apple, quince, and pear trees, a wild bird garden, areas for chickens and ducks, berries, a prickly pear maze, citrus and stone fruit gardens, a bee garden, a native plants garden, and a medicinal plants garden. Each of these gardens is thoughtfully designed to be simultaneously aesthetic, functional, and educational, displaying a multitude of climate-adapted species that are organized, shaped, and combined in novel ways. The prickly pear maze, for instance, is artfully arranged in staggered rows and pruned for easier harvesting. Visitors enjoy a playful experience of being lost within unusual sculptural forms that are managed as a crop. The stone fruit garden, with its square quadrants bordered by nectarine trees, is planted with

14.8
The transverse irrigation channel, aligned with the garden grid, is centered on an existing specimen tree.

flowering aromatic lawns of thyme, Roman chamomile, and native cocoonhead, recalling the medieval flowering mead.

As a working farm and a botanical collection, the geometric garden embraces biodiversity as an inheritance that is at once historical and indigenous. Inspired by the history of medicinal plant-growing at the VOC garden, the healing garden features beds of native and adapted medicinal plants arranged according to the part of the human body treated or health problem remedied. Tea ceremonies of healing herbal infusions from the garden are conducted in two pavilions connected by a water rill. The native plant garden celebrates indigenous plants with an emphasis on edibles historically foraged and adapted to the climate. The four biomes of South Africa are represented by plants native to the Thicket Biome of the Eastern Cape, the Hantam Karoo Biome of the North West Cape, the Succulent Karoo Biome of the Western Cape, and the Simonsberg Mountain Biome.

Overlaid across these gardens is an irrigation system conforming to the overall grid, delivering water collected from the "Tigris" stream through a system of gravity-fed channels above and below ground. (Fig 14.7) A four-meter grade

14.9a–b
The wild bird garden provides birdhouses and bird habitat as well as sculptural human-scale "nests" for bird-watching.

change across the garden directs water from the highest point in the northwest to the lowest point in the southeast. The garden *leiwater* delivers water along the northern edge of the garden to a transverse channel providing flood irrigation to the citrus garden, and to the three fishponds at the garden entry. (Fig 14.8) Water flow in the citrus garden is controlled by wooden sluice gates and directed to trees via small channels in stone pavement. Overflow from both the fishponds and citrus garden is returned to the stream via surface canals.

The design of Babylonstoren privileges biodiversity as the primary means of achieving ecological health and economic stability. The formal garden includes over 300 varieties of edible and medicinal plants, organized in complex layered structures of groundcovers, shrubs, trees, and vines. Beyond the formal garden, the farm grows eleven varieties of plums, twenty varieties of citrus, eight varieties of olives, and thirteen different varieties of grapes – a stark contrast to the typical monocrop of many farms. All of these crops benefit from the beneficial insects and birds that are encouraged to inhabit the formal garden within spaces intentionally designed for them. The wild bird garden invites in species such as Cape Robins, Olive Thrushes, Cape Bulbuls, Pin-tailed Whydahs, and Common Waxbills for pest control. Planted with flax and linseed, Jerusalem artichoke, sunflowers, and bamboo, with bird houses for nesting, the space provides a welcome habitat for the birds and a unique resting spot for the humans who wish to observe them. (Fig 14.9a–b) Pollinators are undoubtedly supported by the garden, invited to inhabit the insect hotel, a place for spiders, wasps, beetles, earwigs, carpenter bees, small lizards, centipedes, and toads. Native Cape honey bees are raised in rustic, English, and American Langstroth hives that dot the bee garden's macadamia orchard. The poultry area houses ducks, employed to remove snails in the vineyard, and chickens, who supply eggs and manure for compost.

The enhancement of two primary natural resources, the "Tigris" stream and the Babylonstoren *koppie*, underpins the ecological health of the farm while supporting ongoing efforts of botanical collection. Flowing from the Simonsberg to the Berg River, the stream forms a riparian corridor providing important habitat for insects, birds, and animals. Understory planting added to the existing wild

14.10
A collection of South African cycads draws visitors to the "Tigris" stream.

olives, oaks, and gums creates a varied walking experience along the stream. Collections of forty-one species of South African cycads, including the rare Wood's Cycad, extinct in the wild, and seven thousand native clivias add a botanical dimension that draws visitors to the stream. (Figs 14.10, 14.11) The puff adder, a seventy-meter-long slatted wood tunnel located within the stream corridor and named for its serpentine meander, displays changing plant collections in its protective shade. (Fig 14.12) The *koppie* is preserved as a natural area for native species of the Western Cape. Visitors walking to the *koppie* can experience the regional fynbos vegetation and observe animal species such as steenbok, duikers, mongoose, cobras, tortoises, peregrine falcons, and owls. (Fig 14.13)

The future of farming and the challenges of climate change are being explored actively at Babylonstoren. In 2018, the Western Cape experienced the worst drought in four hundred years. And since 2015, rainfall has been between 50 and 68 percent of the typical annual average. Agricultural restrictions on the use of municipal water, supplied by a series of rain-fed dams, have been as great

14.11
Understory planting along the stream includes seven thousand native clivias.

14.12
The seventy-meter-long "puff adder" displays collections of plants requiring shade.

14.13
The *koppie* preserve features the regional fynbos vegetation.

as 60 percent, following four years of lower-than-average rainfall. The effect of this cumulative reduction in available water is significant; low levels in the current year impact water levels the following year. The water crisis in South Africa has spurred an exploration of alternative sources such as groundwater extraction, and conservation techniques such as water reuse. Babylonstoren employs both strategies, relying solely on a borehole source and using no municipal water on the property. A recirculation system permits the reuse of water up to three times, greatly reducing the drawdown of groundwater. Within only one year, the farm achieved a 50 percent reduction in water use.

Under the guidance of Ernst van Jaardsveld, a longtime curator and botanist at the Kirstenbosch National Botanical Garden in Cape Town, the farm has expanded its botanical collections with an emphasis on native and water-conserving species. Bringing an expertise in drought-adapted plants, van Jaardsveld has been instrumental in developing gardens devoted to native plants adapted to challenging climates such as the garden of the four South African biomes. Future plans include a *veldkos* garden featuring native edible plants traditionally foraged in the wild.

The Cape Floristic Provence is a global biodiversity hotspot with twenty vegetation types critically endangered in the Western Cape alone. Eighty percent of the land with the most rare and threatened vegetation types is cultivated for agriculture. Babylonstoren demonstrates that biodiversity and agriculture are not mutually exclusive when integrated thoughtfully through design. Supporting a robust program of agritourism and agricultural production simultaneously, biodiversity is critical to the future of Babylonstoren, ensuring the economic and ecological health of the farm in an uncertain and changing climate.

Note

1 Theodore Hiebert, "The Tower of Babel and the Origin of the World's Cultures," *Journal of Biblical Literature* 126, no. 1 (Spring 2007): 29–58.

Overlook

Waverly, Pennsylvania

Olmsted Brothers, 1903–1924

Nelson Byrd Woltz, 2012

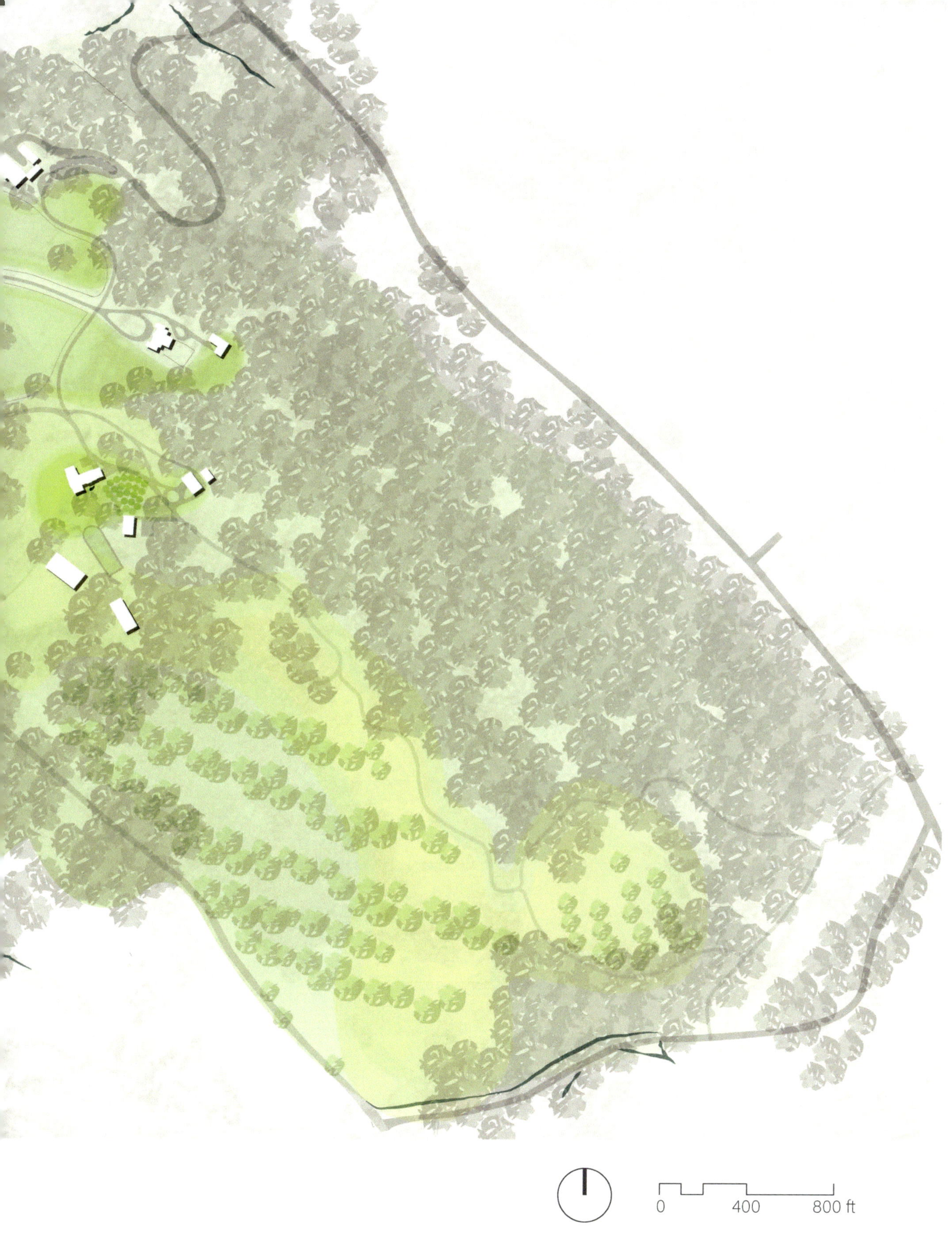
0
400
800 ft

15.1
Overlook farm seen from the central ridge, looking west towards the stable and pastures, c. 1920.

15.2
The Olmsted Brothers designed a *ferme ornée* with carriage roads designed and planted to stage views across the farm.

At Overlook farm in northeastern Pennsylvania, an Olmsted Brothers design for a summer estate is being reimagined as a site of agricultural, cultural, and ecological productivity. Nelson Byrd Woltz Landscape Architects used the cultural landscape to guide a new stewardship plan in which farmers and biologists actively manage the land together, using agricultural activity to enhance ecological function, and conversely, using ecological improvements to create agricultural opportunities.

In 1903, Edward Fuller hired the Olmsted Brothers to design a master plan for Overlook, transforming the property into a country home for his family. Like Moraine Farm and other Olmsted designs, Overlook was designed as a picturesque *ferme ornée*, interweaving the agrarian, domestic, and pleasure landscapes by framing views of the fields, pastures, and orchards along densely planted pleasure roads and bridle paths. The landscape is defined by a long northeast–southwest ridge, with a lake to the south and views to distant hills, the Endless Mountains. (Fig 15.1) The Olmsted Brothers found a site with rolling hills, wooded north slopes, forested lake edge, and open pastures, and a large stone home, known as The Cottage, sited at the brow of the west-facing slope. They designed the farm as a picturesque landscape with serpentine roads that accentuated the geomorphology and brought the visitor through a sequence of enclosed woods and sweeping, framed views, culminating in a proposed new house at the hilltop. While much of the ambitious plan, including the new house, was not built, the agricultural and residential framework was implemented and continuously updated over a twenty-year period. (Fig 15.2)

For the first half of the twentieth century, agricultural production at Overlook sustained the family and staff and supported recreation, especially equestrian activities. Overlook contained acres of pastures, training rings, and hay and grain fields to provide food and bedding for horses, as well as vegetable gardens, orchards, and livestock to provision the family.

The farm had three main productive centers: a large greenhouse and crop complex at the east entry, a livestock area near the west entry, and a smaller garden by the main house. The Olmsted firm had intended to locate the table crops at the bottom of the southern slope, but found the soils "exceedingly stony and poor with rock close to the surface."[1] The flat, sunny soils had been compacted by hogs for seventy-five years and runoff had washed the topsoil off the preferred location. The firm altered the design to locate the large kitchen garden near the east entry where soils were better.

Showing their usual vision, although perhaps not attention to the client's desires or budget, the Olmsted firm proposed an entry complex that included a 2.5-acre vegetable garden, greenhouses and cold frames, berries and tree fruits, cutting gardens, and orchid and palm houses, all underlain with agricultural drainage tile. (Fig 15.3) The family built a more practical garden, with greenhouses, cold frames, and nursery areas to provide both vegetable starts and shrubs and flowers for the extensive roadside plantings the Olmsted firm designed. (Fig 15.4)

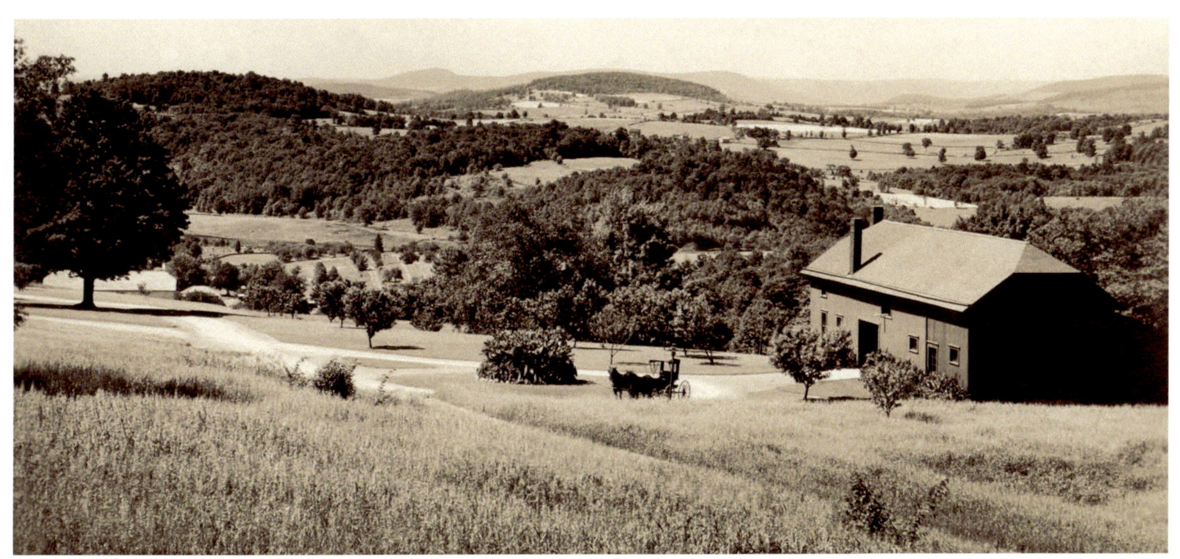

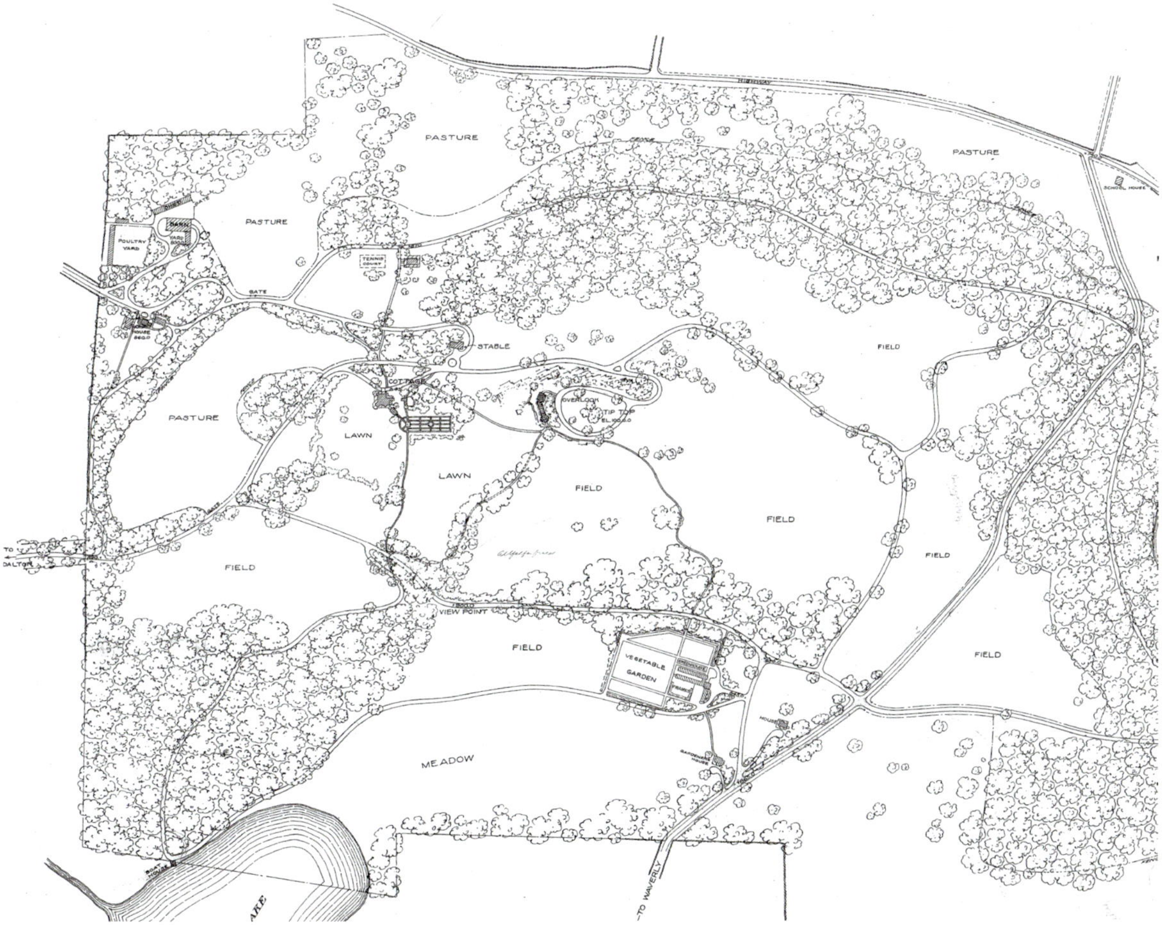
PASTURE
PASTURE
PASTURE
POULTRY YARD
BARN
TENNIS COURT
GATE
STABLE
COTTAGE
OVERLOOK
TIP TOP
PASTURE
LAWN
LAWN
FIELD
FIELD
FIELD
FIELD
TO DALTON
FIELD
VIEW POINT
FIELD
VEGETABLE GARDEN
FIELD
MEADOW
TO WAVERLY

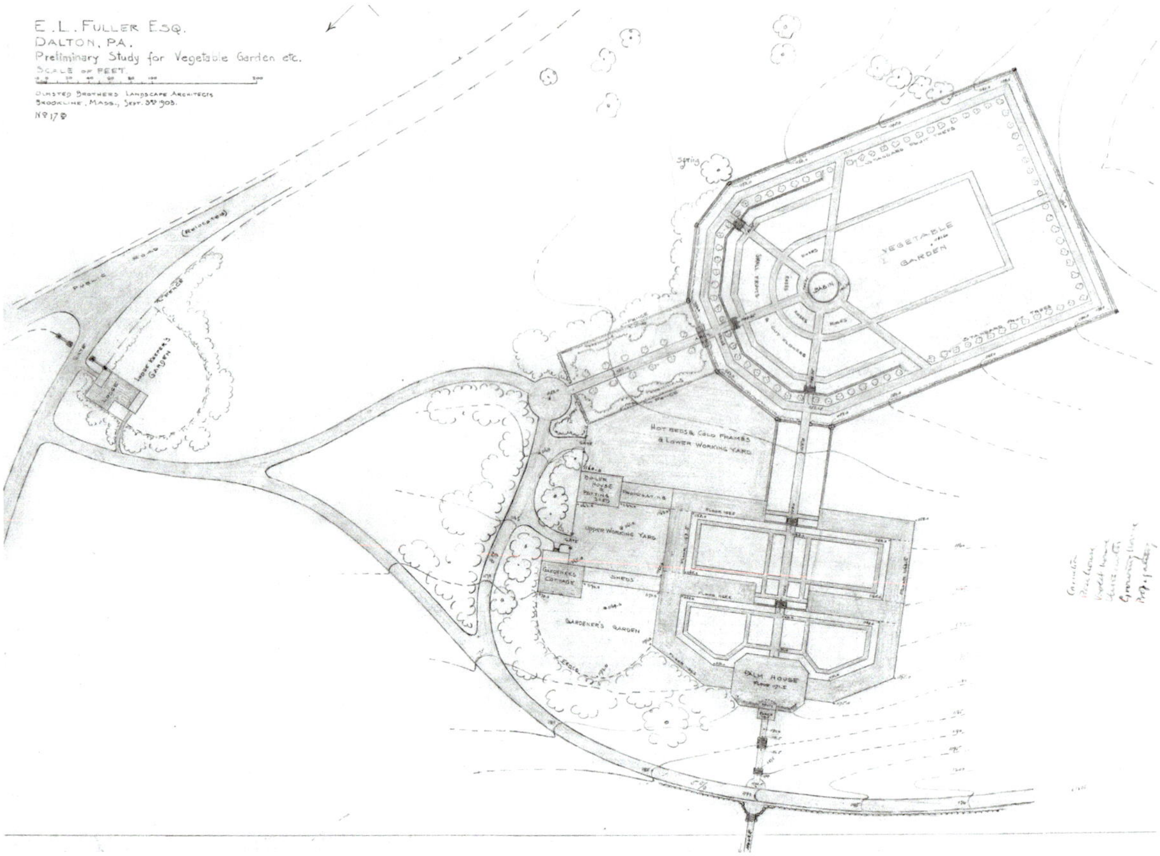
E. L. FULLER ESQ.
DALTON, PA.
Preliminary Study for Vegetable Garden etc.
SCALE OF FEET.
OLMSTED BROTHERS LANDSCAPE ARCHITECTS
BROOKLINE, MASS., SEPT. 3RD 1903.
Nº 17
VEGETABLE GARDEN
BASIN
HOT BEDS & COLD FRAMES & LOWER WORKING YARD
UPPER WORKING YARD
GARDENER'S COTTAGE
SHEDS
GARDENER'S GARDEN
PALM HOUSE
PUBLIC ROAD

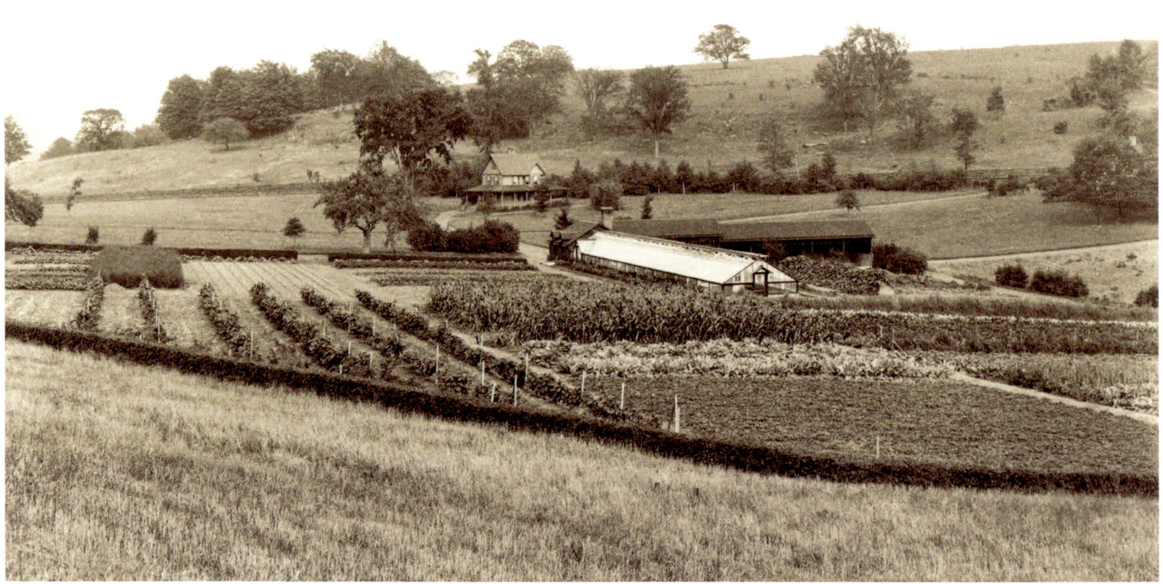

15.3
A 1903 preliminary study for the vegetable garden included extensive greenhouses, a palm house, work yards, fruit trees, and flower and vegetable gardens.

15.4
The vegetable garden and greenhouse, c. 1920.

A three-acre farmyard by the west entry, slightly hidden from view at the base of a northwest slope, was the livestock center for the farm. In addition to a small orchard, the livestock area contained buildings for meat poultry and laying hens, Black Angus beef cattle, dairy cows, and horses, as well as a dairy building. At the main house, the Olmsted firm designed a one-acre cutting garden that evolved into a flower and vegetable garden. (Fig 15.5)

The Olmsted Brothers design contains three frameworks: concentric layers of program, drift plantings framing views, and a planting strategy that takes advantage of natural processes. The Olmsted plan radiates from a residential core surrounded by highly geometric domestic elements. This was ringed with lawn, then crop fields and hay meadows, and framed by wooded clumps and woodlots. In the outermost layer, livestock buildings, yards, and pastures were hidden from view on the north side of the ridge.

Carriage roads and bridle paths weave through these layers to provide carefully choreographed views from fixed viewpoints and along roads. This scenographic strategy uses plantings of trees and shrubs on approach roads first to enclose viewsheds then open to reveal sweeping views of the lake or the rolling fields. This is a form of Southcote's ornamented walk, albeit with a less floral display, with a densely planted road border containing a wide range of ornamental plants. A similar tactic is used from key locations, primarily the main house and a planned future house, to frame views of gardens, lake, woods, pastures, rock outcrops, and the distant hills. (Fig 15.6)

Finally, the plan was intentionally designed to evolve, taking advantage of time as a resource and of the economic and ecological benefits of forestry as an agricultural pursuit. This tactic, which F. L. Olmsted had tested at Moraine Farm and implemented at a large, experimental scale at George Vanderbilt's Biltmore estate in North Carolina, uses a careful sequencing of tree plantings to stabilize and improve thin, rocky, or weak soils while providing a crop – wood – on a twenty- to forty-year cycle. The plantings at the house and along the roads include short-lived, fast-growing trees such as birch and white pine to quickly frame views and form a shading canopy. Long-lived, slow-growing trees such as oak and beech would be shaded by these rapidly growing trees, encouraged to develop sturdy, straight trunks. When the short-lived trees died, the long-lived trees would be able to grow quickly into a mature canopy.

A century later, many mature trees remained, including a magnificent stand of century-old katsura trees. Although there had been significant die out of shorter-lived tree species, many had apparently reseeded, and some of the birch and pine plantations remained. But almost all of the shrub layer had been lost to death and deer browsing, and deer browsing was preventing natural regrowth of the wooded areas. Throughout the property, extensive mowing was restricting grassland habitat and the attendant meadow species.

Taking the same long view as Edward Fuller, the fourth-generation owners want to preserve the ecological function of the land in a way that is economically sustainable and resilient to changes, using a dynamic stewardship plan rather

15.5
A garden near the Cottage, seen c. 1920, included both flowering perennials and vegetables.

than a static master plan. Working with a team that includes landscape architects, conservation biologists, and agricultural consultants, they are transforming the property into a productive farm, an ecological reserve, and a laboratory for education and research.

One of the challenges at Overlook is to design at the emerging edge of science. F. L. Olmsted's work was grounded in scientific inquiry, especially his experiments in scientific farming and the evolving profession of forestry. Yet many of the species his sons' firm planted at Overlook are now known to be invasive, and much of the firm's work lacked a grounding in ecology because that was an emerging field in the early twentieth century. Nelson Byrd Woltz has similarly engaged this challenge – designing at the experimental edge of the discipline. They based their design on the historic principles of framed views, concentric program, and time-based design, and added considerations of ecological function and agricultural productivity.

In 2013, Dr. James Gibbs, Dr. Donald Leopold, and a team of biologists completed a bioblitz of the property, a four-day baseline ecological analysis of the flora and fauna, including mammals, birds, fish, amphibians, and insects. Members of the team returned in 2014 for a second round of biological surveying. The team

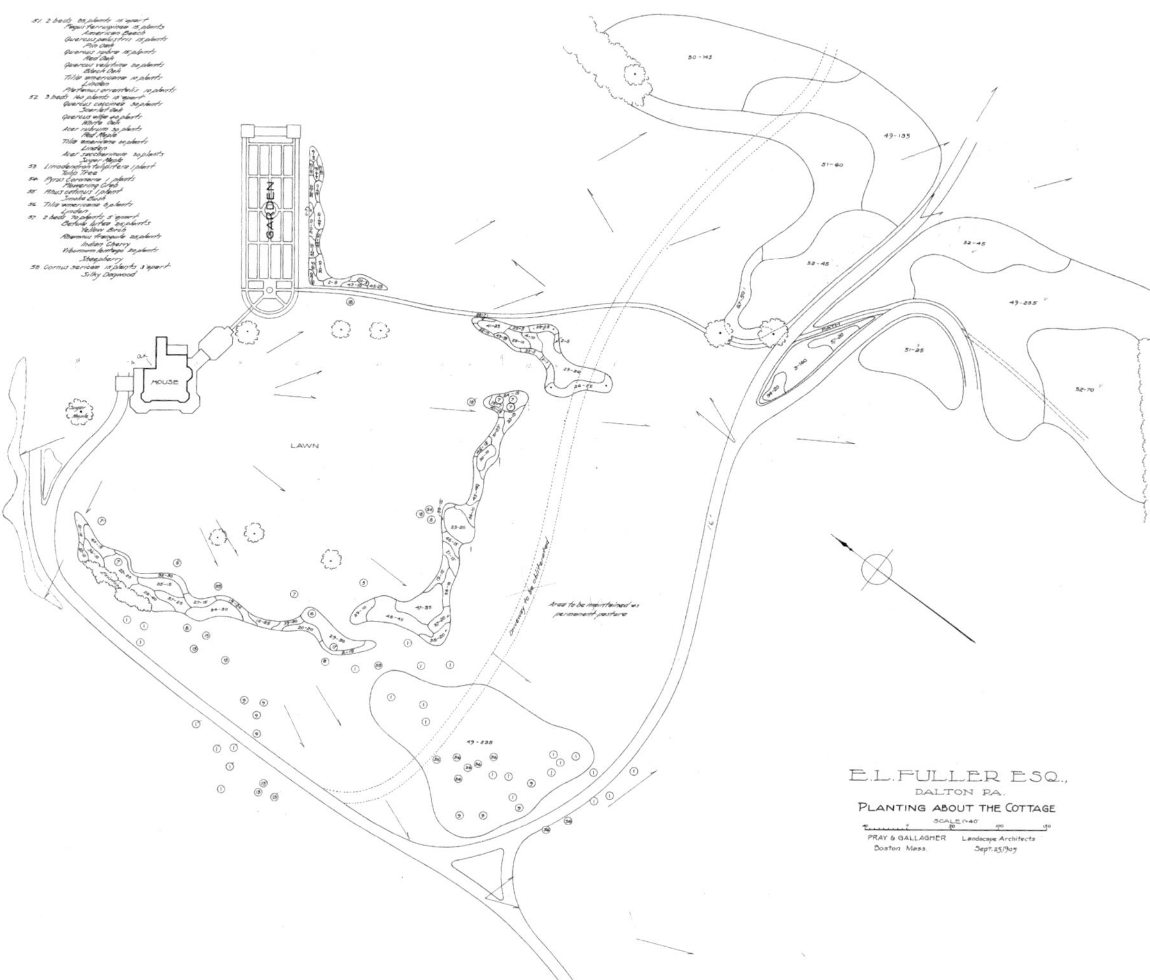

15.6
A 1905 planting plan for the lawns around the Cottage indicates significant views to be framed and accentuated.

found fairly healthy communities of flora and fauna, with some few species of concern, and several invasive or pest species. Their report provided a basis for the landscape architects to design a plan that optimized for ecological function as well as agricultural productivity and cultural stewardship.[2]

The property is banded into ecological zones of forest on the northwest slopes; a matrix of open woodland, pasture, and meadow along a ridge; and wetland and lake to the southeast. (Fig 15.7) In the various districts, the team observed abundant birds, amphibians and reptiles, insects, and mammals, and over 350 species of vascular plants.[3] Most plants and animals were expected species, although three bat species observed are critically imperiled, and Virginia rose, a species of special conservation concern in Pennsylvania, was found. Notably, no non-native species of birds were observed and the majority of the vascular plants are native to Pennsylvania. Several invasive species were observed to be spreading, including glossy buckthorn, common buckthorn, privet, and Amur

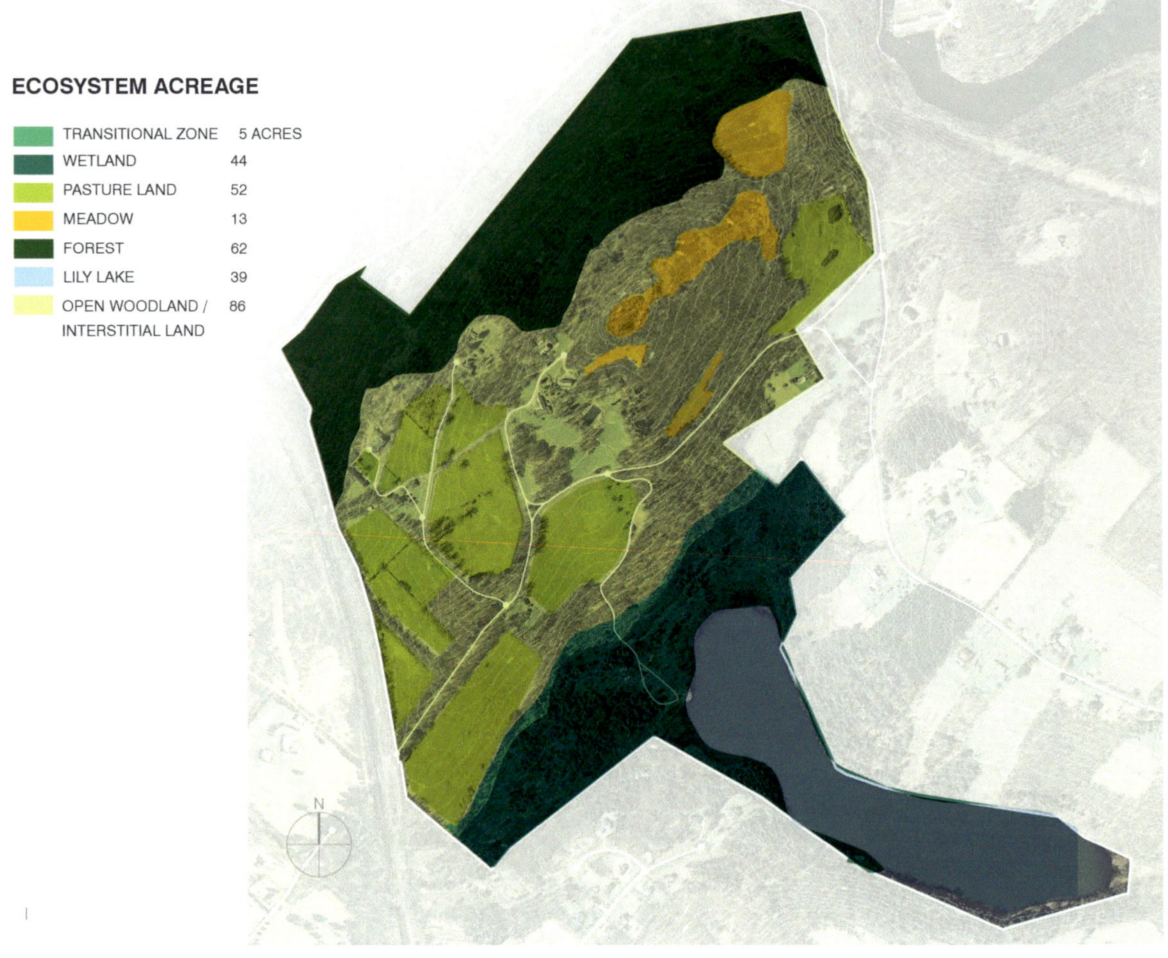

15.7
An ecosystem analysis by Nelson Byrd Woltz Landscape Architects shows bands of habitat following the topography.

maple, interestingly, all noted on the Olmsted planting plans. Wooly adelgid and emerald ash borer were noted on the property; both insects will eventually kill the hemlock and ash stands, respectively.

The biologists defined a three-pronged approach at Overlook: manage current problems, provide increased ecological opportunities, and perform ongoing monitoring to evaluate the impacts of the tactics and adjust them as necessary.[4] Based on the biological opportunities and concerns, the team recommended several strategies with the overarching goal of combining approaches wherever possible, for example harvesting vulnerable ash trees and using the cleared land for agricultural functions such as sugar maple production or silvopasture, as well as for ecological structure such as wildflower meadows.

One of the most significant problems at Overlook was an overabundance of deer. They browsed the mid-story of the forest, eliminating habitat for many species of birds; ground species and canopy species were observed, but almost no mid-story species. And in many areas, there was a low diversity of plant species, dominated by species that are unattractive to deer such as hay-scented fern. A second problem was the presence of wooly adelgid and emerald ash borer, and the certain death of hemlock and ash trees. And a third concern was the presence of invasive species that limit the biodiversity of the property. To address these, the team recommended deer exclosures to improve the ecological diversity of certain areas of the property; protecting desirable hemlock and ash trees, and harvesting less culturally significant stands; and removal of invasive species to the extent possible.[5]

Ecological opportunities included increasing habitat for nesting and foraging, and providing travel habitats for various species. For species such as salamanders and bats, adding water bodies at springs or digging areas for vernal pools would provide seasonal habitat and feeding grounds. Wildflower plantings at field and forest edges, altered mowing regimes to increase grasslands, and forest management would improve biodiversity and successional habitat for insects and birds, while adding a shrub layer would improve nesting opportunities for birds and mammals. The design team also highlighted the need to protect pathways preferred by salamanders over their life cycle from open water to wetland to upland forest. (Fig 15.8)

These broad ecological strategies provided a framework for the landscape architects to develop tactics that would also benefit agricultural production. Alongside the biological analysis, agricultural consultant Zach Wolf studied the property to determine the best locations and types of agricultural production. The team identified areas with low slope and southern exposures, with eastern and western exposures identified as adequate for crop production. After identifying areas with good slope and solar aspect, the team evaluated soil samples from those areas to determine soil depth and fertility, the preferred locations for vegetable production, and potential soil improvement regimes.[6]

Based on this analysis and recommendations for the most suitable agricultural production, Nelson Byrd Woltz designed an agricultural plan that creates a framework for economic viability and ecological robustness, integrating both short- and long-term strategies with the goals of biodiversity, symbiosis between organisms, and soil fertility, using plant and animal rotation to accomplish many of the goals. The plan includes minimal vegetable production on suitable areas, with the majority of the property used for livestock, orchards, nutteries, and forestry. (Fig 15.9)

In the first summer of farming, one priority was to protect crops and stop the ongoing damage to meadows and forests through a perimeter deer exclosure. Farm managers prepared a five-acre area for crop production to provide an economic base for the farm through community-supported agriculture (CSA) memberships, farmers market sales, and direct sales to local restaurants. And the farmers planted pollinator buffers at the edge of the table crop area and along the eastern meadows, and perennial flower beds for market sales, to improve pollination of orchard trees and other plants.

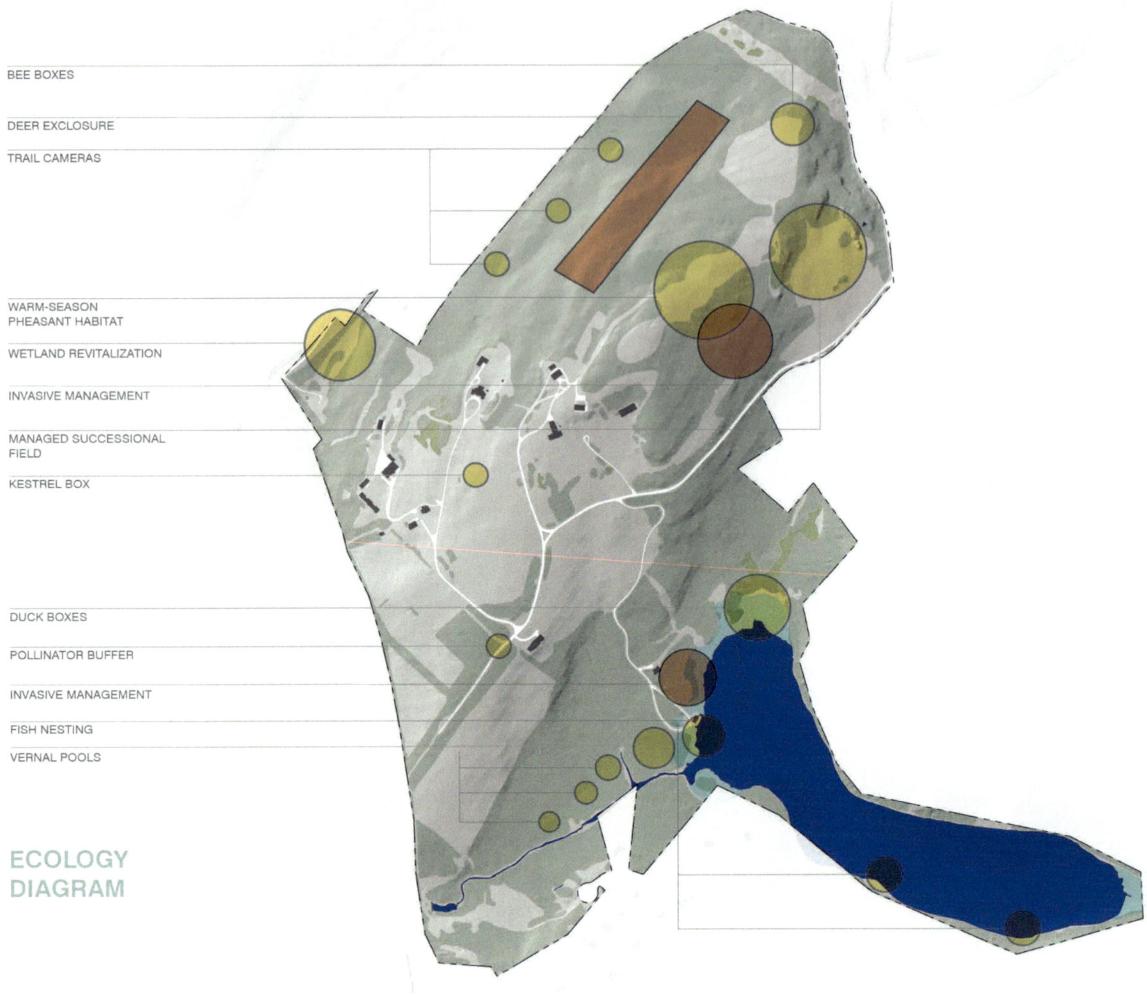

15.8
A proposed ecology diagram shows areas of key habitat potential.

In the second summer, the team added animals to assist with ecological improvements. Using mobile fencing, the farmers moved market pigs through the southern forest, changing their location every two weeks to avoid depleting or compacting the soils. The pigs cleared invasive ground covers, added manure to the soils, and dug wallows that add microtopography that improves water retention and absorption. Chickens in mobile coops were used to help improve soils in pasture areas; they aerate the compacted soils through scratching and grazing, and they add manure to the soil. The introduction of livestock allowed the farmers to begin closing material loops, using waste materials from one realm as a productive material in another. The pigs consume most agricultural excess; composting yard, forest, and agricultural trimmings provides fertilizer for fields; and livestock rotation improves soils in pastures and woods. (Fig 15.10)

Also in the second summer, the team began increasing landscape complexity, especially around the lake where plowing and hog raising in the past had flat-

15.9
An agricultural diagram proposes a diversity of agricultural production suited to the soils and hydrology of the farm.

15.10 (pages 230–231)
The farm managers at Overlook move the pigs through areas needing clearing and tilling.

tened the landscape and eliminated microtopography. Biologists located springs and areas with appropriate soils for excavating vernal pools to aid the seasonal migration of reptiles and amphibians. Eight artificial pools were dug, and biology students continue to monitor the water quality in the pools and the presence of frogs and salamanders, as well as animals visiting the pools for water and feeding.

In the third summer, work began on restoring a native, warm-season grass and wildflower meadow by the house. The meadow, designed by Larry Weaner Associates, is meant to enhance the designed aesthetic of the residential areas, enhance the overall ecological health of the property through native pollinator food sources and bird and mammal habitat, and prevent the incursion of problem weeds throughout the property. (Fig 15.11)

The farmers are experimenting with honey production, maple syrup production, and mushroom production, all high-value retail items. Longer term, they intend to add tree-based agriculture, including mast production for pigs, nutteries

15.11
The restored meadow in 2018, with warm-season grasses and native wildflowers.

and orchards, and timber forests, harvesting at-risk trees and planting and harvesting stands of oak, hickory, walnut, or cherry.

While the Olmsted plan contained a single, residential core ringed by a productive landscape with several nuclei of activity, the Nelson Byrd Woltz plan incorporates three distinct districts. The house and gardens are the historical and cultural center, and are designed as a private, residential area. The farm complex to the west is a relatively public area, open to CSA members on certain days, and is conceived as a productive site where experimentation and innovation will produce food and also accumulate nutrients and increase biodiversity. And in the former livestock area, educational experiments are occurring, with the horse barn repurposed as classroom and display spaces. This will become the educational heart of the property as well as the orientation point for visitors. Currently used by landscape architecture and biology students for field work, the barn programming is intended to expand to include experimental gardens coordinated with farmer training programs and agricultural organizations, as well as monitoring stations for ecological function. The farm is in the first stages of growth towards an ambitious goal of becoming economically viable, educational, and innovative.

The Nelson Byrd Woltz plan stitches a contemporary design onto a historic landscape, integrating current agricultural production and ecological research within a cultural landscape framework. The Olmsted plans are integrated as guiding principles rather than as a structure for historic restoration or preservation. Within these guiding principles, the native ecosystem provides the framework for agricultural practices seeking overlaps and symbiosis between the two goals. The plan sets the stage for improving the soil, the aquatic, terrestrial and aerial habitat, and the function of ecological processes, while using agriculture as an integral aspect of those ecological goals.

Notes

1 Charles Olmsted, site visit notes, 1903.

2 The Roosevelt Wildlife Station, SUNY-ESF, *Report on Ecological Survey of the Overlook Estate* (Syracuse, NY: SUNY-ESF, 2014).

3 Michael Hough, *Vascular Plants of Overlook Estate, Dalton, PA* (Syracuse, NY: SUNY-ESF, 2014).

4 Nelson Byrd Woltz Landscape Architects, *Overlook: Conservation Agriculture Strategic Masterplan* (Charlottesville, VA: Nelson Byrd Woltz, 2014), 10, 30.

5 Ibid., 24, 43.

6 Ibid., 119, 123, 126.

Los Poblanos Historic Inn and Organic Farm

Los Ranchos de Albuquerque, New Mexico

Rose Greely, 1932–1934

OLIN Studio, 2008 and 2015

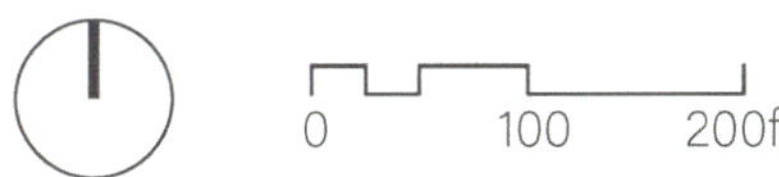
0
100
200ft

The Los Poblanos Historic Inn and Organic Farm is set within the Los Poblanos Historic District located in the village of Los Ranchos de Albuquerque, New Mexico. The District, comprised of historic agricultural lands and significant works by architect John Gaw Meem and landscape architect Rose Greely, lies between the Rio Grande River to the west and the Sandia Mountains to the east. Los Poblanos demonstrates how experimental agribusiness can support the preservation of a cultural landscape and its agricultural heritage. The development of regional crops and new agricultural products, combined with a robust program of hospitality driven by the land, underpin future economic viability while creating a unique experience of place integrating history, architecture, and productivity.

The farm is named after early settlers called *Poblanos* who came from Puebla, Mexico. The land was deeded from the Spanish colonial government to Diego de Montoya in 1694, later conveyed to Elena Gallegos, who left the grant to her son Antonio Gurulé when she died in 1731, and subsequently purchased by Ambrosio and Jaun Cristobal Armijo in the nineteenth century. In the 1930s, Congressman Albert Simms and his wife, Congresswoman Ruth Hanna McCormick Simms, assembled an 800-acre tract, marking the transformation of what was once a small farming community into a vast country farm estate.

The Simms created a model experimental farm that was also a center of culture and community, integrating art, architecture, landscape architecture, and farming to realize a unique cultural expression tied to the land. Architect John Gaw Meem expanded the existing house, now the Los Poblanos Inn, and designed La Quinta, a new cultural center containing an art gallery and ballroom for meetings, lectures, and concerts. Landscape architect Rose Greely designed six acres of gardens, including the Los Poblanos courtyard, a formal garden west of the main house, and an entry allée. Local artisans and artists contributed detail elements. Patron saint of farming San Ysidro appears at La Quinta in a large portal fresco by Peter Hurd (Fig 16.1), in a wooden beam above the fireplace carved by Taos artist Gustave Bauman, and in the wrought iron door fixtures by Walter Gilbert. Scenes of farm life painted by Santa Fe artist Harry Miller grace La Quinta's portal windows. Folk artist "Pop" Shaffer created a unique pebble paving featuring animals within the formal garden. These elements express the centrality of agriculture at Los Poblanos as an integrated agri-cultural enterprise.

With the commission to design the landscape at Los Poblanos, Rose Greely (1887–1969) had a rare opportunity to pursue her interest in the planning and design of agricultural communities. The first woman to be licensed as a landscape architect in Washington, DC, Greely had a thriving practice designing residential gardens and country estates.[1] But her 1920 thesis, "Report on a Proposed Cooperative Farm Community," indicated an early interest in preserving cultural resources and fitting agricultural communities to the existing conditions of the land.[2] In her proposal for transforming an existing village outside of Boston into a farming community, "the spirit of the old village has been retained as far as possible."[3] Greely recommends the preservation and adaptation of existing buildings

16.1
Patron saint of farming San Ysidro at La Quinta. Fresco by Peter Hurd.

and the enhancement of existing roadway infrastructure. These strategies, paired with an approach considering "the value of each type of land ... from the agricultural standpoint,"[4] are threads reappearing at Los Poblanos, seen in the repurposing of existing architecture, adaptation of infrastructural elements, and integration of gardens within a working farm.

As in her thesis work, Greely was sensitive to the historic and cultural resources of the site. Her design incorporated the historic patterns of acequia irrigation and responded to the unique climate of New Mexico's North Valley. The formal west garden situated between the main house and the Griegos Lateral, a significant regional irrigation canal, and the long linear gardens and outdoor spaces between the main house and La Quinta were designed to connect to an existing system of acequias. In the west garden, terra cotta roof tiles form channels delivering water to planting beds of flowering perennials. (Fig 16.2) South of the main house, channels defined by low stone curbing heighten the sense of geometry and legibility of water infrastructure. (Fig 16.3)

Greely addressed the need for cooling outdoor spaces using vegetation for shading and small water features. Strategically located trees and arbors planted

16.2
Terra cotta roof tiles create channels delivering water to plantings in Rose Greely's west garden.

16.3
Long linear channels defined by stone curbing deliver water via the existing system of acequias.

16.4
A small water feature in the west garden is bordered by low seat walls, providing a respite from the heat of the sun.

16.5
Greely designed small water features, such as this focal point in the main house placita, to create cooling microclimates.

with vines such as wisteria and lady banks rose shade gathering areas from the hot New Mexico sun. Small water features were designed as focal points in both the formal garden (Fig 16.4) and the main house placita (Fig 16.5), providing direct access to the sound and cooling touch of water. These elements create significantly cooled microclimates, domestic and cultural spaces distinct from the sun-loving open fields of the farm.

Farming operations under the direction of the Simms in the 1930s and 1940s were experimental and opportunistic, expanding local production for the growing city of Albuquerque. In a 1937 article for *Country Life* magazine, noted photographer Laura Gilpin described the farm at Los Poblanos as a "far-reaching civic vision,"[5] intended to improve agriculture in the state. The farm operated both as an economic enterprise and as a laboratory for new regional crops, techniques, and markets. Creamland Dairies, developed undoubtedly with Ruth Simms' expertise in raising dairy cattle, provided a new local supply of milk to Albuquerque. Sugar beets were grown to ensure a domestic supply of seed when shipping was strained and sugar in short supply following the attack on Pearl Harbor. Purebred rams were raised to improve New Mexico flocks. Turkeys were employed as a

new method of pest control. New varieties of roses and chrysanthemums were developed for commercial production.

The Simms' legacy of experimental agriculture synthesized with art, design, and community has been embraced by the Rembe family, the current owners who acquired the property in 1976. Wanting to preserve the architectural and agricultural history of Los Poblanos while also developing a sustainable plan for the future, the Rembes engaged OLIN Studio to develop an overall design for the farm that accommodated maximum acreage for the farm's existing lavender production with an expanded visitor experience. OLIN commenced a master planning process in 2008, collaborating with architect Stephanos Polyzoides. This first phase resulted in the addition of twenty hotel units north of the existing Los Poblanos Inn, a new swimming pool, and new landscape areas and parking associated with La Quinta. In 2015, OLIN returned for a second design phase to rethink the master plan to accommodate additional guest suites, a retail store, and a field-to-fork restaurant. Building architecture in the second phase was designed by Atkin Olshin Schade.

The designers were challenged to integrate additional buildings and gardens with the original farmstead and historic structures. New buildings harmonize in scale and material with the agricultural vernacular, adapted where possible for new use, and are nestled within the larger patterns of the acequia network and farm fields. The overall effect is one of seemingly organic growth, a contemporary adaptation that knits together the historic buildings and gardens of the Inn and La Quinta, new guest suites and parking, the farm fields, and the borrowed landscape of the Sandia Mountains to the east.

The OLIN design provides a formal organization sensitive to the existing historic fabric using a suite of strategies including preservation of the existing Greely gardens, careful insertion of new program in areas outside of the Greely gardens, an overlay of agricultural patterns and forms, and a blending of the historic 1930s planting with a contemporary native and adapted palette. The Rose Greely courtyard and gardens remain intact with original paving, fountains, and terra cotta water runnels. Much of the original planting remains, with new species added for climate change resilience and use in the restaurant and shop.

Original rose species have been replaced with new varieties for apothecary purposes and a new Chinese Pistache provides additional shade in the paved area of the formal garden. The long linear acequia gardens and lawn areas between the Inn and La Quinta are still flood irrigated (Fig 16.6) and include a planting palette diversified over the years with additions such as columbine and pitcher sage. The Siberian elms of Greely's main entry allée, nearing the end of their life cycle, have been interplanted with walnut trees. In the future the new allée will produce a crop that can be harvested for use in the restaurant and bar, while maintaining the character and form of the historic entry.

Expanding the programmatic capacity of La Quinta as a space for weddings in addition to cultural events, OLIN inserted a new ceremonial lawn in an area previously modified from Greely's original design. On axis with La Quinta and

16.6
The regional practice of flood irrigation is retained at Los Poblanos to water lawn areas.

16.7a-b
Framed views across the La Quinta pool terrace and the wedding lawn capitalize on the Sandia Mountains to the east.

16.8
Wilderness gardens offer a space of privacy and reflection.

flanked by rows of lacebark elms aligning with the building's outer columns, the wedding lawn extends the area of La Quinta's pool terrace eastward, directing views towards the distant Sandia Mountains. (Fig 16.7a–b) Along the eastern edge of the lawn, a low wall planted with lavender, roses, and juniper hides the new parking area beyond from view, providing a backdrop for ceremonies while permitting views to the mountains bathed in dramatically shifting light during the late afternoon.

Two wilderness gardens recalling the eighteenth-century baroque precedent and bounded with an unclipped hedge, offer spaces for privacy and reflection adjacent to the wedding lawn. (Fig 16.8) These gardens take advantage of existing plantings of trees and shrubs whose exuberant growth and dark multi-layered density contrasts sharply with the spare minimalism of the bright, open wedding lawn. Roses and peonies have been strategically located in shady conditions beneath existing trees for greater drought tolerance. These plants are well suited as a groundcover for thirsty trees, matching water needs and keeping trees healthy.

Agricultural patterns and forms are used to define parking areas and a series of outdoor spaces associated with the new guest suites and restaurant. Two new parking areas, the main entry parking and the La Quinta parking, are situated between the historic core to the west and the agricultural fields to the east. Both areas incorporate the design language of their agricultural context, mediating between farm and garden with the linear geometry of crop fields and irrigation and carefully selected plantings. The northern parking area is defined by a central walkway shaded by a grape arbor and several large shade trees. A swale under the walkway captures stormwater. The La Quinta parking area is planted as an orchard of flowering trees, extending the pattern of orchard trees in the adjacent farm fields. Drought-tolerant Russian hawthorn and crabapples are located between parking spaces. Stormwater from the compacted gravel parking areas drains to the tree planters. (Fig 16.9) Acequias define the northern and southern boundaries of the parking areas, flowing under the pavement and across the site from east to west, knitting together the historic core, newly developed areas, and

16.9
The La Quinta parking area is designed as an extension of the adjacent orchard.

agricultural fields. Water provides connectivity and historic continuity, as well as life-supporting irrigation, across the property.

16.10 (pages 246–247)
New guest suites extend into the lavender fields.

The new guest suites sited at the edges of farm fields place visitors in direct contact with the agricultural landscape. (Fig 16.10) Courtyard spaces open to the crop fields to the east and feature board-formed concrete water troughs and regular grids of square concrete pavers. (Fig 16.11) The garden area between the guest suites just east of the new restaurant features beds of herbs in steel planters whose geometry shows a clear relationship to crop row patterns just beyond. Here visitors can play pétanque, a game similar to boules originating in Provence, France. The overt reference to the famous lavender-producing region connects Los Poblanos to the expansive history and tradition of cultivating lavender but also acts as a hinge between the working landscape and a landscape of community and culture. At Los Poblanos, the agricultural landscape is multifunctional, a place to be inhabited and experienced, a place for work and play.

Landscape designer Judith Phillips worked in collaboration with OLIN to develop a planting design across the property that draws upon the 1930s historic planting palette while integrating new plant species appropriate to anticipated future climatic conditions and usable for restaurant and distillation operations. The historic planting designs reflect a time when there was less concern for water scarcity. Phillips chose only those species from the historic core that have proven adaptability to increasingly hot and dry conditions, adding additional low water species to support water conservation.

Species within the historic gardens adaptable to the shifting climate include peonies, burkwood viburnum, roses, lady banks rose, figs, wisteria, yarrow, and weeping mulberry. These plants have been integrated with new species such as rosemary, yucca, hops, yerba manza, escarpment live oak, Texas sage, jujube, cardoons, lavender, mullein, and persimmon. This blended palette selected for low-water adaptability, edibility, and the capacity to self-sow creates the effect of a slow transition in the character of gardens as one moves from the historic core to the inn expansion to the renovated milking barns.

In the area east of the restaurant, surrounding the north and south guest suites, the gardens fully transition to a contemporary palette of native and adapted New Mexico planting. The pétanque court garden includes herbs for the restaurant – sage, thyme, rosemary, bronze fennel, giant hyssop – and red yucca. Fruit trees and Mexican feather grass shade garden areas to the north and south. Gardens at the new guest suites display xeric species such as spineless prickly pear and Maverick mesquite trees. An area intended for botanicals, plants harvested for distillation as flavorings and infusions, is currently seeded with bluestem, blue grama, sacaton, and prairie clover, grasses that will improve the soil for future use.

Los Poblanos continues as a model experimental farm, carefully navigating the impacts of climate change while expanding territory for agriculture in New Mexico. Lavender has proven ideal as a sustainable crop largely for its low water requirements and because few insect pests and fungal diseases affect the crop

16.11
Guest suite courtyards open to crop fields, capitalizing on the distant view of the Sandia Mountains.

in arid climates. The variety of lavender cultivated at Los Poblanos, *Lavendula x intermedia 'Grosso,'* has excellent winter hardiness and produces high yields of oil. The significant challenge of weeding is met with the aid of alpacas, who dine on problem volunteers such as bindweed, leaving the lavender untouched. (Fig 16.12)

While lavender is well suited to an arid climate, with good heat and drought tolerance, increasingly unpredictable weather and drought in recent years have required adaptive farming practices. Significant variation in harvest dates requires greater flexibility to time the harvest with peak oil content. Temperature increases and drought conditions place greater demands on the two wells that supply drip irrigation, resulting in a coordinated effort to manage and schedule water use needs across the property, balancing lavender irrigation with guest use, vegetable irrigation, and garden irrigation. At the tipping point for heat tolerance, the farm is exploring strategies that will keep the soil cool, like interplanting to shade plants and developing a soil mix able to retain water. Cuttings are taken from lavender plants that are thriving to advance the development of adapted varieties.

16.12
Alpacas weed the fields, leaving the lavender untouched.

Along with expertise in cultivating lavender, Los Poblanos has become known for its expertise in distillation. Oil extraction occurs on site and high-quality value-added lavender products are available for purchase at the farm store, located in the renovated milking barns. Future areas of experimentation and expansion include cultivating beets for vodka distillation, a twist on the farm's history of sugar beet cultivation.

The culinary talent of Los Poblanos chef Jonathan Perno provides the ultimate experience of the farm through the gifts of the plate. At Los Poblanos, the collaboration between Perno, farmer Judy Hartline, and landscape manager Wes Brittenham results in an evolving and experimental farm-to-table menu that emphasizes the connections between food, the land, and regional context. Perno's interest in the historical and cultural traditions of medicinal and culinary plants in New Mexico has resulted in the cultivation of crops like epazote and tepary beans grown in the region for centuries. Los Poblanos is a participant in Row 7 Seeds, whose mission is to develop regional specific crop varieties through collaborations between chefs, plant breeders, and farmers. Seeds of new varieties provided by the company are improved at Los Poblanos through a dynamic process privileging flavor, yield, and disease resistance specific to place.

For nearly a century, Los Poblanos has balanced agricultural experimentation with cultural preservation, adapting the crops and livestock to both respond to and predict societal change. Two-thirds of Los Poblanos' twenty-five acres has been placed by the Rembe family in permanent agricultural trust, ensuring the preservation of farming so critical to the cultural and environmental traditions of Albuquerque's North Valley. Still an experimental farm today, Los Poblanos retains its historic character while seeking new ways to realize economic and environmental sustainability. The development of agritourism facilitated by the OLIN design connects a population of locals and visitors from afar to the ever-evolving experimental farm while situating these new experiences in relation to the site's rich history.

Notes

1 See Joanne Seale Lawson, "Remarkable Foundations: Rose Ishbel Greely, Landscape Architect," *Washington History* 10, no. 1 (Spring/Summer 1998): 46–69.

2 See Rose Greely, "Report on a Proposed Cooperative Farm Community" (Thesis, School of Domestic Architecture and Landscape Architecture, Cambridge, MA, 1920).

3 Ibid., 18–19.

4 Ibid., 15.

5 Laura Gilpin, "Los Poblanos Ranch," *Country Life* (March 1938): 83.

Composition, meaning, and practice

A framework for designing agriculture

The projects in this book illustrate the long history of landscape architecture integrating farm and garden and using that hybridity to explore the expansive margins of the field. The projects were selected to highlight the shifting relationship between landscape design and agriculture. Early projects reveal a close integration in the eighteenth century when many garden designers were also gentleman farmers and amateur botanists. Nineteenth-century farms reflect a period of farming-design praxis and scientific exploration, while twentieth-century projects often highlight a mechanistic, functionalist approach to both agriculture and design, and especially in the decades around the two world wars, designs often reflect a desire for individual or communal self-sufficiency. Contemporary projects tend to be highly site-specific, with designs emerging from the ecological, cultural, and economic understanding of the site, and integrating these changing systems in a holistic way. For the designer interested in farmscape design, the case studies reveal an eight-part framework for considering the design of agricultural sites: compositions of form and time; polemics of politics and health; and practices of technology, ecology, economic markets, and labor.

Composing the farm spatially and temporally

J. B. Jackson memorably described the evolving meaning of the word landscape from a painting representing a composed view of a place, to the physical reality of such a view, and eventually to a place itself, whether aesthetically conceived or not.[1] Aesthetics are intrinsic to landscape architecture, and the sensory experience of designed works remains a significant consideration for landscape architects even as designers are increasingly asked to predict and quantify the economic, environmental, or social performance of a project and to consider landscape designs as systems in flux with unpredictable formal outcomes.

Landscape architects often incorporate agriculture into the spatial composition of their works in one of two ways. Either the agricultural realm of a project is ordered on an internal spatial logic that is distinct from, or perhaps informs, the surrounding realms, or the agriculture is seamlessly integrated into a larger aesthetic vision for the design.

In the first mode, the design is divided into related, sometimes overlapping or nested, but distinct realms, each with its own formal structure. Many of these projects use the framework of first, second, and third nature – wilderness, productive landscapes, and pleasure gardens – to organize the farm and the user's experience of the land into three types of landscapes, wild, cultivated, and designed.[2] This conception of the farmscape manifests itself in two ways. The cultivated lands and pleasure grounds are sometimes designed as conceptually and experientially distinct, with the pleasure gardens even at times masking the productive aspects of the farm. Middleton Place illustrates this aesthetics of distinction, with geometrically composed gardens and hydrologically organized rice fields, with very little stylistic or physical interaction between the two, although the river rice fields provide a productive foreground to the pleasure gardens when seen from the river approach. Alternately, the conceptually distinct realms are woven together, often with the agricultural landscape as a painterly backdrop for the pleasure landscape. This interwoven mode is seen in the *ferme ornée* of Woburn and Moraine Farms, with lushly planted pleasure routes traversing the productive landscape and using the fields and meadows as a cinematic backdrop for walks and carriage rides. Similarly, Merchiston Farm borrows the long views of agricultural fields and pastures into the design of the pleasure gardens around the house, and Babylonstoren uses the agrarian landscape and views of the nature preserve – second and first nature – as part of the visual composition of the resort gardens.

In the second broad category of agricultural aesthetics, a unified design approach connects all parts of the design, the natural, productive, and recreational areas and elements, without clear distinctions in form between the realms. This holistic approach to the design of the farmscape sometimes uses a functional aesthetic based on the processes and patterns of husbandry, or the design can be more artistically inspired. In the early twentieth century, designers like Sørensen in the Nærum Allotment Gardens intentionally and visibly designed across the entire productive landscape. Those projects with more legible designs have tended to survive better than those with less formal clarity. In the open-ended design of Welwyn Garden City, the designers provided space for farms and gardens but the layout was not explicit and changed over time, often driving out the agricultural production. Similarly, in the kit-of-parts functionalist approach used at Ziebigk, families selected the layout that suited their needs, and as individual needs shifted, often it was the agricultural program that was pushed out.

In addition to concerns of form, designing with agriculture requires landscape architects to engage temporality and change over time. While designing with time is inherent to designing with landscapes, the nature of agriculture, with distinct activities associated with the growth cycles of plants and animals, preferred sequences of events over time, and the inherent feedback loops of cultivation, foregrounds the role of time and the different forms and senses of time. Ancient Greeks used two words for time: *chronos* and *kairos*. Chronos is sequential, linear time, the inexorable movement from one moment to the next, leading towards entropy. Kairos is numinous, circular time, the notion of a right time or moment for events to unfold.[3] In the Bible's lines "To every thing there is a season, and a time to every purpose under the heaven,"[4] the repetitions of time – a time to reap, a time to sow – were originally translated into Greek as *kairos*, the right moment for each activity. Agriculture engages both forms of time. Seasons, weather cycles, sowing and harvest, growth, death and decay, and maintenance are all inherent to the productive landscape which is not merely designed but is spatially produced and enacted over time. Yet our understanding of this temporal engagement is ruptured by the global food market, which disconnects food from both place and time, "ensuring the year-round provision of fresh fruit and vegetables irrespective of their seasonality or the distance between their sites of production and consumption."[5] Agriculture provides a site for designers to mend that rupture, to reconnect people with the place and time in which they live.

While some designs create neutral realms for the temporal work of the farmers, others explicitly integrate linear and cyclic time into the conception of the project. At Shenyang, two temporal systems operate in the same space: the spring-to-fall cycle of rice harvest, and the fall-to-spring cycle of education. Although the two rhythms occupy the same physical space, they only interact on two days of the year, when students plant and harvest rice as a way to learn regional agrarian traditions. Similarly, at Green Gulch, the growing and harvest season is conceived within a liturgical calendar, with agricultural work understood as spiritual practice through labor mirroring the winter season of spiritual practice through meditation or exercise.

Meaning and use

The subject of meaning in landscape architecture is much contested, and yet designers work within a cultural milieu and ideology, clients have motivations, and visitors seek to make sense of the intent or message of the work.[6] Agriculture is particularly ripe with the potential to be leveraged by designer, client, or both as polemic or propaganda, whether to reinforce or to challenge cultural norms. Middleton Place expressed the dominant economic and political system, serving as the corporate headquarters for the Middleton family's international rice business. The gardens displayed the family's wealth, power, and sophistication to visitors, while masking the slave ownership that made those traits possible. Montpelier operated as a physical manifestation of Madison's written political manifestos, positing a new social order with the yeoman farmer as an ideal American citizen, capable of self-sufficiency and stewardship of his own real estate as well as the commonwealth. Later projects echo this ideal of self-sufficiency, especially those designed during wartime deprivation. Migge's built works reflect his polemical writing calling for German self-colonization. His and Sørenson's gardens were critiques of global capital and a praxis of familial economic independence and food self-sufficiency. Similarly, Welwyn and Village Homes critique global capital systems, but with a proposition not of family independence, but of communal interdependence. In a slightly different vein, Merchiston Farm served as a testing ground for theory, exploring the potential for women's work as a form of women's agency, an expansion of the idea of family self-sufficiency. These projects all make ambitious claims towards meaning and significance, with agriculture at the heart of social and economic change. Other projects embrace the potential for education through agriculture, as at Shenyang, Los Poblanos, and Babylonstoren, where regional patterns and traditional practices are displayed for visitors as a didactic exhibition of cultural heritage.

Agricultural projects highlight another persistent theme in landscape architecture: the connection between ideas of nature and ideas of health. Woburn

Farm represents an early model of this idea, echoing pastoral and bucolic ideals popularized in poetry and painting of the era. Rural, agricultural landscapes were commonly seen as morally and physically restorative, ideal locations for city dwellers to visit and rejuvenate their mind, body, and spirits. In the Modern era, this idea of healthy landscapes shifted slightly while still framing the city as polluted and unhealthy and agriculture as clean and wholesome. Welwyn sought to hybridize city and nature, while Nærum inserted the garden into the city, and Ziebigk used the garden as the building block of the city. All three emphasized the physical importance of health-improving recreation in the garden through agricultural labor, and the garden as a site for access to beneficial sun and air, all intended to counter the tensions resulting from industrial labor. This continues in a modified way at Village Homes, with the added intention of improving social cohesion and mental health through shared labor. And the ideology at Green Gulch is similarly expansive, with agricultural labor viewed as an integral element in a spiritual practice, improving the land inextricably connected to spiritual renewal and refinement. These views of agricultural lands as a source of physical, mental, ethical, and spiritual restoration become somewhat problematic in the post-industrial era, as we recognize the deleterious effects that extractive practices, including some agriculture, can have on land. Winslow Farm, and Green Gulch to a lesser extent, invert the model set by the other projects. In these projects, the land itself is in need of restoration and health and agriculture is part of the practice of recuperation. At Winslow Farm, the staging and practice of agriculture restore and renew the soils on site, while the material production of dune grass is exported to restore regional landscapes damaged through increasingly violent seasonal storms. Rather than conceiving of agriculture and nature as limitless sources of human renewal, these projects recognize the potential negative impact of cultural practices on the land and seek to reposition agriculture as ameliorative of the place itself.

The practice of agriculture

Farming is an environment of engagement that produces a landscape over time, countering a visual trend in the Modern era. A farm is also a physical nexus of cultural and economic trends that impact that production. Inventive technology and evolving scientific theories change the practice of agriculture and the design of agricultural sites. And changes in food and labor markets alter the selection of livestock and crops that are raised, with subsequent local impacts on environmental conditions.

During the European agricultural revolution, in the 150 years centered on the eighteenth century, European agricultural production increased three to fourfold, a result of sustained research and invention that led to better understanding of soils and nutrient cycles, plant growth and hybridization, and resulting innovations in agricultural technology.[7] Over the Modern era, Western culture sought a rational, mechanistic understanding of the world. Through that understanding, scientists sought to identify objective laws that could allow the control of nature, and through that control, allow freedom from scarcity and from the vicissitudes of natural devastations.[8] In the case studies, we see this Modern belief system emerge then retreat, as the farms reflect vernacular, mechanistic, and holistic management approaches.

Scientific agriculture emerged and gained strength at the turn of the eighteenth century and flourished in European horticultural gardens and the Prussian Gärtner-Lehranstalt, the Royal Gardener's Institute in the Potsdam court. There, Peter Joseph Lenné, the Institute's first director, merged design and scientific knowledge in a three-year course of study. The Institute used the gardens to expand Prussian knowledge of natural resource cultivation. The gardens were both epistemological and didactic – both generating and displaying knowledge of the world through scientific gardening that combined nature, art, and the sciences of botany, horticulture, and chemistry.[9] The practices and findings of the gardens echoed throughout Europe as gentleman farmers combined scientific experimentation with aesthetic design on their productive lands.

The practice of agriculture fundamentally displaces natural flora and fauna with food crops.[10] This specialization often leads to limited species plantings or even monocrops; it is inherent to farming to transform a landscape from a complex, biodiverse state to a more simplified, organized state, or agro-ecosystem,[11] with the monoculture as an extreme example. Many cash crops, such as rice and tobacco, are notorious for depleting soils or creating unhealthy environments,[12] and the impact of monocrops was recognized fairly rapidly in the eighteenth century. Scientific farmers like James Madison sought to understand the connection between plant biology, nutrient and mineral cycles, and soil vitality. Madison and his Virginia peers tried to both adjust their husbandry techniques and shift their primary crops to increase soil fertility, decrease erosion, and increase profits. A half a century later, Frederick Law Olmsted was similarly implementing state of the art technology such as tile drainage to increase soil productivity and using the latest scientific knowledge to replenish depleted soils and preserve healthy soils. At both Moraine Farm and George Vanderbilt's Biltmore Estate in Asheville, NC, he proposed forestry as a long-term investment in the restoration of farmlands, depleted at Moraine Farm through over-cultivation and at Biltmore through hog droves. Mid-twentieth-century projects similarly looked to the soil and saw resource extraction: both Welwyn Garden City and Ziebigk explicitly addressed soil fertility and proposed early forms of closed-loop agriculture, returning nutrients to soils through composted food, livestock, and human waste.

This focus on systems thinking expanded over the twentieth century, with projects that explicitly connect productive landscapes not only to food systems, but also to the restoration of animal habitat, to the renewal of damaged post-industrial landscapes, and to regional, multi-scale material exchange. Green Gulch continues to evolve from its former design as a cattle ranch with the ongoing transformation of its hydrologic systems for salmon habitat, balancing the irrigation needs of the farm with the habitat needs of the fish. Village Homes similarly incorporates multiple systems into the agricultural landscape, with multi-scalar agriculture from the residential lot to the communally owned orchard, seeking to connect the house and landscape, minimize energy use, and contribute to regional groundwater recharge. And perhaps the most quietly ambitious project, Winslow Farms is explicitly situated between two scales of landscape restoration, ameliorating human degradation of the land through multi-scale material exchange. Clearing forested areas for growing fields provides material to remediate the former quarry; additional fields provide plant material to repair storm-damaged dunes.

Specialization, the shift from low-input, self-sufficient farms to few or single crops, creates market risk as well as environmental risk,[13] and the economic market is a second external consideration that deeply impacts the conception and design of agricultural projects. When steam engines became widely used in the nineteenth century, they fostered the long-range transport of fertilizers and food products across land and oceans. Wheat from the United States, Canada, and Argentina flooded the European market and undercut the market for locally grown wheat.[14] Similarly, in the United States, Midwestern crops flooded the eastern seaboard market. This was also a moment when international markets were rewarding large-scale agriculture. Commercial farmers could match crops to regions with preferred soils and climates, and export them to markets regionally, nationally, and globally. This idea extends nineteenth-century political economist David Ricardo's principle of comparative advantage to connect natural resources to fungible products, and proposes that regions or countries should specialize in foods that grow best there and trade regionally and internationally, rather than attempt to fully provision a population locally.[15]

Smaller, regional farms responded to this influx of cheaper crops by shifting farm activities. Rather than competing in those larger markets, farms such as Moraine Farm and those in Welwyn focused on perishable provisions aimed for a local market, especially livestock-based or value-added foods such as meat, eggs, and dairy products. As food consumption was increasingly separated both temporally and spatially from food production, a response strategy of re-localizing and re-temporalizing can be achieved through a focus on highly perishable foods. Rather than the temporal cycles of the land, the transportation times and shelf life of goods were considerations for the design proposal.

The ideal scale and location of lands for crops or livestock is often a function of the projected market. Designers must understand these intended markets before organizing the farmscape. At Village Homes, almonds were intended for the local farmers' market while grapes were intended for community or family use and also used as shading structures in the individual gardens. With a weak market for grapes and an oversupply in the neighborhood, the vineyard is frequently unharvested. The high value market for the almonds, meanwhile, originally made the expense of harvest feasible. Residents could harvest for home use and sell the excess. But as that expense grew the motivation to keep harvesting has declined.

And at Winslow Farms, the ability to sell the crop produced was a deciding factor. The originally intended crop, echinacea and bayberry, did not have a viable market, and so production was completely shifted to a different crop, dune grass.

But the market impacts agricultural designs in ways beyond the sale of the plants and animals grown. Development pressures and the real estate market frequently impact the lifespan of farms. At Welwyn, Howard tried to predict and mitigate those development pressures and also use them to the advantage of the development corporation. Some lands were to be protected and held communally in perpetuity, to protect the character of the city and the resulting land values. Other lands were leased to farmers in the early years of the development, generating revenue for construction, then gradually some agricultural land was to be developed into neighborhoods and industrial lands. At Moraine, Nærum, Green Gulch, Winslow Farms, and Los Poblanos, later owners similarly saw the potential for encroaching development and increased land values to endanger the farms and gardens, and they also used covenants and easements, often through a land conservancy, to protect the gardens. In some cases, the land itself or the design heritage was viewed as significant enough to merit preservation, indicating the value of design in agricultural lands. And the structure of landownership also connects to development pressures. At Ziebigk, each garden is privately owned, and over time, almost every farm has been converted to a recreational yard, while the Nærum gardens are regulated by the Allotment Garden Association of Denmark (*Kolonihaveforbundet for Denmark*) and listed on the National Register of Cultural Heritage by the Danish Agency for Culture, providing a measure of institutional protection. Los Poblanos has conserved the agricultural use of the land and important historic buildings while developing a small portion for hospitality to ensure economic sustainability. In contrast, communally owned lands, such as at Welwyn and Village Homes, can become contested as different groups within the community hold different values and can force a decision that may be unpopular with some owners. Green Gulch is a notable exception, with communal values explicitly encoded; the property is protected by the "Covenant Running with the Land," and the Zen Center purchased the property with the stipulation that the agricultural use be maintained.

Ziebigk hints at a final, critical aspect of agriculture: labor. When Migge designed the neighborhood, food shortages were endemic and the labor required to maintain a family farm was acceptable to almost all residents. Over time, as the food system recovered from wartime shortages, people grew less interested in spending hours farming, and owners converted the gardens into leisure yards. The same pattern occurred at Welwyn and, to a lesser extent, Nærum. Several projects were not sustainable based on their labor models. At Woburn, the labor of both the agricultural landscape and the densely planted shrub and flower border was masked, not part of the aesthetic experience. But the expense of upkeep was too much for later owners and the ornamented walks were abandoned. At Middleton Place and Montpelier, slavery underpinned the economic viability of international market agriculture, and even with enslaved workers, Montpelier still sometimes struggled to turn a profit. Without the economic prop of forced labor, these large-scale operations weren't sustainable. It is troubling to read Madison's Address to the Agricultural Society of Albemarle, with its emphasis on utilitarian philosophy's "greatest good for the greatest number," and reflect on the inhumane practice of slavery operating at his home. When Madison and his correspondents discuss slavery, it is largely through the pragmatic lens of economics, not a philosophical lens of freedom. Letters note the annual expense of enslaved workers ("twenty-five or thirty dollars a year")[16] and that "Slave labor is notoriously the most expensive of all labor."[17] More recent projects include unusual labor models that support agricultural models outside the global market: Green Gulch has the volunteer labor of the Zen community members, and Village Homes operates upon communal cooperation.

Composition, meaning, and practice

One-quarter of the world's terrestrial surface is occupied by cultivated systems.[18] Yet as the world urbanizes, with 68 percent of the global population projected to live in urban areas by 2050,[19] most people are disconnected from those physically and culturally sustaining landscapes. Publicly accessible agriculture, at a variety of scales, can produce not only food, but also a broader urban ecosystem of production, education, sustainability. Small-scale, regionally specific agriculture may provide only a small percentage of a community's food need, but hybrid typologies of farm-park or farm-garden produce and sustain community, reinforcing the social, educational, recreational, and economic connective tissue of the city.[20] At the same time, publicly accessible agriculture is also a resistive act, creating an environment of engagement that resists a purely visual environment, and an environment of connection that resists an isolated, minute analysis of the world, what Samuel Taylor Coleridge called "the little-ists."[21]

With the framework of composition, meaning, and practice in mind, designers can approach the farmscape as a physically, ecologically, and culturally productive landscape with the potential for education and sensory engagement: to reconnect the literal and metaphoric sense of cultivation.

Notes

1 J. B. Jackson, "The Word Itself," *Discovering the Vernacular Landscape* (New Haven, CT: Yale University Press, 1984), 1–8.
2 John Dixon Hunt, *Greater Perfections* (Philadelphia: University of Pennsylvania Press, 2000).
3 Paul Chan, "A Time Apart," in *Time*, Amelia Groom, ed. (Cambridge, MA: MIT Press, 2013), 53–55.
4 Ecclesiastes 3:1–8.
5 Colin Sage, *Environment and Food* (London: Routledge, 2012), 15.

6 Cf. Marc Treib, ed. *Meaning in Landscape Architecture and Gardens* (London: Routledge, 2011).
7 Sage, *Environment and Food,* 33.
8 David Harvey, *The Condition of Postmodernity* (Oxford: Blackwell Publishers, 1990), 12–14.
9 Björn Brüsch, "The Garden as a Laboratory. Nineteenth-Century Scientific Gardening," in *The Shape of Experiment, Preprint 318* (Berlin: Max Planck Institute for the History of Science, 2006), 165–174.
10 Sage, *Environment and Food,* 68.
11 Ibid., 68.
12 Philip J. Pauly, *Fruits and Plains* (Cambridge, MA: Harvard University Press, 2008), 12.
13 Sage, *Environment and Food,* 36.
14 Ibid., 34.
15 Ibid., 22.
16 Richard Beale Davis (editor) and Augustus John Foster (author), *Jeffersonian America, Notes on the United States of America Collected in the Years 1805–6–7, 11–12* by Sir Augustus John Foster, Baronet (San Marino, CA: The Huntington Library, 1954), in Hilarie M. Hicks, "'To Introduce Principle & System into a Profession Hitherto Conducted Without Much of Either:' James Madison's Approach to Agriculture at Montpelier" (Orange, VA: The Montpelier Foundation, December 2012, updated February 2018, MRD-S 41872), 41.
17 Francis Corbin to James Madison, October 10, 1819 (James Madison Papers, Library of Congress, Washington, DC), in Hicks, *Madison's Approach*, 68.
18 Sage, *Environment and Food,* 71.
19 UN 2018 Revision of the World Urbanization Prospects, 16 May 2018.
20 Pierluigi Nicolin, "The Beauty of Urban Agriculture," *Lotus International* 149: 42–46, 46.
21 Thomas L. Hankins and Robert J. Silverman, *Instruments and the Imagination* (Princeton, NJ: Princeton University Press, 1995), 86.

Operationalizing the farmscape

The farmscape case studies, particularly those projects spanning the past fifty years, offer many transferrable lessons for contemporary design. Though wide-ranging in scale and scope, these case studies share characteristics that are determining factors in their success. A comparative analysis can be distilled into five themes, identified as being critical to current and emerging practice: 1) interdisciplinary collaboration, 2) motivated clients, 3) economic viability, 4) climate adaptive strategies, and 5) powerful aesthetic expressions.

Interdisciplinary collaboration references the complex, interdisciplinary nature of farmscape design and the benefit of ensuring the long-term involvement of the design team. *Motivated clients* and *economic viability* draw attention to aspects outside of the designer's control, but critically significant nonetheless – the agency of the client and the influence of the market. *Climate adaptive strategies* illuminates emerging experimental practices that are both responsive to a changing climate and predictive of increasingly extreme conditions requiring flexibility in the face of uncertainty. And finally, *powerful aesthetic expressions* highlights the significance of aesthetic experience, not only as a core contribution of design, but also as a mechanism operationalized in the farmscape through design, connecting human beings to the land through the senses.

Interdisciplinary collaboration

Collaboration between designers and consultants is critical in the design of food-producing landscapes. Agricultural projects have specific requirements associated with crop production and animal husbandry that necessitates farming expertise. But as the case studies demonstrate, the agricultural landscape is increasingly multifunctional and project goals encompass more than food production alone, with additional objectives including remediation, ecological restoration, conservation, and historic preservation. Large interdisciplinary teams, often led by the landscape architect, frequently include ecologists, biologists, horticulturists, engineers, and historians, in addition to farming expertise provided by a farm consultant or the client's inhouse team.

Overlook is exemplary in respect to interdisciplinary collaboration. The project illustrates a working model developed by Nelson Byrd Woltz Landscape Architects that brings together a tripartite team including the designer, farm consultant, and biologist to work with the client in a collaborative process. The early contributions of farm consultant Zach Wolf and biologists from SUNY-ESF provided important data and recommendations informing Nelson Byrd Woltz's design master plan. SUNY-ESF scientists continue to provide ongoing monitoring, an important feedback loop for the designers, who use the data to calibrate future work. The collaboration with SUNY-ESF gives Nelson Byrd Woltz the capacity to measure ecosystem improvements and provide real data supporting the efficacy of their designs.

One of the factors for success among the consultant team at Overlook has been continuity from the planning stages to implementation and beyond.

SUNY-ESF have carried their work forward from the early phases of analysis and design, continuing to study and monitor the property to assess conservation success. On the other hand, the recommendations of Zach Wolf, essential to the design framework plan, have been handed off to two farm managers hired to realize and manage the farm, who now face the inevitable challenges of adapting the plan according to their knowledge and practices. Where farming expertise is provided by the client, as at Green Gulch Farm and Los Poblanos, or in partnership between existing farm managers and outside farm consultants, loss of continuity can be avoided, easing the translation from design to implementation and future adaptation.

In addition to science and farming expertise, many farmscape case studies involved the participation of horticulturists, botanists, or planting experts during the design phase. A growing niche area of landscape architectural practice, plant specialists are increasingly desired on interdisciplinary teams where their expertise is needed to address specific challenges. At Overlook, Larry Weaner Associates consulted on the design and realization of meadow areas, a complex undertaking requiring horticultural knowledge and implementation expertise. At Winslow Farms Conservancy, ecologist David Smart and the Cape May Plant Materials Center helped to develop a planting palette providing wildlife habitat and suitable for hostile environments like the regraded quarry landscape. Los Poblanos planting designer Judith Phillips provided expertise in planting adapted to New Mexico's changing climate. And Babylonstoren has engaged a host of plant specialists, including botanist Ernst van Jaardsveld, who contributes his knowledge of indigenous, water-conserving species for the design of gardens featuring native and edible plants.

Client motivations

The role of clients is often underestimated in landscape architecture projects. In our desire to honor the creativity and innovation of the designer, we sometimes fail to recognize the significance of the client in originating, guiding, funding, and ultimately stewarding the designed landscape. The case studies in this book indicate that the farmscape is no exception. These projects are exemplary in large part because of the clients who made them possible, clients who are motivated by their own values and ethics to develop groundbreaking new work. Ultimately, it is the client who stewards the farmscape through its cycles and seasons, with adaptations and transformations certain to occur. Where designers establish long-term relationships with clients, as at Overlook, there is the capacity to recalibrate and adjust the design throughout an extended period of implementation.

Almost without exception, farmscape clients are motivated by an ethic to protect and improve land health. For Hank McNeil, the Fullers, and the San Francisco Zen Center, remediation and restoration was a primary initiative. McNeil's environmentalist ethic guided the remediation of a degraded landscape that would become Winslow Farms Conservancy, as well as the decision to respond to the devastating impacts of climate change by farming beach grass for the restoration of coastal lands miles away. The San Francisco Zen Center, guided by Buddhist principles, also sought to repair a vulnerable ecosystem by restoring the health of creek ecosystems and developing an overall long-term vision that maximizes land health while supporting farming and inhabitation of the property. The Fullers have made a multi-generational commitment to stewarding their land at Overlook in a way that improves ecological health over the long-term.

A secondary client motivation is the development of self-sufficiency through local production. At Welwyn Garden City, Ziebigk Siedlung, Nærum Allotment Gardens, Village Homes, and Green Gulch Farm, clients wanted to provide communities with the opportunity to gain a measure of self-sufficiency by growing their own food. Concerned about the volatility of the global food market, Ebenezer Howard and Leberecht Migge wanted to create local market. Later in twentieth-century America, this concern took an environmental turn, reflecting the desire to reduce food miles and ensure a food supply free from harmful chemical inputs. The desire for self-sufficiency, of individuals, communities, and even regions, can be identified today in the emphasis on local production, a trend that will undoubtedly strengthen with the development of more sustainable food systems.

Economic sustainability

Another critical factor in the design and long-term management of the farmscape is economic viability. Profitability ensures the farmscape's future, sustaining productive use of the land. Where the land is not currently in operation as a farm, particularly if the land was used agriculturally in the past, the initial choice to integrate productivity into an overall design provides an economic advantage, either in the form of a tax benefit or as a low budget alternative maximizing existing land resources. At Shenyang Architectural University, the limited project budget was met by retaining agricultural use of the land, making use of existing irrigation infrastructure and soils suitable to the low-cost rice landscape.

While the reuse of land formerly or currently in agricultural production minimizes costs, the development of profitable farming operations offers a path to economic sustainability. Strategies exemplified by the case studies for maximizing profitability in a competitive global market include agritourism, the development of products for niche markets, and community-sourced labor. At Los Poblanos and Babylonstoren, farming is an integral aspect of an agritourism experience, supporting overall profitability through hospitality that includes visitor accommodation, a farm-to-fork restaurant, private events, and educational programming. Green Gulch Farm also offers a guest experience, albeit one that is limited to a small number of guests at any one time, with overnight accommodation, meals, and optional work on the farm.

The case studies reveal new alternatives to traditional small-scale fruit and vegetable markets like community-supported agriculture and farmers' markets, with the sale of edible and non-food products to rapidly expanding, high-profit markets. At the time of this publication, Winslow Farms Conservancy has yet to meet the demand for beach grass production for coastal restoration, a market that could continue to grow given future predictions of increasingly frequent coastal storms. Los Poblanos and Babylonstoren have developed markets for their value-added farm products, accessing the global marketplace through their e-commerce websites which expand sales beyond the reach of their brick-and-mortar stores. Profit is maximized by processing crops on-site, through the distillation of lavender in the case of Los Poblanos and olive oil production and wine-making in the case of Babylonstoren. As reflected in the case of Village Homes' neglected almond orchard and vineyard, the absence of a market for sale can undermine the success of the agricultural landscape even in a residential setting.

A final strategy for maximizing profitability is community-sourced labor, implemented to varying degrees in several case study projects. At Green Gulch Farm, for example, economic viability is dependent on the labor of the resident community, whose work serves a double purpose, integral to both Buddhist practice and for-profit farming operations. The Shenyang Architectural University campus also makes use of free labor, inviting the academic community to participate in planting and harvest, but relies on paid farmers to maintain the rice landscape at all other times.

Climate adaptations

The farmscape case studies demonstrate the imperative of addressing the challenges of climate change. More than a matter of ethics and values, this attention to a shifting climate is a matter of survival; the future of the farmscape, both its profitability and productivity, is dependent on adaptations responsive to changing weather patterns resulting in water scarcity and biodiversity loss.

Water scarcity is of primary concern in many of the case studies, including Village Homes, Green Gulch Farm Zen Center, Babylonstoren, and Los Poblanos. Green Gulch Farm demonstrates the difficult balance between ecological restoration and agriculture when water resources are limited. The community continues to study how it can share its water supply to support a healthy creek ecosystem while still providing for the needs of the farm. Recent design projects have adapted both farm and garden to make space for creek restoration, but thoughtful implementation of Mithun's long-term vision plan will be required to resolve future competing needs.

Village Homes is also experiencing the effects of water scarcity, questioning the viability of maintaining high water use plantings, despite its surface stormwater system designed to recharge groundwater. While there is at least one native low water garden in the community at the time of this publication, it remains to be seen how the community will adapt its edible landscape to meet climate challenges in the future and if it will be possible to retain the original design intent and character as inevitable adaptations are made.

The future certainty of water scarcity demands new water-conserving approaches including water recycling, farming low water crops, and a shift in planting design aesthetics. Two case studies, Babylonstoren and Los Poblanos, demonstrate a dedicated effort to conserve water, modeling approaches that will need to be replicated and advanced in future farmscapes. Located in dry climates where recent droughts have increased the urgency for water conservation, these projects show how designers have responded by adapting planting palettes and agricultural crops. Experimental practices include the development of drought-tolerant regional crop varieties adapted to local conditions, in the case of Los Poblanos, and the exploration of water-conserving indigenous edible plants in the case of Babylonstoren. Notable in both projects is the successful design integration of xeric species in landscapes with diverse planting palettes and the role these plantings play in demonstrating for the public a new water-conserving aesthetic. Both projects have also made efforts to reduce overall consumption of water, balancing the demands between hospitality needs and agriculture, through recycling of water in the case of Babylonstoren, and through the careful coordination of flood and drip irrigation with guest usage in the case of Los Poblanos.

A second climate-related issue that rises to the fore in a comparison of the case studies is biodiversity loss. Outstanding examples of conservation agriculture are illustrated by the case studies of Green Gulch Farm and Overlook, where the agricultural landscape is designed with express goals for habitat remediation and conservation, while Babylonstoren and Shenyang Architectural University demonstrate how biodiversity can be achieved in agricultural landscapes by modeling ecological and educational approaches.

Green Gulch Farm and Overlook reveal the long-term investment necessary to achieving ecological conservation in a meaningful way. Collaboration between designers and biologists is critical, from the start of the project through construction and into the future as monitoring and design adaptation continues. Both projects are guided by an overall framework – Mithun's long-term vision plan in the case of Green Gulch Farm and Nelson Byrd Woltz's master plan in the case of Overlook – and rely on phased implementation and feedback loops where data collection informs design, leading to more data collection, the next phase of design, and so on. Clients need to be made aware that the master plan is but a guide, that the design must necessarily evolve, and change will be incremental. New contractual models, like those of meadow consultant Larry Weaner Associates, which specify design and management over a number of years, will need to be adopted to manage client expectations and ensure long-term engagement of the design team.

Agricultural ecosystems benefit from biodiversity, but where conservation is not a primary intent, biodiversity can still be valuable not only in supporting healthy agricultural crops, but also in providing educational benefits. The rice campus of

Shenyang Architectural University, forgoing the use of pesticides, supports a biodiverse aquatic ecosystem, providing a harvest of both rice and aquatic species like frogs and crabs. The integrated agriculture–aquaculture system serves an educational purpose for the academic community, modeling traditional agricultural methods and their adaptation to an urban environment.

Biodiversity at Babylonstoren likewise facilitates educational programming. The organization of plant diversity across the formal garden serves a dual purpose of easing the work of managing farm operations and of educating the public about typologies of edible plants and their horticultural requirements, serving both functional and educational goals. The diversity of crops makes the garden more resilient while creating opportunities for educational offerings that keep guests returning.

Powerful aesthetic expressions

The farmscape is designed to maximize aesthetic experience, with a multi-sensory dimension unique to food-producing landscapes. The cycles and operations of the working landscape, from tilling to planting, harvesting, and composting, as well as daily and seasonal rituals related to animal husbandry, intimately connect humans with the sights, sounds, smells, and tastes of the farm. Designers amplify these sensorial qualities through formal, ecological, and programmatic strategies, choreographing an aesthetic experience that is legible and meaningful. A powerful aesthetic expression has cultural value, offering the potential for meaningful connection between humans and the land, but as the case studies demonstrate, it can also facilitate economic success, educational value, and the likelihood that the farmscape will be preserved.

As seen in the Nærum Allotment Gardens, form can be an aesthetic expression that creates cultural value, and landscapes valued culturally are more likely to endure. The elliptical hedge, an atypical form for allotment gardens, repeated across the rolling terrain, creates a unique perceptual experience both inside and outside individual gardens. Ultimately, it is this that has ensured its preservation more than its value as a producer of food.

Aesthetic value can also be understood as essential to economic success, in case studies like Village Homes, where elevated housing prices from time of construction to the current day reflect the value placed upon the aesthetic experience of a lush edible landscape.

Case studies such as Babylonstoren and Los Poblanos also rely on aesthetic expression for economic success to support high-end agritourism. Guests are drawn to Babylonstoren and Los Poblanos precisely for the kind of aesthetic experiences they provide. At Babylonstoren, formal organization makes the garden legible as a series of discrete experiences, juxtaposed visually with the significant natural features that lie beyond the garden gates. Paths, walls, and water provide visual, tactile, and auditory sensations. The diversity of plant life broadens the sensory experience with a rich tapestry of colors, textures, scents, sounds, and flavors expressing the agricultural landscape as a place as variable as life itself. At Los Poblanos, design decisions such as the insertion of guest suites into the fields, the extension of the orchard across the parking, the extension of acequias across the property, and the framing of views across the La Quinta lawn and fields of lavender, connect guests to the land through aesthetic experience. Farm-to-fork restaurants at both Babylonstoren and Los Poblanos use the culinary arts as a tether back to the land, a multisensory experience of the farm condensed on the plate.

Design for agroecosystem health enriches aesthetic experiences, often supporting educational goals by facilitating learning through the senses. At Shenyang Architectural University, the decision to forgo pesticides supports a robust aquatic ecosystem of creatures visible to the academic community. The nightly cacophony of frogs and other creatures inhabiting the rice landscape would not exist were the campus managed as a conventional rice paddy. Conservation measures at Overlook have resulted in an increase in songbirds. Planting design, in the shape of meadows and new understory plantings, is calculated to fill a void in the soundscape. At Green Gulch Farm and Winslow Farms Conservancy, the restoration of degraded lands likewise makes space for new species and an entirely new aesthetic expressing the transformative effects of regeneration. The sinuous designed hydrology of Green Gulch Creek contrasts with the regular forms of the farm fields, providing a new sensory experience of a meandering creek ecosystem where there was once a concrete channel. The quarry water basins and rolling open fields of Winslow Farms Conservancy reflect the dynamic qualities of light and wind, seasonal shifts of color, and the comings and goings of wild turkeys, a living landscape for the senses where there was once barren ground. These are not timid aesthetic expressions. The farmscape is powerfully legible, highly organized, and sensory rich.

The farmscape is in a constant state of flux, a form of landscape that is never static, composed as a series of mutable processes. Design success requires long-term involvement, as designers evaluate and respond to the evolution of land health over time through implementation of plants and animals as agents of incremental, choreographed transformation. The design of productive landscapes is a testing ground for experimentation in shaping the land. Increasingly multifunctional, the farmscape demands new strategies to resolve competing uses in the face of limited resources. Future practice integrating agriculture will continue to demonstrate the cutting edge of design, expanding connections between disciplines, providing new long-term contractual models, advancing knowledge about climate adaptation through design research, and developing new aesthetic expressions that build upon cultural heritage while enriching daily life.

Index